ILLUSTRATIONS IN
CHILDREN'S
BOOKS

literature for children

Pose Lamb
Consulting Editor
Purdue University

Storytelling and Creative Drama—*Dewey W. Chambers, University of the Pacific, Stockton, California*

Illustrations in Children's Books, Second Edition—*Patricia Cianciolo, Michigan State University*

Enrichment Ideas, Second Edition—*Ruth Kearney Carlson, California State University at Hayward*

History and Trends—*Margaret C. Gillespie, Marquette University*

Poetry in the Elementary School—*Virginia Witucke, Purdue University*

Its Discipline and Content—*Bernice Cullinan, New York University*

Children's Literature in the Curriculum—*Mary Montebello, American University, Washington, D.C.*

Second Edition

ILLUSTRATIONS IN CHILDREN'S BOOKS

Patricia Cianciolo

Michigan State University

WM. C. BROWN COMPANY PUBLISHERS
Dubuque, Iowa

Conformity in taste in the realm of art (be it graphic art and/or literary art) or politics or religion is not a virtue but a vice.

contents

foreword

This series of books came to be because of the editor's conviction that most textbooks about literature for children had not been written for elementary teachers, regardless of the anticipated audience suggested by the titles. The words, *Literature for Children,* preceding each individual title indicate not only the respect for the field held by the authors and the editor but our evaluation of the importance of this type of literature, worthy of consideration along with other categories or classifications of English literature. However, it is *what happens* through books, and the *uses* of literature which are of concern to the authors of this series, as well as the provision of an historical perspective and some knowledge of the writer's and the illustrator's crafts. Our work, then, is directed primarily to the elementary classroom teacher who wants to design and implement an effective program of literature for children.

Because entire books have been devoted to specific topics, for example, the history of literature for children, it is hoped that such topics are covered in greater depth than usual. They are not merely books *about* children's literature; the focus in this series is on helping teachers see what literature for children has been, the direction or directions pointed by scholars in the field, and some ways in which a teacher can share with children the excitement and joy of reading. The authors have tried to share with teachers and prospective teachers their enthusiasm for children's literature, today's and yesterday's; for an unenthusiastic teacher, though well-informed, will not communicate enthusiasm to his pupils.

The author of each book was selected, first because he has demonstrated this enthusiasm in his teaching and writing, and secondly because of his competence in the field of children's literature in general. It is hoped that the thoroughness and depth with which each topic has been explored and the expertise which each author has brought to a topic in which he has a particular interest will serve as sufficient justifications for such a virtue.

Children's literature courses are among the most popular courses in the professional sequence at many colleges and universities. It is rewarding and exciting to reenter the world of literature for children, to experience again the joy of encountering a new author or of renewing acquaintance with a favorite author or a character created by an author.

The editor and the authors of this series have tried to capture the magic that is literature for children, and to provide some help for teachers who want to share that magic with children.

Art and design, as they are reflected in books for children and adolescents, are fascinating fields of study. Illustrators do not agree as to the best answers to these questions, and the readers of this book probably won't agree either!

> Should the art in children's books be representational or abstract? How does one decide what techniques, what media are most appropriate for conveying the artist's and writer's messages?
>
> Are illustrations in children's books primarily adornments, an attractive and enticing "extra," or do they contribute to whatever the content is?
>
> When the author and illustrator are not the same person, which one answers the questions suggested above, and what if the answers are not the same?

In this second edition, Patricia Cianciolo includes, in updated form, much of the material which proved to be so valuable in the first edition. She discusses, in detail, the wide variety of techniques and materials available to the artist and illustrator, and the many different types of illustrated and picture books from which parents, teachers, media specialists, and child and adolescent readers might choose.

There are a number of books without text and the story line or plot is relayed entirely through the artwork. Are such "wordless" books literature? This question has generated some controversy. The author discusses the several issues involved and states her own position very clearly. Visual literacy is viewed as a major educational objective, and illustrated books can serve as an invaluable means of achieving this objective.

Dr. Cianciolo makes a strong plea for accepting diversity in artwork and illustrations. There is not now, and is not likely to be, agreement among experts on the criteria by which illustrations might be judged. The author concludes that conformity is a vice, not a virtue. However, there are several very general considerations which can be helpful in determining the quality of illustrations in a book, and these are discussed.

The sections dealing with surrealism and naive art are new in this edition. The editor found this material informative as well as interesting and predicts readers will have similar responses.

After completing this book, readers should have much more insight into the illustrator's craft and the significant contribution of illustrations to literature for children and adolescents. They should be able to look at and to perceive the artwork which is an integral part of most books for children with increased appreciation. They should also be better equipped to share some of these perceptions with young readers in order that they, too, may read and look with more pleasure and understanding.

POSE LAMB, EDITOR

preface

Examination of children's books that have been published in recent years will reveal that these books are illustrated with pictures that vary widely in style and in artistic quality. Many of the books are illustrated by most competent graphic artists who have mastered aspects of design and the handling of media. The action and plot are illustrated with pictures that are imaginative and beautiful. Unfortunately, however, there are some recent publications that are illustrated by less talented artists.

Illustrations can contribute much to help children grow in their interest in reading and in their appreciation of fine books. This is likely to be the case if the book illustrations interpret and extend the story in an artistic manner and in a style that is suitable to the young reading audience. Hopefully, this book will help bring together children and well-illustrated books.

It is intended that the various facts about the illustrations in children's books which the writer has included in this manuscript will help the student of children's literature (whether this student is an elementary-school teacher, a school librarian, or an undergraduate student in a teacher education program) to become familiar with the varieties of illustrated books that are available for children; to acquire the rudiments of information about the styles of art in the pictures that contemporary artists use in their illustrations; to appreciate the impact that the artist's media have on his creations; and to acquire some insight into the methods that can be used to create in children a keener awareness and an attitude of critical evaluation of the illustrations in the stories that they read. It is hoped that the readers of this book will be led to discover and to appreciate new and better-illustrated children's literature so that their young pupils can be helped to find joy in good books and to develop a love for them.

P.C.

chapter 1
appraising illustrations
in children's books

Visual impressions tend to prevail in contemporary society. Yet many of our children, and adults too, are "visually incapacitated." They do not *see* in the fullest sense of the word; oftentimes they fail to realize the significance of what they see. They look at things in a stultified, singular way, unaware of the many facets of what could be seen in and felt about the reality in which they live.[1] Their sensibilities would be sharpened considerably if they were granted the privilege of reading, from early childhood on through adulthood, books that were illustrated by courageous and creative book artists.

If an individual has numerous opportunities to examine artistic visuals that are part and parcel of the contemporary scene of illustrated books and has the benefit of the unique literary experience which is offered by the illustrated books (especially the picture books), it is conceivable that he will make better use of his imaginative faculty and will tend to see his reality in more fresh and vital ways. It is quite likely that once a child has "experienced" the marvelously unique impressionistic abstract watercolor paintings and poetic text that Chihiro Iwasaki created for *Staying Home Alone on a Rainy Day*, he will see and respond to rain (and the other elements too, perhaps) in a refreshingly subjective, poetic manner. If one is open-minded enough to accept surrealism in art and in fiction, Mercer Mayer's surrealistic paintings that illustrate Barbara Wersba's surrealistic creation entitled *Amanda, Dreaming* will help him to resist the cliché makers that surround him in our "conformity-cloistered society." The naive graphic and verbal statements that William Kurelek made in *A Prairie Boy's Winter* will serve to add a newness to one's comments about and reactions to winter, be it on the prairie or elsewhere. And so it goes.

1. J. W. Creber, *Sense and Sensitivity* (London: University of London Press, 1967), p. 23.

1

These are only three of the many books available to today's children that are created by truly creative people who can effectively "convert substance into metaphor"[2] and because none of these book artists slavishly followed models or rules when creating their pictures, they were able to produce visuals that could enlarge the personal experience of their viewers. Their illustrations evoke personal feelings and imagery about some human experience. More importantly, they all express some new way of reacting to these experiences; they can serve as a catalyst to bring about the release of imaginative powers that are so often inert or stifled. Book illustrations worthy of distinction may be realistic or abstract. They may be done in traditional or conservative art styles or in modern or unconventional forms. They have the potential to help their viewers become visually sensible and visually literate.

There is little agreement among the critics of children's literature about the criteria one should use to evaluate the illustrations that appear in books read by children. The critics are unable to remain objective in their appraisals and cannot reach unanimous decisions about the styles of art that are most appropriate for illustrating stories for children. There is little accord as to which of the many illustrated books should be designated as the most creative or artistically graphic and/or literary accomplishments. They cannot agree as to which of the illustrated books constitute the most innovative, inventive, or original graphic efforts. This is as it should be. Conformity in taste is a vice rather than a virtue. To accomplish conformity in taste, especially in the realm of art, is to violate and demean human nature; it squelches development in thought and sensitivity to experience and feelings. This is not to deny that there is room for judicious decisions about the worth and quality of book art. It does mean that criticisms of illustrations are not based merely on impressions. Judicial decisions about book art are to be made on the basis of generalizations, tentative values, some precedents or conventions, and a variety of traditions. These are the type of criteria which are put forth and discussed in the pages that follow.

It must be emphasized that appraisal of the art in children's books should be in terms of the needs of today's children, and today's children have many and varied needs. The young modern needs and is likely to be appreciative and accepting of pictures done in a variety of art styles. He will soon recognize the beauty of each, if only given the opportunity to experience them in the context of relevant and quality literary selections.

2. Robert E. Samples, "Kari's Handicap—The Impediment of Creativity," in *Readings on Creativity and Imagination in Literature and Language,* ed. Leonard V. Kosinski (Champaign, Ill.: National Council of Teachers of English, 1968), p. 81.

Whether the illustrations are made by the author himself or by a book artist, the function of the illustrator is to use the graphic art form to help tell the significant aspects of the story and to extend the text. This very general rule applies to the picture book where author and artist share almost equally the responsibility for telling the story. It also applies to the illustrated novel which has only a few pictures.

Types of Illustrated Books

There are extremes in the ways in which illustrations are used in books. There are children's storybooks which consist only of pictures and have no text at all. There are books which contain illustrations that serve primarily to decorate the pages and neither depict or expand on the text. In some cases illustrations reinforce and expand upon the mood of a literary selection but do not actually depict the actions described therein. There are many books in which the illustrations are an essential part of the book but the proportionate number of illustrations is small when compared to the length of the text and the number of situations and characters included in the story itself. Finally, there is the longer book, the junior novel, which contains only a few illustrations and these serve to highlight the major situations or incidents.

The proliferation of books without words within the last decade constitutes an interesting development in the juvenile trade-book scene. Storybooks in which the illustrations carry the complete load in the way of literary connotation are addressed to children as young as three years of age and as old as the most sophisticated teenager. The nursery school- or kindergarten-aged child will delight in the surprises and will quickly identify the concepts about size from the simple black-and-white sketches that are offered to him in *Elephant Buttons* by Noriko Ueno. He would also enjoy the situations and recognize the theme presented by Edward Ardizzone in *The Wrong Side of the Bed*. It would take a far more mature and perceptive person to recognize that Fernando Krahn's book *A Flying Saucer Full of Spaghetti* may be interpreted as a commentary about social inequities. About *The Inspector*, a macabre tale created by George Mendoza and illustrated in carefully detailed line drawings by Peter Parnall, some will say the theme in this story is: "Don't become too bogged down with the little details in life; take the broader view if you want to get a true perspective of what is happening." Others may say that its message is: "Even your best and most trusted friend may become your enemy." So, depending upon one's attitude about life, any number of themes may be read into this dramatic and controversial wordless book.

Illustration by Lynd Ward for *The Silver Pony* by Lynd Ward. Copyright © 1973 by Lynd Ward. Reprinted by permission of the publisher Houghton Mifflin Company.

Lynd Ward's *The Silver Pony: A Story in Pictures,* which was included in the 1974 Children's Book Showcase, is the longest and most involved of the wordless books. Gray and white tempera paintings tell this episodic story. They depict the things that happen as a farm boy flies over the world on a magic horse: he presents an apple to an Eskimo child, a sunflower to a girl living in an isolated lighthouse, and another to a girl on an urban rooftop; he rescues a lamb stranded on a mountain cliff and after a flight among missiles he returns home to be presented with a pony.

Contrasted with the books which consist primarily of pictures are those which contain marginal drawings that decorate the pages and do not have the slightest connection with the accompanying text. These pictures are not book illustrations in the truest sense, however. The pictures that accompanied the chapbooks, so popular during the eighteenth century, served primarily to decorate these books. They did not *illustrate* them in the sense in which the term is usually defined.

A superficial examination of the illustrations by Maurice Sendak that appear in *The Bat-Poet,* which was written by Randall Jarrell, would lead one to say that this book belongs in this category. Not so. The illustrations are imaginative and decorative, but they do not rest upon the text. They are in themselves an extension of the text, because each says things visually that were not said in words. The illustrations do indeed elucidate the story of a little brown bat who cannot sleep during the day and who makes up perceptive poems about the owl, the mockingbird, the chipmunk, and his own bat boyhood. In a very sophisticated manner, Sendak's pen drawings extend text and masterfully depict the mood, the tones, and the overtones of this lovable fable. *The Bat-Poet* was among the ninety-six titles that were shown in the American Institute of Graphic Arts Children's Book Show in 1965. The full-color photographs in the compilation of original haiku in *Haiku: The Mood of Earth* by Ann Atwood reinforce and extend the human experience and the emotional response to the moods of nature which are expressed in the poetry; they do more than merely literally interpret the content of this beautiful and perceptive poetry.

The story, the pictures, and the graphic presentation are all one when the worth of an illustrated book is being evaluated. So far as the pictures are concerned, it is not the amount of illustration that matters. It is how the pictures integrate with and complete the story. The illustrator has an artistic responsibility to concern himself with the *significance* of the story when he prepares the pictures. This is exactly what Sendak and Atwood have accomplished in the total design of *The Bat-Poet* and *Haiku: The Mood of Earth* respectively. This type of book is properly termed an illustrated book to differentiate it from a picture book.

There is yet another kind of illustrated book, one with a longer text and a more complex plot than is generally available to the preschool child. There are numerous pictures included in this second type of illustrated book. But in proportion to the length of the text and the number of situations and characters included in the main plot and subplots, there are fewer illustrations than there usually are in the picture books for the very young reader. Books that are of this type demand a longer attention span, for the story takes longer to read.

An example of this second type of illustrated book is *The Jazz Man* by Mary Hays Weik which is illustrated with numerous superb woodcuts made by Ann Grifalconi. Both text and pictures express a black family's struggle for understanding and love. It is a story for readers from ages nine through twelve. The story of Zeke, a crippled boy living in Harlem; his parents' love for him; the family's experience of finding moments of happiness in hearing the jazz played by their neighbor and his friends; the reality of the cold, hunger, and loneliness realized by Zeke when his mother and dad leave him are some of the aspects depicted by Mary Hays Weik and Ann Grifalconi in this well-written and uniquely illustrated book. This moving story could not be told as effectively by way of an abbreviated text or fewer illustrations. Nor is it one that would be fully appreciated or even understood, for that matter, by an immature child. *The Jazz Man* is a fine illustrated book for an older, mature child. It is perfect proof that profusely illustrated books can be appealing to children in the age range that, wrongly, we tend to assume has long since outgrown them. *The Jazz Man* was a runner-up for the 1967 Newbery Award, a medal awarded annually to the author of an original, creative work that is considered a distinguished contribution to American literature for children. There is little question about Mary Weik's writing in *The Jazz Man*, for it is exquisite, but Ann Grifalconi's illustrations are unquestionably an essential part of this book. So it is with *Black Pilgrimage* by Tom Feelings. Both the forthright text and the many representational drawings and paintings, in full color and black and white, are necessary to make the emphatic and persuasive comment about this man's decision to live permanently in his ancestral home and to help the reader gain an insight into black consciousness.

Picture Books Described.   The picture book is a special form of an illustrated book. Traditionally, educators and publishers do have some specific elements in mind when they speak of a picture book. Typically, the picture book usually contains a rather uncomplicated plot developed by way of a brief text which the youngster enjoys having read to him, and numerous pictures which enable him to comprehend the story independently of the text. The text is an important part of the book and worthy of the pictures that accompany it. The text alone is not the "heart" of the story and neither are the illustrations. The two must be together.

Any number of titles well exemplify this type of picture book. Those created by Ezra Jack Keats and Robert McCloskey, although the styles of the texts and illustrations in each differ markedly, are the sort that properly fit this type of illustrated book. In their books there is thorough fusion of pictures and words. Both the stories and the illustrations in the books created by these author-artists are typified by a creative artistic expression which serves to extend the reader's experiences, experiences which are intended to heighten the child's awareness of the world about him and help him gain a more complete understanding of himself. Included in this type of picture book are Taro Yashima's *Crow Boy*, John Schoenherr's *The Barn*, and Leo Lionni's *The Biggest House in the World*. Also included in this type of picture book are those in which the alphabet, the numbers, Mother Goose rhymes, and other poems are pictorially depicted. The Mother Goose books done by Feodor Rojankovsky, Celestino Piatti, and Tasha Tudor fall into this category of picture books, as do the number books by Ed Emberley and Brian Wildsmith.

Traditionally, the picture book was addressed primarily to the young child, but that practice is changing. Currently, numerous picture books which are geared to children as old as fourteen, sixteen, and even the mature adult are available. And the number of picture books designed for the older reader is increasing with each publishing season. Exemplary are *The Pigeon Man* written by Jean-Pierre Abraham and illustrated by Alan E. Cober, *The Ballad of the Burglar of Babylon* written by Elizabeth Bishop and illustrated by Ann Grifalconi, and *The Geranium on the Window Sill Just Died but Teacher You Went Right On* written by Albert Cullum and illustrated by twenty-eight artists. Society's intolerance of different and unusual individuals is the commentary expressed in *The Pigeon Man;* the pursuit of a black burglar and killer by soldiers on the hill of Babylon in Rio de Janeiro is the story told in verse with depth of understanding, intense emotion, and stunning woodcut prints in *The Ballad of the Burglar of Babylon*. A classic example of surrealism in verse and in book illustration is found in *The Geranium on the Window Sill Just Died but Teacher You Went Right On* and constitutes a cynical commentary about life in some of our classrooms.

It is for the picture books that the Caldecott Medal is awarded each year. This annual award, a medal, is presented by the Children's Services Division of the American Library Association to the artist who has created the most distinguished picture book of the year. The award is in honor of Randolph J. Caldecott, the nineteenth-century English illustrator of books for children. In order to be eligible for the Caldecott Medal, books must meet the following criteria: the text must be worthy of the book but need not be the work of the artist; the pictures rather than the text are the most important part of the book; there are no limitations as to the age level of the intended reading audience of the picture book, but traditionally the Caldecott Medal has been awarded for the art work in the books that are addressed to young children; the artist must be a citizen or resident of the United States; and the book must have been published in the United States during the year preceding the presentation of the award.

The Children's Book Showcase consists of titles which are judged by a committee to be the best designed and/or illustrated children's books that have been published in the United States during the preceding year. A catalog of pertinent information about the production and design elements of each is prepared and accompanies an exhibit of these books. The Showcase is sponsored by the Children's Book Council for the main aim of arousing interest in and providing information about high graphic quality in children's books among teachers, librarians, students, and those professionally involved in graphic design. The first Children's Book Showcase was in 1972.

Illustrations for Young Readers

Both the text and the illustrations in an illustrated book are important. Each is a unique creative accomplishment; together picture and word must blend so well that it will seem as if one person had been responsible for both.

It is not particularly unusual for an author to illustrate his own story; examples abound of illustrators who have experienced considerable success in creating the pictures for their own books. Beatrix Potter included her own exquisitely detailed, pastel-tinted illustrations in her tales about Peter Rabbit, Jemima Puddle-Duck, Tom Kitten, Squirrel Nutkin, and Benjamin Bunny, to name only a few of her delightful creatures. Ludwig Bemelmans wrote the five widely known *Madeline* books and made happy, colorful, espressionistically styled pictures for them, using watercolor as his medium. His illustrations give the impression that he lost no time with details in drawing, but close examination will reveal that details are there. Robert McCloskey wrote quite a number of picture books. The Caldecott Medal winners, *Time of Wonder* and *Make Way for Ducklings*, were his own stories, illustrated by him in his inimitably humorous and gently satirical fashion. He has used varied media to make the pictures for his books, but watercolor was used for *Time of Wonder*, and lithographic pencil on grained zinc was used for *Make Way for Ducklings*. Most often, however, an artist chooses to make pictures that illustrate stories created by someone other than himself.

There are no tangible or quantitative bases upon which one can objectively evaluate a piece of art. There are no certain constants or certain factors present in all or most works on the basis of which they may be declared good or bad, successful or unsuccessful. We cannot state in absolute terms that one book artist is a better painter or woodcut artist than another. Nevertheless, one can and should have some pertinent but not final views about book art; he should have some values, some preferences, and some degree of enthusiasm about the art.[3] If he had none of these he "would be about as useful as the editorial writer with no opinions."[4]

Before the revolt by the impressionist artists, craft itself was an inflexible, relentless standard in art. Today, it still involves mastery and is considered an artist's responsibility. But the means by which he accomplishes mastery, deftness of touch, is his own personal problem and is not measured against a set, established style. No serious artist can be without craft, mastery, and deftness. These are necessary to "free the spirit," to realize a private sense of perfection; these are necessary if style is to result. Undoubtedly the subconscious may exert considerable influence on the shape or style of one's art, but it cannot create art. The very act of making a painting is an intending one. The artist renders his impression of an object or an experience (in the case of a book artist, it is his interpretation of a literary statement) by means of imaginative vision. Nonetheless, he is obliged to express his own responses to that subject matter (object, experience, literary statement) under controlled and weighty *objective* compulsions.[5] Thus one can become an artist if he consciously masters his craft and uses it in a way which will express his individualism and his variety.[6]

Some *general* criteria that one might consider when attempting to appraise book illustrations are identified below. Subjective and variable as they well may seem, they should allow one to *react* to book art (and art in general) and to *enjoy it*.

Something of Significance Is Said. Picture books have long been among the first steps in a child's learning. They have served as an illus-

3. Ben Shahn, *The Shape of Content* (Cambridge: Harvard University Press, 1957), pp. 92-98.

4. *Ibid.*, p. 98.

5. John Dewey, *Art as Experience* (New York: Minton, Balch and Company, 1934), p. 306.

6. Shahn, *Shape of Content*, pp. 43-123.

trated informant and guide to the world about him. Picture books have introduced new ideas to the reader. Concepts gained previously are often reinforced or extended by the illustrations. Children have the intellectual capacity and the imaginative powers to enjoy picture books that express a variety of ideas and concepts, but the picture and text must portray ideas and concepts that are within the realm of the reader's understanding and interest. It would take a reader well within the ten to sixteen year age range (maybe even older) to recognize the intensity of purpose and the persuasive techniques used by Betty Jean Lifton (author), and Eikoh Hosoe (photographer) in *Return to Hiroshima,* a dramatic detailing of the immediate and long-lasting effects of the atomic bombing of Hiroshima in 1945. The reader of *Wildfire* would probably have to be within the age range of eight through twelve years to appreciate fully the text and pictures that tell the important story of a small flame that secretly kindles a gigantic fire. The poetic prose, written by Evans G. Valens, Jr., and the effective, exquisite pictures done by Clement Hurd typify this book. Yet neither the story nor the illustrations would impress the immature or inexperienced reader to any significant extent. On the other hand, the very young child would be delighted by the text and the pictures of Maurice Sendak's *Where the Wild Things Are* and Ezra Jack Keats' *Peter's Chair.* The fantasy in the one and the reality in the other are of the type a young reader can imagine or has already experienced. The original and imaginative pictures and brief text of *Where the Wild Things Are* portray a story about a little boy's adventure with fanciful monsters, a story that would thoroughly thrill children within the three to five year age range. The illustrations in the book depict a roguish little boy and big, ludicrous beasts and would stir the creative imaginations of young readers. They are done in dark green and blue tempera contrasted with shades of purple. Pen-and-ink cross-hatching is used effectively to achieve texture and shading. Different from *Where the Wild Things Are,* but still of interest to readers in the same age range, is *Peter's Chair,* which conveys a young boy's reaction to having to play more quietly than has been his habit, and to having to give up the belongings he has outgrown to his baby sister. Keats uses collage and pen-and-ink with skill.

The story and the illustrations that make up a picture book will be appreciated and enjoyed by the reader if the contents have significance to him, if they have integrity, and if they extend his experience and heighten his awareness of the world around him. All of the books mentioned above can accomplish these very things when they are given to the right child at the right time. But a child's interests are infinite, and he has a fondness for a world that is filled with the tiniest of details, as well as one that is

Illustration for *Peter's Chair* written and illustrated by Ezra Jack Keats. Copyright © 1967 by Ezra Jack Keats. Reprinted with permission of Harper & Row, Publishers.

filled with the biggest of forms. Thus, he must be given illustrated books that will cause him to look for and see many things. He needs books that will lead him toward many imaginative adventures. Most young people enjoy picture books about serious as well as humorous things, and so would probably like the ones that are discussed below.

The sportive and fun-filled picture story entitled *An Anteater Named Arthur* by Bernard Waber is illustrated with charming cartoon-styled drawings done with felt-tipped pens and Magic Markers. The young reader will find much of himself in Arthur who is described as being "helpful, understanding, well-behaved, sensible, orderly, and responsible; yet messy, argumentative, forgetful, finicky, indecisive, and irresponsible."

This same reader would also very likely enjoy the serious and touching story of *Salt Boy* by Mary Perrine. This picture book, illustrated by Leonard Weisgard, tells the story of a Navajo Indian boy's harrowing experience as he is forced to lasso a lamb swept away in a flash flood.

The young reader wants stories about ordinary things as well as the very unique. And so he would probably appreciate McCloskey's *One Morning in Maine*. Great satisfaction may be experienced upon introduction to the characters of *One Morning in Maine*. Both text and illustrations realistically tell of a child's reaction to losing her first tooth. It is a story that brings joy and excitement to everyday living and to just growing up.

The Burning Rice Fields by Sara Cone Bryant and illustrated in pastels by Mamoru Funai, or Margaret Hodges' *The Wave*, illustrated with cardboard cuts and color overlays by Blair Lent, are two versions of a Japanese legend which portray a unique situation in which an old man burns the rice fields on the mountain in order to bring the people away from the shore village that is about to be engulfed by a tidal wave.

Our young reader enjoys books about the real as well as the imaginary. A very real situation is described in *Evan's Corner* by Elizabeth Starr Hill. The text and Nancy Grossman's illustrations, which are done in soft watercolors, portray a vivid and sympathetic story of a little boy who lives in a two-room Harlem apartment with his family. He is given a corner in which he can be "lonely" in his own way.

Contrasted with this story of reality is the modern, fanciful tale entitled *The Country Bunny and the Little Gold Shoes*, by Du Bose Heyward, an interesting account telling how the Easter Rabbits are chosen and how Easter eggs are delivered. The matter-of-fact illustrations by Marjorie Flack make this charming fantasy even more believable.

Each of the aforementioned books varies in content, in writing style, and in the type of illustrations. The contents of the text and illustrations in each book will help the child to envision his two worlds—the real and the imaginary, the actual and the ideal—in a new and vital way.

Audience Is Understood and Respected.   If the book is addressed to children, the book artist must have a feeling for children as people. He must be aware of, and have respect for, their likes and dislikes. This quality of keen sensitivity to what children are like, and also to what they like, is apparent in *One Morning in Maine*—or in any of McCloskey's books, for that matter. In this picture book, the story line and the beautiful dark blue, double-page spreads enable the child to read about things that are important to him. In a genial satirical manner such meaningful realities of childhood as the following are considered: one must learn how to squeeze toothpaste onto the toothbrush, one must realize that a loose tooth means that one is growing up, and one must consider the fact that the vanilla ice cream cone (as opposed to a chocolate one) should be given to a little sister "so the drips won't spot."

The book artist must be aware of children's capacity to understand and to make judgments about the story and its accompanying pictures. He needs to know when and in what way children's tastes differ from adults' tastes. Children are dependent upon adults to offer them books. We should offer them in word and art our intelligent best, offer them reading fare that will entertain and extend. With these statements most publishers, authors, and book selectors will probably agree. Some people claim that we should incorporate into the books we offer our children (in ideas, words, designs, art, and packaging of books) the concept that life is unpredictable. It is sometimes, but seldom, sweet; often it is cruel; occasionally it is rewarding.[7] Others tend to believe that rather than tell it "like it is" we should provide literature that depicts the memory of childhood life as it ought to be and not what it is. One can readily see the controversy that exists in these points of view about what kinds of books should be made available to children. Each point of view represents a different interpretation of what life is "really" like; each represents an attitude about life in general and about children in particular.

These contrasting points of view are exemplified in books that are available to children today. Compare Arnold Adoff's *Black Is Brown Is Tan*, which is illustrated by the line-and-wash illustrations of Emily A. McCully, with Albert Cullum's *The Geranium on the Window Sill Just Died but Teacher You Went Right On*, illustrated in various art styles and media by twenty-eight artists. Both are poetry books, but so very different in tone and attitude. The Adoff story is warm and affectionate and depicts the vivacious activities and feelings of an interracial family. The Cullum book is a cynical commentary about life in some of our classrooms and emphasizes the harsh realities and unpleasant conditions that exist in them. There are few children within the age range which usually enjoys the Mother Goose rhymes who could appreciate the offbeat humor depicted in the illustrations that fill *The Chas. Addams Mother Goose*. However, there is little doubt that this oversized, colorful picture book would be enjoyed by the sophisticated teen-ager and adult. Conversely, *The Tall Book of Mother Goose* by Feodor Rojankovsky interprets the rhymes as most modern younger children would imagine

7. Harlin Quist, "Children's Book Production in the U.S.A.," *Graphis* 23 (1967): 312.

them. Rojankovsky's characters are natural-looking youngsters dressed in contemporary clothes, and the animals are delightfully appealing and expressive.

Fortunately, some books are multileveled. Readers within several age ranges could read *A Flying Saucer Full of Spaghetti* by Fernando Krahn; the level of maturity of the individual children within each designated age range will determine their interpretation of this wordless book. The child of kindergarten or primary-school age will recognize this as a story about a small girl and mischievous, snoopy, and scheming elves. The child around ten or so, who is likely to have acquired a little knowledge and perceptivity about some of the ills of society may recognize this picture story as a commentary about social inequities. The reader of primary-school age would very likely recognize the tragedy that occurs when runaway horses kill Old Soap's dog in *Through the Window*, written and illustrated by Charles Keeping. He would probably be a few years older before he would recognize the symbolism which this talented expressionistic artist employed so effectively in his paintings to emphasize that the little boy in the story refused to come to grips with the hard realities of life, preferring to stay safe and warm at home behind the window curtains.

The integrity of the young reader must not be violated by an interpretation that is coy or condescending. Instead, the artists must radiate a rich, human warmth and a depth of emotion. The charming, unpretentious picture book by Ezra Jack Keats, entitled *The Snowy Day*, is worthy of mention in this respect. The colorful pictures done in collage and paint, and the simply-written, brief text constitute an appealing and youthful portrayal of a little boy's pleasure on a snowy day. The youngster joyfully crunches in the snow, makes tracks with his feet and a stick, makes a snowman and snowballs, and makes angels in the snow. An artist such as Keats knows (as must any book artist) how to use his artistic talents to reach and challenge young readers. He knows how to use his talents to help his readers relax and enjoy their illustrated books.

Artistic Talent Prevails.   Only really good illustrations can bring the conceptions of an author to completion. They should not merely decorate the book. Nor should they be merely a compilation of independent pictures in which the artist's only concern is to have *his* say. Ideally, there is a harmonious combination of textual and pictorial elements in any book that includes illustrations. Each component is significant and, in a picture book, each is of relatively equal importance. Admittedly, the story idea or theme in any book must come first. This rule is applicable to the picture book, too.

When creating pictures he intends to use to illustrate a story, the artist's role is to make pictures that have storytelling qualities. He has to reveal in visual form the characters and setting of the story. This is especially important for the young child who "reads" the story through the pictures. An effective picture must be made out of each page. Each page must reveal action; each must be a change of scene. When one looks through a picture book, one should have the feeling that he is sitting through a theatrical spectacle.

In his acceptance speech when he was awarded the Caldecott Medal for his illustrations in *May I Bring a Friend?* by Beatrice Schenk de

Copyright © 1964 by Beatrice Schenk de Regniers. Illustrated by Beni Montresor from *May I Bring a Friend.* Used by permission of Atheneum Publishers.

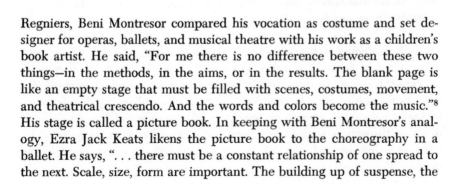

Regniers, Beni Montresor compared his vocation as costume and set designer for operas, ballets, and musical theatre with his work as a children's book artist. He said, "For me there is no difference between these two things—in the methods, in the aims, or in the results. The blank page is like an empty stage that must be filled with scenes, costumes, movement, and theatrical crescendo. And the words and colors become the music."[8] His stage is called a picture book. In keeping with Beni Montresor's analogy, Ezra Jack Keats likens the picture book to the choreography in a ballet. He says, ". . . there must be a constant relationship of one spread to the next. Scale, size, form are important. The building up of suspense, the

8. Beni Montresor, "Caldecott Award Acceptance," *The Horn Book Magazine* 41 (August 1965): 370.

dramatic effect of one big drawing, one small one, are important in the turning of the pages. Each drawing is considered not in itself, but in relationship to the rest of the book. The artist must keep in mind drama, continuity, contrast, mood."[9]

A whole succession of pictures in a book must make an effective, clear, and simple design that will get the reader's attention and set the mood of the story. This was done aptly in Janice Udry's *The Moon Jumpers*, in which Maurice Sendak's luminous illustrations capture the joyous feeling of four children dancing in their bare feet in the moonlight of a quiet summer evening. The illustrations in this stunning book, which was a runner-up for the Caldecott Medal in 1960, are done in full color.

One might ask at this point, "Will children appreciate and grasp the meaning of a well-designed book?" Children crave something that is inspired and attractive; nonetheless, they will take whatever is at hand. Good taste can be acquired, but if children are to get on the path that will lead them to recognize beautiful things, they must be given those that are well-designed, are pleasing to look at, and will enrich their lives. Handsome books must be placed within their sight and reach, and then they must be encouraged subtly and gently to read these books. A child can develop an appreciation of beauty through his handling of well-illustrated books. One need not settle for the lifeless illustrations that crowd the pages of many children's books when quantities of beautiful and vital illustrations are available at libraries and book stores merely for the asking. It is not expecting too much that the books published for children of all ages should include drawings that are made by the greatest artists. It is never too early to give a young child books that are illustrated with the best and most substantial pictures so that his inborn tendencies to be imaginative and curious do not dwindle into dormancy or that his creative spirit becomes stunted by lack of nourishment.

Illustrations Go Beyond the Text.   Book illustrations should constitute a work of decoration and reflect a well-planned design, but they must accomplish still more than this. Whether the artist is making pictures for a picture book or for a book which is to contain only a few illustrations, he must help the reader to understand and visualize the text, to recreate the significant scenes and ideas from the story. The illustrations must be the equivalent of each significant emotion and thought expressed in the text.

9. Erma Perry, "The Gentle World of Ezra Jack Keats," *American Artist* 35 (September 1971):49-50.

Woodcuts by Gil Miret from the book *Wigwam in the City* by Barbara C. Smucker. Copyright © 1966 by Barbara C. Smucker. Reproduced with permission of E. P. Dutton & Co., Inc.

There are only about seven illustrations in Barbara C. Smucker's story, *Wigwam in the City*, yet the superb woodcut prints of the artist, Gil Miret, depict so well the experiences and the emotions of Susan Bearskin and her family when they leave their reservation home in Lac du Flambeau, Wisconsin and move to Chicago. These few illustrations do indeed have relevance to the text, but they accomplish much more than merely help the reader interpret the text. Gil Miret, as should any accomplished book artist, created illustrations that do more than serve as a neutral vehicle for transmitting the text of the story. The illustrations encourage the reader to exercise his own imagination and go beyond the text. This is an essential and admirable goal of the book artist, for the awakening and strengthening of the imagination is one of the chief factors in the development of a child's mind.

Frequently, the artist is called upon to create illustrations that will cause the reader to enlarge on story elements that were only hinted at in the text. In order to do this, the artist must offer a sufficient number of pictures with enough detail in each so that the reader can use them as a guide to extending the text and recalling the story. Once he has heard the story, the young reader should be able to retell it by studying the details in the pictures. Robert Quackenbush has accomplished this with his illustrations for Jane Yolen's *The Wizard Islands* which is a collection of factual, legendary, and fanciful tales about various new and ancient islands throughout the world. Photographs, facsimiles of old documents and maps, plus many original black charcoal pencil drawings by Quackenbush enrich and enlarge on Ms. Yolen's host of spine-tingling stories. *The Wizard Islands* was included among the 1974 Children's Book Showcase titles.

Beatrix Potter, who seems to have been a natural book illustrator, created what some authorities consider to be almost perfect picture books. She expressed herself freely in her drawings and her brief texts. Ms. Potter's books have a colored picture on every spread, and on each page the text is limited to concise, simple sentences. Stories and pictures in *The Tale of Peter Rabbit* and *The Tale of Jemima Puddle-Duck,* as well as in her other tales of creatures of the farm and field are evidence of her sense of beauty, imaginative approach, and feelings for the countryside she loved.

There are innumerable good illustrators of children's picture books. Certain graphic designers whose names quickly come to mind because their illustrations carry far more detail and more substance than appears in the text, have brought fresh life to children's books over the last few years. For example, one such artist is Celestino Piatti, widely known in Switzerland as an outstanding graphic designer, who authored and illustrated *The Happy Owls.* His work has the essential quality of communication and is brilliantly decorative as well. In his designs, the white paper is as important as the flat, colored poster illustrations. One might mention here Jacob Lawrence's *Harriet and the Promised Land,* a landmark among familiar titles dealing with black history. Eloquent and powerful expressionistic paintings (many of them surrealistic!) accompany this ballad about Harriet Tubman. When accompanied by the simple and vigorously rhythmic verse, the grotesque and disproportionate size of body parts, especially the hand of the scrub woman, the deathlike skulls, bony appearance of the heads, and the stark, white teeth expressing the agony of the oppressed, can only create an unforgettable and consuming spiritual experience. These paintings would rank as perhaps the most powerful that have been used to illustrate a picture book.

Leo Lionni, an Amsterdam-born American, is another graphic designer who devotes much time and effort to finding new methods of visual communication. A talented painter and graphic designer, Lionni has created several stunning picture books. Two of his most widely acclaimed books are *Inch by Inch* and *The Biggest House in the World.* Each book has a rather brief text. Each is illustrated with original and imaginative, beautifully colored pictures. *Inch by Inch* is done in rice paper collage. The pages of *The Biggest House in the World* are filled with dramatic paintings, bold in design, rich in color.

There are the sumptuous, gloriously colored works of Alois Carigiet, a Swiss artist, who illustrated *A Bell for Ursli* and *The Snowstorm,* both of which were written by Selina Chonz. Carigiet's paintings are large, done in full, radiant color, and filled with alluring detail. His books have the appearance of the classic picture book, and yet Carigiet's art is exquisitely modern. He was awarded a Hans Christian Andersen International Children's Book Medal in 1966.

Among the most productive and successful of the contemporary illustrators are Alice and Martin Provensen. Their drawings in *The Charge of the Light Brigade* are comparable to an early illumination or a Mogul painting. This picture book is a stunning graphic interpretation of Tennyson's poem. The double-spread paintings are among the most beautiful and most dramatic pieces of illustration to appear in recent years and should be considered a significant contribution to book art.

Color and Shading May Be a Goal.   Plenty of rich, harmonious color has been an important goal in children's literature. Color can be one way to attract children's attention to a book. More important, perhaps, is the fact that a major aim of color is to serve an expressive rather than a representational color sense. According to some art critics, absolute imitation of color can scarcely by called art for it expresses so little of the human mind.

Examination of the colored illustrations that are included in children's books will reveal that few of the contemporary artists and lithographers do try to present a sketch of a subject as it *really* is. Even the representational artists seem to go to great length to avoid the imitation of nature. Most book artists use tones and shades of color to express form as they see it, not as an attempt to imitate that form. Thus, the artist should be encouraged to use color freely.

If one agrees with this attitude toward color, he will ignore the association of color, and he will not feel the need to copy the color of an object literally in order to aid realism. Free use of color will permit the artist (and the reader of a text illustrated with colored illustrations) to express his own feelings and emotions toward the subject.

It is extremely difficult to be objective when evaluating the book artist's use of color. Perusal of some of the critical reviews of children's picture books will reveal that by no means is there agreement among graphic artists or authorities in children's literature as to color harmony or "suitable" colors for children's books. There is very little agreement as to whether or not the colors used in any one book have helped to tell the author's message clearly. Each book reviewer will have a different opinion as to what he sees in the illustrations—or in the story, for that matter. For instance, one critic may feel that the colors Jacob Lawrence has used in *Harriet and the Promised Land* are "out of harmony" and unsuitable for children. Another will find the contrasting color combinations bold and angry, but completely appropriate for the author's message and for the audience to whom this moving narrative verse is addressed. Likewise, one may find that the colors used in Edward Lear and Ogden Nash's *The Scroobious Pip* are in delightful unity with the text. He may welcome the subtle distinctions between the warm and cool shades that Nancy Ekholm Burkert has used. Another reviewer may find that the combination of color shades used in *The Scroobious Pip* are too quiet, much too subtle to move the young reader.

In an article in which she reviewed the AIGA Children's Book Show that opened at the New York Public Library on March 6, 1961, Edna Beilenson stated that such color combinations as cerise, yellow, and clear blue against a background of black and white, or shades of blue-green and violet, are not suitable for young children. Indeed, they are much more suitable, says Ms. Beilenson, for a new perfume by Channel or for a gown by Schiaparelli or Oleg Cassini.[10]

Acceptance or rejection of Ms. Beilenson's comment about colors "appropriate" for young children will depend largely upon personal opinion. One might bear in mind that a child is a product of his times, and that today these color combinations are considered by some art educators to be appropriate for children as well as for adults. Furthermore, each artist brings his unique perceptions to a story. His interpretations and the colors he finds appropriate to express his thoughts and feelings about the subject will, and should, differ from those of another artist. This individuality should be respected.

Antonella Bolliger-Savelli and Brian Wildsmith make exquisite use of brilliant colors in their illustrations. Ms. Bolliger-Savelli's collage illustrations are created by clever arrangements of flat, deep, and brightly colored paper cutouts. The two stories about an adventure-prone striped knitted cat which will delight the younger child are *The Knitted Cat* and *The Mouse and the Knitted Cat*. Brian Wildsmith's works, painted in gouache, are usually full color, and his style is representational with abstract ten-

10. Edna Beilenson, "The AIGA Children's Book Show," *Publisher's Weekly* 180 (6 March 1961): 69-72.

dencies. For example, in *Brian Wildsmith's 1, 2, 3's*, the numbers one through ten are illustrated with simple basic forms of the rectangle, the triangle, and the circle. His books employ a splendor of color combining most beautifully and effectively, clear and bright shades of orange, blue, black, chartreuse, fuchsia, purple, and yellow. Today's young moderns thoroughly enjoy these combinations, despite the opinions of some graphic critics to the contrary.

Rich, strong watercolors with pen and india ink are used by Tony Chen for the meticulously conceived and executed illustrations in *Honschi*. Chen studied the habits and habitats of the chickadee in preparation for this book. He found it to be a staunch, beautiful "jewel of nature" and that is exactly the way he paints it. The birds move gracefully and continuously from left to right, from page to page. The three dimensional qualities in his Japanese landscape paintings and his marvelous sense of color and patterns help his viewers to get a sense of song and feeling of the tiny creatures, even the smells of each and every flower as they read about this fragile but staunch chickadee who wins his battle for survival and freedom.

Contrasting the use of brilliant color found in Wildsmith's and Tony Chen's books are the soft, soothing colors found in *The Scroobious Pip*, illustrated by Nancy Ekholm Burkert, and mentioned previously. Ms. Burkert's exquisite brush-and-ink drawings, which would also appeal to young readers, delineate the teeming forms of life celebrated in this rhythmic poem in which all the animals in the world gather around a strange inscrutable creature that is part bird, part beast, part insect, and part fish. The drawings are representational, with emphasis on craftsmanship and particularization. Ms. Burkert's concept of Pip is based on Edward Lear's own small pen drawings that were included in his incomplete manuscript, which is now available in Harvard University's Houghton Library in Cambridge, Massachusetts.[11]

All four of these artists, Bolliger-Savelli, Chen, Wildsmith, and Burkert, make wide use of marvelous color combinations, and the writer does think they are suitable for children growing up in today's world. None of the artists referred to overstrains the use of color, nor does he use it as superficial decoration. Admittedly, there are some children's books which contain paintings in heavy garish colors. Some contain illustrations that are done in painting techniques that overwhelm the narrative they are supposed to depict. But quantities of beautiful books are available and should be read to children and examined by them.

11. Edward Lear and Ogden Nash, *The Scroobious Pip*, illustrated by Nancy Ekholm Burkert (New York: Harper & Row, Publishers, 1968), foreword.

Children enjoy books illustrated in monochrome (in one color and white), if the figures stand out enough and express action and vitality. There are several picture books done in monochrome, for example, *The Biggest Bear* by Lynd Ward, *Picture Bible* by Felix Hoffmann, and *The Silver Pony* by Lynd Ward. Robert McCloskey's Caldecott Medal book, *Make Way for Ducklings,* is monochromatic (sepia) and his delightful story, *One Morning in Maine,* is done in blue and white. A tense drama in animal life, the compelling story of a skunk and an owl's struggle for survival, is told in John Schoenherr's *The Barn,* with text and black-and-white pictures. These artists do not depend upon color to state their messages. Instead, they make use of shading to suggest light, dark, and color. The illustrations in each of the books cited above are good and are fully enjoyed and appreciated by children who see them.

Sizes and Shapes Should Vary.   The contents of the illustrated books for children vary, as do the style of writing and the illustrations. It is desirable, also, that there be considerable variation in the sizes and shapes of the books that are made available to the young reader. Children delight in handling the very big, the tiny, the thick, the square, the rectangular, and the tall picture books. Oftentimes, the very shape of the book adds more credibility to the story line. The size and shape of the book can also emphasize the mood of the story or can make the setting more explicit and believable.

Included in a good picture-book collection would be books such as the following. Feodor Rojankovsky's *The Tall Book of Mother Goose* is a tall slim book whose characters illustrating these beloved rhymes are natural-looking and appealing. *The Book of Nursery and Mother Goose Rhymes* by Marguerite de Angeli is just the opposite of Rojankovsky's book. It is thick and broad and contains numerous full-page illustrations painted in soft pastels. The characters are beautiful, delicate creatures. Maurice Sendak's *Nutshell Library* is a package of four wonderfully humorous books. Measuring only 3¾ inches in height, each little book offers much to the young reader. Illustrated with pen drawings in Sendak's wonderful cartoon style, the books interpret the months of the year, the alphabet, the numbers from one through ten, and a cautionary tale. Captivating picture books by Beatrix Potter, such as *The Tale of Jemima Puddle-Duck* or *The Tale of Peter Rabbit,* contain full-color spreads and are only an inch or so bigger than the four volumes of the *Nutshell Library* and are also a must in a picture-book collection. Another must is the big rectangular book by Issac Bashevis Singer, entitled *Mazel and Schlimazel or the Milk of a Lioness,* which contains strong, heavily-lined, colored illustrations by Mar-

Illustration for "Alligators All Around" from *Nutshell Library*, written and illustrated by Maurice Sendak. Copyright © 1962 by Maurice Sendak. Reprinted with permission of Harper & Row, Publishers.

got Zemach. Pictures in this book effectively underlie the humor and the tradition quality of this Yiddish folktale.

Other Considerations.   Writers of good children's books do not depend entirely upon help from the graphic artists, for literature has its own forms of expression. Whether or not illustrations accompany the text, the language in the text must create its own conceptions. When illustrations are used, the artist may not impose his conceptions of the story with definitiveness, or precise literalness, for this would "interfere in a very unpleasant way with the readers' own dreams."[12] The illustrations must be created in a manner that permits the reader to be completely free to use his own creative and imaginative powers when interpreting the words and the pictures.

A succession of flashy, experimental, or unusual pictures in a book may very well attract a child's attention, but the attention of the reader will not be held long by the illustrations alone. The story that is told by both the text and the illustrations must be a good one. It may be long or short, but it must be a story that is of interest to the reader. The language used to tell the story must be rich in imagery. It must be void of cliches, and it must encourage the reader to sense, in his own youthful way, the composition, the perspective, and the use of color in the illustrations. Janice Udry's *The Moon Jumpers* is an excursion into the beautiful world

12. Roger Duviosin, "Children's Book Illustration: The Pleasure and Problems," *Top of the News* 22 (November 1965):30.

of quality literature and genuine art, an expression of beauty which should be in every illustrated book, for beautiful expression denotes quality.

Beautiful expression can be found in other illustrated stories too, but in each case, the stories must be told with language that is precise, colorful, and descriptive. Seldom is beauty of expression found in a book in which the vocabulary is controlled, for then the writer is too restricted to create a beautiful story. The vocabulary control does not permit him the freedom and range necessary for imaginative creative writing.

Wingfin and Topple, a large handsome picture book, is written in exquisite poetic form by Evans G. Valens, Jr., and is illustrated by Clement Hurd with linoleum-block prints on the grain of weathered wood. Both text and illustrations create fascinating images that capture the beauty and vastness of the sea, sky, and water. Both forms of artistic expression complement the other; each is made more beautiful by the presence of the other.

The text and the illustrations are not the only factors to be considered when appraising an illustrated book. There are several other important elements that can enhance the beauty of a volume and result in a fine illustrated book (as being distinguished from a book with fine illustrations). As we stated earlier, decisions must be made as to such aesthetic concerns as the shape and size of the book, whether the illustrations will be in color or in black and white, and the number of colors, if the decision is made to have color illustrations. Typeface that is compatible with the style and color illustrations must be selected, too. As a rule, these decisions are made by the artist, together with the art director and the editor of the publishing company. This is the team that must interpret the story and produce a book which will be of interest to young readers, a book which they can read and look at with pleasure.

Summary

The illustrated book is defined as any book in which the text is accompanied by illustrations that are pertinent to the text. The picture book is a special form of an illustrated book. In the picture book, there is a thorough fusion of pictures and words.

Qualities which should characterize the illustrations in children's books have been cited. The contents of the story and the illustrations must have significance to the young reader. The illustrations should heighten and extend the reader's awareness of the world around him. They should lead him to an appreciation of beauty. The style and content of the illustrations should be childlike; that is, they should be neither coy nor condescending, nor should they be adultlike in the level of sophistication. The illustrations should have storytelling qualities so that such literary components as action, mood, theme, setting, and story line are revealed. They should enlarge upon the story elements that were hinted at in the text and should include details that will awaken and strengthen the imagination of the reader and permit him to interpret the words and pictures in a manner that is unique to him.

Rich and harmonious color should be used to serve an expressive, rather than a representational, purpose. Monochrome and black-and-white illustrations are appropriate for use in children's books, too, if the shading and contrasts are used so that the figures stand out, so that action is expressed, and so that an adequate degree of warmth and vitality is reflected. Sizes and shapes of the illustrated books for children should vary, as should the style of writing and the styles of art that are used to tell and interpret the story.

SELECTED REFERENCES

ABRAHAM, JEAN-PIERRE. *The Pigeon Man.* Illustrated by Alan E. Cober. New York: Harlin Quist Books, 1971.

ADDAMS, CHARLES. *The Chas. Addams Mother Goose.* Illustrated by Charles Addams. New York: Harper & Row, Publishers, 1967.

ADOFF, ARNOLD. *Black Is Brown Is Tan.* Illustrated by Emily A. McCully. New York: Harper & Row, Publishers, 1973.

ARDIZONNE, EDWARD. *The Wrong Side of the Bed.* Illustrated by Edward Ardizonne. New York: Doubleday & Co., 1970.

ATWOOD, ANN. *Haiku: The Mood of Earth.* Illustrated with photographs by Ann Atwood. New York: Charles Scribner's Sons, 1971.

BEMELMANS, LUDWIG. *Madeline.* Illustrated by Ludwig Bemelmans. New York: Viking Press, 1939.

BISHOP, ELIZABETH. *The Ballad of the Burglar of Babylon.* Illustrated by Ann Grifalconi. New York: Farrar, Straus & Giroux, 1968.

BOLLIGER-SAVELLI, ANTONELLA. *The Knitted Cat.* Illustrated by Antonella Bolliger-Savelli. New York: Macmillan Co., 1972.

———. *The Mouse and the Knitted Cat.* Illustrated by Antonella Bolliger-Savelli. New York: Macmillan Co., 1974.

BRYANT, SARA CONE. *The Burning Rice Fields.* Illustrated by Mamoru Funai. New York: Holt, Rinehart & Winston, 1963.

CHONZ, SELINA. *A Bell for Ursli.* Illustrated by Alois Carigiet. New York: Henry Z. Walck, 1953.

———. *The Snowstorm.* Illustrated by Alois Carigiet. New York: Henry Z. Walck, 1958.

CULLUM, ALBERT. *The Geranium on the Window Sill Just Died but Teacher You Went Right On.* Illustrated by twenty-eight artists. New York: Harlin Quist Books, 1971.

DE ANGELI, MARGUERITE. *The Book of Nursery and Mother Goose Rhymes.* New York: Doubleday & Co., 1954.

DE REGNIERS, BEATRICE SCHENK. *May I Bring a Friend?* Illustrated by Beni Montresor. New York: Atheneum Publishers, 1964.

FEELINGS, TOM. *Black Pilgrimage.* Illustrated by Tom Feelings. New York: Lothrop, Lee & Shepard Co., 1972.

GLASGOW, ALINE. *Honschi.* Illustrated by Tony Chen. New York: Parents' Magazine Press, 1972.

HEYWARD, DU BOSE. *The Country Bunny and the Little Gold Shoes.* Illustrated by Marjorie Flack. Boston: Houghton Mifflin Co., 1939.

HILL, ELIZABETH STARR. *Evan's Corner.* Illustrated by Nancy Grossman. New York: Holt, Rinehart & Winston, 1967.

HODGES, MARGARET. *The Wave.* Illustrated by Blair Lent. Boston: Houghton Mifflin Co., 1964.

HOFFMANN, FELIX. *Picture Bible.* Illustrated by Felix Hoffmann.

JARRELL, RANDALL. *The Bat-Poet.* Illustrated by Maurice Sendak. New York: Macmillan Co., 1964.

KEATS, EZRA JACK. *Peter's Chair.* Illustrated by Ezra Jack Keats. New York: Harper & Row, Publishers, 1967.

———. *The Snowy Day.* Illustrated by Ezra Jack Keats. New York: Viking Press, 1962.

KEEPING, CHARLES. *Through the Window.* Illustrated by Charles Keeping. New York: Franklin Watts, 1970.

KRAHN, FERNANDO. *A Flying Saucer Full of Spaghetti.* Illustrated by Fernando Krahn. New York: E. P. Dutton & Co., 1970.

LAWRENCE, JACOB. *Harriet and the Promised Land.* Illustrated by Jacob Lawrence. New York: Windmill Books, Simon & Schuster, 1968.

LEAR, EDWARD and NASH, OGDEN. *The Scroobious Pip.* Illustrated by Nancy Ekholm Burkert. New York: Harper & Row, Publishers, 1968.

LIFTON, BETTY JEAN. *Return to Hiroshima.* Illustrated with photographs by Eikoh Hosoe. New York: Atheneum Publishers, 1970.

LIONNI, LEO. *The Biggest House in the World.* Illustrated by Leo Lionni. New York: Pantheon Books, 1968.

———. *Inch by Inch.* Illustrated by Leo Lionni. New York: Ivan Obolensky, 1960.

MCCLOSKEY, ROBERT. *Make Way for Ducklings.* Illustrated by Robert McCloskey. New York: Viking Press, 1941.

———. *One Morning in Maine.* Illustrated by Robert McCloskey. New York: Viking Press, 1952.

———. *Time of Wonder.* Illustrated by Robert McCloskey. New York: Viking Press, 1957.

MENDOZA, GEORGE. *The Inspector.* Illustrated by Peter Parnall. New York: Doubleday & Co., 1970.

PERRINE, MARY. *Salt Boy.* Illustrated by Leonard Weisgard. New York: Houghton Mifflin Co., 1968.

POTTER, BEATRIX. *The Tale of Jemima Puddle-Duck.* Illustrated by Beatrix Potter. New York: Frederick Warne & Co., 1908.

———. *The Tale of Peter Rabbit.* Illustrated by Beatrix Potter. New York: Frederick Warne & Co., 1902.

ROJANKOVSKY, FEODOR. *The Tall Book of Mother Goose.* Illustrated by Feodor Rojankovsky. New York: Harper & Row, Publishers, 1942.

SCHOENHERR, JOHN. *The Barn.* Illustrated by John Schoenherr. Boston: Little, Brown & Co., 1968.

SENDAK, MAURICE. *The Nutshell Library.* Illustrated by Maurice Sendak. New York: Harper & Row, Publishers, 1962.

———. *Where the Wild Things Are.* Illustrated by Maurice Sendak. New York: Harper & Row, Publishers, 1963.

SINGER, ISAAC BASHEVIS. *Mazel and Schlimazel or the Milk of a Lioness.* Illustrated by Margot Zemach. New York: Farrar, Straus & Giroux, 1968.

SMUCKER, BARBARA C. *Wigwam in the City.* Illustrated by Gil Miret. New York: E. P. Dutton & Co., 1966.

TENNYSON, ALFRED LORD. *The Charge of the Light Brigade.* Illustrated by Alice and Martin Provensen. New York: Golden Press, 1964.

UDRY, JANICE. *Moon Jumpers.* Illustrated by Maurice Sendak. New York: Harper & Row, Publishers, 1959.

UENO, NORIKO. *Elephant Buttons.* Illustrated by Noriko Ueno. New York: Harper & Row, Publishers, 1973.

VALENS, EVANS G., JR. *Wildfire.* Illustrated by Clement Hurd. Cleveland: World Publishing Co., 1963.

——. *Wingfin and Topple.* Illustrated by Clement Hurd. Cleveland: World Publishing Co., 1962.

WABER, BERNARD. *An Anteater Named Arthur.* Illustrated by Bernard Waber. Boston: Houghton Mifflin Co., 1967.

WARD, LYND. *The Biggest Bear.* Illustrated by Lynd Ward. Boston: Houghton Mifflin Co., 1952.

———. *The Silver Pony: A Story in Pictures.* Illustrated by Lynd Ward. Boston: Houghton Mifflin Co., 1973.

WEIK, MARY HAYS. *The Jazz Man.* Illustrated by Ann Grifalconi. New York: Atheneum Publishers, 1966.

WILDSMITH, BRIAN. *Brian Wildsmith's 1,2,3's.* New York: Franklin Watts, 1965.

YASHIMA, TARO. *Crow Boy.* Illustrated by Taro Yashima. New York: Viking Press, 1955.

YOLEN, JANE. *The Wizard Islands.* Illustrated by Robert Quackenbush. New York: Thomas Y. Crowell Co., 1973.

chapter 2
styles of art
in children's books

Literature is an art form which has its own means of expression. The content as well as other narrative elements of literature provide the materials with which the graphic artist builds an attractive page and gives order and visual qualities to that page.[1] It is in the order, in the arrangement of line and color, that the style of art can be identified.

The art in our modern picture books must say something to children and must say it in a loose way so that the reader is free to bring his own interpretation to the writing and to the book illustrations. Uri Shulevitz, noted illustrator who has been cited by the Society of Illustrators and the American Institute of Graphic Arts, stated that he usually tries to suggest and evoke rather than state rigidly, so as to encourage the child to participate actively, filling in with his own imagination. Shulevitz emphasized that this approach is based on the belief that his audience is intelligent and active rather than passive.[2] Furthermore, the children's book artist should express his ideas in a manner that is so original and interesting to the reader that the book cannot be ignored.

Inventive book design and book illustration can be found in many of the children's books that have been published in recent years. Consider the emphatic typography and cheerful assortment of soft, bright colors for the wood engravings in Antonio Frasconi's *See Again, Say Again.* This delightful, inventive approach to book design extends an irresistible invitation to the young reading audience. Tasha Tudor's series, *A Is for Annabelle, 1 Is One,* and *Around the Year,* with their charmingly delicate pastel illustrations, are quickly recognized as books that would be cherished by children

1. Roger Duvoisin, "Children's Book Illustration: The Pleasure and Problems," *Top of the News* 22 (November 1965):31.

2. Lee Kingman, Joanna Foster, and Ruth Giles Lontoft, "Uri Shulevitz," *Illustrators of Children's Books, 1957-1966* (Boston: The Horn Book, 1968), p. 174.

the world over. The illustrative art in these books, as in quantities of other children's books, is imaginative, dramatic, and expressive. The art in each book is typified by originality. It is an orginality which is not at all super- ficial as so often happens when an artist is too conscious of making his illustrations "new," when his attention has been directed toward making the expression different rather than on the thoughts he was supposed to express. There is little room for the children's book artist who strives for novelty merely by being different, and who is giving vent to eccentricity through illustrating books. This defeats the purpose of the book. A book is intended to be read, and the illustrations must legitimately help deliver the writer's message.

Whether or not the artist is illustrating his own story or that written by another, the art used throughout the book must reflect the individual- ness of the painter and must vouchsafe and encourage individualness of perception of the viewer of his art.[3] The book artist is expected to go beyond the appeal of the literal level approach to visual communication. He should create illustrations that are not only arresting, captivating, and convincing, but imaginative, dramatic and entertaining as well. Only then has he fulfilled his obligation to his audience and to more personal stan- dards.[4] Only then will he allow his readers one of the most effective methods for esthetic development and eventual enjoyment.

It does not follow necessarily that the personality of the book artist is destroyed, or that he becomes a servant to the writer. The talented illus- trator can still use his own creative powers. His personality can still be preserved through the spirit of the particular literary selection he is illus- trating. Marcia Brown is an outstanding example of a contemporary artist who meets the requirements of each story that she illustrates, but manages to do so on her own terms. Each of her picture books is her very own per- sonal creation despite the fact that many of them contain illustrations of well-known folktales. She used vigorous crayon and gouache drawings to illustrate *The Three Billy Goats Gruff*, bold and graceful woodcut designs in *Once a Mouse*, and delicate drawings in pen line and colored crayon for *Cinderella*. In each book, Marcia Brown retains the mood and period of time peculiar to the traditional text, but she makes her own exquisite pic- tures, using different media and art styles for each story. The story line and the illustrations for each book are undeniably compatible.

3. Ben Shahn, *The Shape of Content* (Cambridge: Harvard University Press, 1957), p. 123.

4. Paul Rand, *Thoughts on Design* (New York: Van Nostrand Reinhold Co., 1970), p. 95.

Style in illustrative art, like style in writing, is a rather elusive quality. It is influenced by the content and the mood of the story. It is also influenced by the age of the reader as well as the artist's concept of his audience. The younger the child, the more representational the art style should be. To some extent, the younger the child, the more conservative the artist will have to be in his use of space, in his use of the combinations and color relations, in the dramatic use of forms and lines, and in his treatment of surfaces. If the artist views children as being only sweet and angelic, if he tends to be condescending in his way with children, in all probability this will be revealed in the style of art used in his illustrations. On the contrary, if he respects his young audience, if he believes they have the maturity and intelligence necessary to appreciate and understand illustrations that are more impressionistic and sophisticated in nature, this will be evident in his illustrations.

There are other factors that influence an artist's style. Among these are interrelated factors such as the basic personality of the artist, his creative talent, the media he uses to make his pictures, and his mastery of the media and techniques employed.

We are witnessing an era in which there is an astonishing wealth of creative talent involved in illustrating books for children. The artists are rapidly breaking away from tradition. Their book designs and styles reveal independent thinking and respect for experimentation. There is an ever-mounting number of artists who speak freely, who refuse to succumb to the pressures of popular taste. Book artists make use of unconventional and contemporary art work as well as of the more conventional.

The influence of the ideas of fine artists is readily recognized in today's styles of art used in children's book illustrations. In fact, practically every artistic style suggestive of famous artists such as Raol Dufy, Wassily Kandinsky, Paul Klee, Marc Chagall, Paul Cézanne, Vincent Van Gogh, and others can be identified in the illustrations of many modern picture books.

All the graphic arts have profited from the discoveries that the painters made as they moved toward abstraction, although the pure abstract painter has never illustrated books. The abstractionist must completely eliminate the subject in conceiving his painting. Thus he cannot apply his art in book illustration.[5] Nonetheless, children's book artists have been influenced greatly by the evolution of painting toward abstraction. Their illustrations often hint at or use symbols, illusions, and imagery to varying degrees.

5. Duvoisin, "Children's Book Illustration," p. 30-31.

A catholicity of taste is often displayed in the pages of modern children's books. Numerous remarkable books can be found in which the modern book artists have assimilated the various art styles—representationalism, cubism, expressionism, impressionism, surrealism, and the pointillist technique. Also, there is a strong movement toward combining folkloristic elements with a modern technique. No one school seems to predominate.

The wealth of shapes and sumptuous colors, the wonderfully original ideas and uninhibited experimentation in book design and art style, indicate how important children's book illustration currently is. This growing importance reveals to some extent, too, that much effort and creative ability is necessarily put forth in the making of good books for children. Each of these books is a reminder that there is much beauty to see in children's literature, and fine books can permit children to experience pleasure from books at an early age.

It is indeed gratifying that one can find well-designed and well-decorated children's books. When beautiful books are placed constantly within their sight and reach, children are more likely to grow to recognize and prefer the things that are beautiful. They will be less likely to settle for the second-rate and lifeless illustrations which crowd the pages of some children's books. There will always be the mediocre books, the ones issued by publishers who do not seem to care what kind of market they find for their books, or who succumb to expediency for temporary profit. Hopefully, if a young child has read and examined books that are tastefully and beautifully illustrated, he will learn to enjoy distinctive art in paintings and in books. Some educators and artists maintain that a child unconsciously learns to appreciate fine art, that is, he learns very early in life to appreciate order, rhythm, and interesting arrangements of color from the picture books he sees. Marcia Brown has emphasized that if a child habitually sees well-designed pages in the picture books, the varied and interesting shapes may start a chain of reactions within him that could continue into adulthood. She maintains that the child's discrimination, along with whatever segments of his individuality he can manage to preserve, will be his main defense against the bombardment of visual materials that he is likely to face during most of his waking hours.[6]

An illustration can show us new ways of seeing; it can give us our perception; it can give us a deeper understanding of the relation between nature and man. Great art is more than a mere record of nature and what

6. Marcia Brown, "Distinction in Picture Books," in *Illustrators of Children's Books, 1946-1956*, ed. Bertha Mahoney Miller et al. (Boston: Horn Book, 1958), pp. 6-10.

one sees. It is an expression of man's thoughts and feelings. However, a work of art must be more than expression of an artist's ideas and emotional responses. It must arouse in the viewer a kind of enjoyment that is long-lasting rather than one that is short-lived. Furthermore, a work of art must cause the viewer to stop and look, and then look again.

An artist's choice of style is a personal one. He needs a good eye for detail and a sensitivity to form. Regardless of the art style he uses to express his ideas and feelings, he needs a good memory for each of these. Artists of every age have interpreted reality in their own language of form and color. Since nature cannot be transcribed onto paper or canvas, it must be translated more simply by way of pictorial technique. Varied art styles have been originated by artists in their attempt to transmit their mental images and their feelings. An individual's taste with regard to literature and art is his own private concern. Be he a creator or a viewer of a work of art, he must be permitted to respond spontaneously and freely to these art forms, elsewise "mental despotism" ensues. For "whatever crushes individuality is despotism by whatever name it be called. . . . It is not by wearing down into uniformity all that is individual in themselves, but by cultivating it, (individualism) and calling it forth, within the limits imposed by the rights and interests of others that human beings become a noble and beautiful object of contemplation; and as the works partake the character of those who do them, by the same process human life also becomes more valuable to himself, and is therefore capable of being more valuable to others. There is a greater fullness of life about his own existence and when there is more life in the units there is more in the mass which is composed of them."[7] In the pages that follow some of the art styles used by contemporary book artists are identified.

Representational Art. The power of the realist, or representational artist, lies in his ability to select from an object or an event exactly what is necessary to tell, only the important facts that typify that object or event (but in a manner entirely different from that used by the photographer). The representational illustration is fairly decorative and transmits a feeling of formality and immediacy. It is concerned with the details and facts of the object itself. Outlines are exact and precise, as if one is viewing the scene closely. To a certain extent, there is a literalism and realism in a representational painting that controls the style, although a limited amount of distortion is permitted to emphasize the artist's message. Thus, a repre-

7. John Stuart Mill, *On Liberty*. Original edition, 1859. (New York: Gateway, 1956), pp. 86-87.

sentational artist may speak freely with color and lines, and with round, smooth, undulating, and living curves. Modern representational artists oftentimes are more concerned with the anatomy and the details of their model than they are with its inner nature. Yet they are experimental enough so that their creative efforts are recognized as original works of art.

The realist stays rather close to the appearance of the objects, but it must be remembered that each of us has a different perception of a single object. Each of us will bring his own interpretation to a particular incident. The book artist, like everyone else, selects or abstracts thoughts from his experience (or from the written word) emphasizing those features that are suitable, essential, and compatible to his purpose and personality.

The watercolor and pencil illustrations by Tasha Tudor are realistic in style, although they reveal the artist's nostalgic attitude toward nineteenth-century Americana. In her beautiful and quaint alphabet book, *A Is for Annabelle*, Ms. Tudor uses an old-fashioned, delicately illustrated doll. In *Becky's Birthday*, the story of a little farm girl of bygone years celebrating her tenth birthday, the artist-author depicts the happy events and surprises of the day in a realistic, and yet nostalgic manner, with charming and pleasing watercolor paintings, as well as with black-and-white pencil sketches. The wonderful candle-lighted, flower-bedecked birthday cake at the evening picnic party in the pasture by the river would bring pure delight to modern young readers.

Adrienne Adams, the creator of meticulously detailed scenes and attractive decorations for such books as Alice Goudey's *Butterfly Time* and *Houses from the Sea*, and the Charles Scribner's Sons edition of Hans Christian Andersen's *Thumbelina*, captures living pictures of a child's world of reality and make-believe. Adrienne Adams is a magnificent draftsman. Her concern for minute detail reveals as much, if not more, information than do the brief texts and stories she so often illustrates.

John Goodall's illustrations for his unique wordless books *Jacko, Paddy's Evening Out, and Shrewbettina's Birthday* are done in the representational art style. His appealing and happy fanciful stories are told with realistic and imaginatively detailed watercolor paintings on interpolated or alternating half and full pages. The first two named titles were included in the 1973 and 1974 Showcase, respectively.

The handsome and vigorous representational lithograph prints made by Lynd Ward to illustrate his own *The Silver Pony* and *The Biggest Bear* and May McNeer's *The Canadian Story* depict animals and the woodlands in a manner that would delight any naturalist. The anatomical detail of the male Indians and of the galloping horses which appear in Lynd Ward's illustrations for May McNeer's *The American Indian Story* are particularly

Illustration by Lynd Ward reprinted with the permission of
Farrar, Straus & Giroux, Inc.
from *The American Indian
Story* by May McNeer, copyright © 1963 by May McNeer
Ward and Lynd Ward.

impressive. The bodies are muscular and sinewy and transmit such a feeling of energy that the reader feels a sympathetic tension in his own
muscles. Ward's figures are creatures of almost perfect, normal propor-
tions, with the one exception that his well-muscled figures are somewhat
distorted about the chest, arms, and legs. It is this very distortion that
accentuates the stunning rhythmic movements of the horse, for example,
and the tremendous power and strength of the Indian. Lynd Ward's distortions serve only to highlight the books' messages. He does not use distortions as a tool of caricatures to attract attention, to satirize, or to provide
pure humor.

Also exemplary of this art style is the work done by John Schoenherr
for the matter-of-fact but emotion-arousing narratives *The Barn* written by
the artist himself and *The Wharf Rat* written by Miska Miles. In both picture books the habits of animals (a skunk and an owl in the first-named
book and a water rat in the latter) are realistically portrayed before and
after they are threatened with disaster. His carefully detailed representational illustrations are beautifully compatible with the forthright style of
writing found in each book.

Expressionistic Art. Expressionism is diametrically opposed to imita-
tional art. It is an expression of the artist's subjective emotion and leans

heavily toward abstraction. Expressionism is a form of impressionism. When compared to impressionism, it may seem to be an undisciplined or a less self-conscious interpretation of the effect that light has on an object. The essential or structural quality of the object, as opposed to the outward aspects of the object, is a primary concern of the expressionist. The artist's subjective emotional expression about his reality (or object) is another, and perhaps major, concern. Oftentimes, the first quick glance at an expressionist's painting will lead one to equate it with the primitivism of children's art. Consider Ludwig Bemelmans' work in the *Madeline* books. His sketches of the girls in the private school, the long-robed nuns, the circus scenes, and the scenes of Paris are typical of one type of expressionistic are and are rather childlike in nature. The influence of Paul Klee's and Raoul Dufy's styles of expressionism can be recognized, although Bemelmans made the expressionistic style his own and applied it in his picture books.

There seems to be a close relationship between the work of Joseph Low and Uri Shulevitz and that of Bemelmens. Low's sketches tend to be bolder and heavier than Bemelmans', but both evidence a rather whimsical tone in their sketches. The line drawings in Joseph Low's *Jack and the Beanstalk* as told by Walter de la Mare, and the line drawings and brush tones in his illustrations for *The Big Cheese* match the folk quality of each of these stories. Like Joseph Low, Uri Shulevitz, talented illustrator of

Illustration by Uri Shulevitz for *Charley Sang a Song* by H. R. Hays and Daniel Hays. Pictures copyright © 1964 by Uri Shulevitz. Reprinted with permission of Harper & Row, Publishers.

Illustration by Alice & Martin Provensen from *The Charge of the Light Brigade* by Alfred Lord Tennyson. Reproduced by permission. © Copyright 1964 by Western Publishing Company, Inc.

Charley Sang a Song by H. R. and Daniel Hays, often uses the reed pen to create his sketches. His figures reveal more action than do Low's or Bemelmans', however. All three artists have minimized the photographic function of painting and have traveled toward abstraction. None of the art by the three is entirely lacking in representative form, for too much of the objective forms is suggested in their style.

In a style suggestive of Vincent Van Gogh, especially his painting *The Starry Night*, Blair Lent depicts stirring action in water, clouds, and smoke. His effective use of swirls to denote the forcefulness of the tidal wave can be noticed in *The Wave*, Margaret Hodges' adaptation of Lafcadio Hearn's *Gleanings in Buddha-Fields*. The expressionistic illustrations in this version of the Japanese folktale were made by Lent with cardboard cuts and watercolor overlays. He has also used this same technique effectively for *Baba Yaga*, a Russian folktale retold by Ernest Small. Baba Yaga, a fascinating and harmless witch who likes only bad children, literally swirls through the pages of this picture book. Although he used different

Storm'd at with shot and shell,
While horse and hero fell,
They that had fought so well,
Came thro' the jaws of Death,
Back from the mouth of hell,
All that was left of them,
Left of six hundred.

media to illustrate the Caldecott Medal book *The Funny Little Woman*, retold by Arlene Mosel, the style is expressionistic. He used two contrasting media to illustrate this book, namely pen drawings to depict the outside world and soft acrylic paintings to designate the world underground.

Often an expressionistic painting or sculpture is marked by elongations and distortions, linearity and pointedness, as in the figures that make up the battle scenes in *The Charge of the Light Brigade*. The men and the horses in the Provensens' paintings typify the nonphotographic quality of an expressionistic work. Intricate ornamentation is stripped away, and the artists appear to be far more concerned with the emotional message of Tennyson's lyrics than they are with the qualities that would imitate the reality of the soldiers' features, garb, and fighting equipment, or with the qualities that would imitate the real shape of the horses or their battle gear. This kind of modern expressionism is also used effectively by Alice and Martin Provensen in the attractive little book entitled *The First Noel: from the Gospel of St. Luke*. Their style of art reflects the acceptance of the directness typical of the primitive or elemental foundation, but it also strongly adheres to the idea that an essential expressive form is basic to the artistic creation. Their work, in *The Charge of the Light Brigade* particularly, is marked by its directness and simplicity. The artists do pleasing color work using gouache.

If we compare the Provensens' paintings with Miroslav Sasek's work, we will see that although their paintings definitely differ in many respects, their style must be grouped under the term "expressionistic art." Sasek's stylized elongations, and the distortions of the human figure, buildings, and animals lean toward the subjective and imaginative. The virile color pattern paintings and the almost bold simplification of his forms bring forth from his readers a strong, almost overwhelmingly forceful reaction to the "personality" of each city he describes in his series of guide books. The art in Sasek's books is evidence of his vitality and creative accomplishment. One quickly recognizes why this series for children delights even adults.

Taro Yashima (Jun Iwamatsu) is one of the most talented expressionistic painters and illustrators of children's books. The tremendously expressive illustrations in *Umbrella* and *Plenty to Watch* were done in brush and pencil, media which Taro Yashima handles to perfection. In each book, the illustrations denote distinctive action and evoke high-powered emotionalism on the part of the readers.

Cubism. The cubist's paintings of the human figure and of landscapes are composed of planes with curved or straight edges, but the figure or landscape is broken into its theoretical components. Each component is analyzed and split into prismatic shapes. The cubist distorts shapes for the intellectual pleasure of seeing them differently and surprisingly, for it is felt this will enable him to get to the "essence of things" and grasp the "realities of life." The cubist uses this technique to cut across or compress time and thus, sees all aspects of a thing at once. One can see the influence of Paul Klee in Erich Fuch's *Journey to the Moon*, which records the eight-day mission in space of Apollo 11. The cubist's work is a construction of abstracted elements with colors used to unify the painting. The styles of Paul Cézanne and Wassily Kandinsky, in whose work the cubists found the basic principle of their formula, are both reflected in the paintings done by Brian Wildsmith. The works of these five artists evidence a quality that is structural and geometric. When their paintings are analyzed, one can only conclude that their works present poised forms and an organized structure. The fundamental idea behind this structure and order is that the artist feels that in his paintings he must rearrange the planes of an object in order to give his emotional or aesthetic response to it. Thus cubism is a form of expressionism. In many of the illustrations of Robert Louis Stevenson's *A Child's Garden of Verses* and throughout all of *Brian Wildsmith's 1 2 3's,* Wildsmith employs a simplified sort of cubism. None of his figures disorganizes the planes of reality or rearranges them in an arbitrary order as was done by Picasso or by Albert Gleizes.

Illustration by Brian Wildsmith for *A Child's Garden of Verses* by Robert Louis Stevenson. © Copyright in this edition. Oxford University Press, 1966. Reprinted with permission of Franklin Watts, Inc.

Most cubists renounce the aid of color and work in tones of brown and gray. Not Brian Wildsmith! He uses brilliant shades of green, lavender, blue, red, yellow, and pink. As Cézanne did, Wildsmith uses color to build structurally and to help with the aesthetic organization of his painting. Perspective in Wildsmith's paintings is largely a matter of colors carefully chosen; it is not a matter of a vanishing point. The greatness of cubist painting usually lies in its structure, in the way in which shapes and masses fit together. Its greatness seldom lies in the use of color. Wildsmith has not mastered the technique of cubism to the extent that Kandinsky, Picasso, or Cézanne have mastered it. His paintings do not evoke the emotional response as do those of the artists just mentioned, probably because he depends too heavily upon color to present his message and is too conservative in his rearrangement of the planes of his objects. Nonetheless, he has introduced cubism to young children in a very adequate and agreeable form.

The influence of the cubists Paul Kandinsky and Kasimir Malevich is evidenced in the pictures made by Paul Rand, particularly in the illustrations that appear in *I Know a Lot of Things* by Ann and Paul Rand. Rand's pictures are in bright colors, and they convey the feeling of wonderment at the things a child can find in the world around him and the delight he experiences with his increasing knowledge.

Surrealism.   The surrealist values intuition above intellection. His work signifies a gleeful freedom of the imagination and a response to life that is suggestive of a childlike wonder and freshness. A surrealist's work contains startling images and incongruities. Often it suggests a spirit or attitude of mockery about conventionalities and moderation. It is not unusual for the surrealist to make use of symbolic references in his paintings. The surrealist in no way intends to use in his paintings form or content with which he or his viewer is comfortably familiar. Surrealism as an art form used by the book illustrator has made its way in the children's book field!

Consider the work of such children's book illustrators as Philippe Corentin, Frank Asch, Mark Stamaty, Etienne Delessert, and William Wondriska. Practically everything about the books in which these surrealistic artists' illustrations appear reflect the "surrealist attitude": content, theme, style of writing, style of art, philosophy, and attitude about life. *Story Number 3* by Eugene Ionesco and illustrated by Philippe Corentin was recognized as an exemplary creative work by the American Institute of Graphic Arts during its 1971-72 exhibition. It was also included in the 1972 Showcase. The artist's expert watercolor illustrations are of a bluish violet and orange cast and effectively establish a dream atmosphere. A sensuous response is created as one involves himself in the child's imaginings and logic and the reality of the girl's fanciful dreams. Frank Asch has created two masterpieces in *Linda* and *Yellow, Yellow*. At first glance Hark Stamaty's zany line drawings for *Yellow, Yellow* and Frank Asch's illustrations for *Linda* look like spontaneous and quick jottings. Close examination of the illustrations will reveal innumerable sly touches; there are many surprises offered in these "scribbles." Wild, imaginative, sometimes slapstick and other-times repulsive things are actually depicted. Often these actions seem to have no relation to the story itself. Yet they do offer something of significance and one will not find it on the surface in the brief text or in the larger illustrations but below the surface in and among the detailed drawings. Children will love these antic illustrations if they only take the time to examine them.

Etienne Delessert illustrated the classic *Just So Stories* by Rudyard Kipling and *Story Number 1* and *Story Number 2* both by Eugene Ionesco. This Swiss surrealistic artist employs the grotesque absurdities typical of this art style masterfully and his uncanny, imaginative illustrations are quite in keeping with the stories he interprets and comments upon.

Suggestive of the master surrealistic oil painter, Giorgio de Chirico and his well-known *The Enigma of a Day* is the work done by William Wondriska in *The Stop*. The pictures in this story about two boys who courageously and determinedly execute the rescue of a wounded colt are positively stunning. The use of contrasts (tiny figures of the boys in a huge landscape, the crashing rain, the blazing hot sun, the cool deep blue of the night, or the gloriously fresh dawn) all happen in the precipitous mountains in Navajo country.

Works of art created by a group of creators was a common practice among the original surrealists. These group efforts would emerge from a common experience and the surrealists believed that it constituted a way to express their theory about a mystical essence common to all individuals. Thus we see the presence of books like *The Geranium on the Window Sill Just Died but Teacher You Went Right On* which was written by Albert Cullum but illustrated by twenty-eight artists and *The 14th Dragon* written by James E. Seidelman and Grace Mintonye and illustrated by thirteen artists. The array of the illustrations in both of these picture books as well as their very content and form may well surprise or annoy the more conservative critic of literature for children and will delight those inclined to follow the surrealist philosophy.

Collage. Collage is a form of synthetic cubism, and Georges Braque and Picasso are the master names of this style. A collage is made by pasting non-painterly materials onto swatches of pages and by completing the image with a linear structure drawn on top of these surfaces. Collage is a form of expressionism. Ezra Jack Keats, Leo Lionni, and Antonella Bolliger-Savelli are three of the many contemporary illustrators of children's books who use this technique. Keats, the recipient of the Caldecott Medal for *The Snowy Day*, has vigor, joyous color, and attractive organizational form in most of his illustrations. When making the pictures for *The Snowy Day*, he used wallpaper, angel hair, cotton, and other materials in addition to the painting. The collage work done by Leo Lionni, author-illustrator of the delightful picture book entitled *Frederick*, is very appropriate for use

Illustration for the *Knitted Cat* by Antonella Bolliger-Savelli. Copyright © 1971 by Benziger Verlag, Zurich, Koln. Reprinted by permission of Macmillan Publishing Company, Inc.

in children's books. His designs are much simpler than those of Keats and are characterized by their simple but sophisticated understatement. The style of his pictures is not quite as vigorous and detailed as the style of Keats, but it does suit the stories it illustrates. A collage artist new to the American children's literature audience is Antonella Bolliger-Savelli. She uses an infinite variety of color, shape, and pattern with flat, deep, and brightly colored paper cutouts for her illustrations. Two books that are illustrated by her in the collage style are *The Knitted Cat*, which is about a lovable, adventure-prone cat whose mistress forgot to finish knitting his tail, and *The Mouse and the Knitted Cat*, which is about this same cat who falls into a lake while chasing after a ladybug, but is rescued by a duck and a mouse.

The collage style is also found in Ed Young's art work for Jane Yolen's *The Girl Who Loved the Wind*. These gaily decorative, exquisitely detailed illustrations are suggestive of Persian miniatures, each one in and of itself constitutes a masterpiece of collage art, and seems so perfect for the author's words. *The Girl Who Loved the Wind* was included in the 1973 Showcase and The American Institute of Graphic Arts Fifty Books of the Year (1972). These honors signify just recognition for this gem in book illustration.

Indicative of the current interest in nostalgia and exemplary of collage art are the illustrations in *The Slightly Irregular Fire Engine or the Hithering Thithering Djinn* written and illustrated by Donald Barthelme and *The Matter with Lucy* written and illustrated by Ann Grifalconi. Both books are illustrated with collage-art pictures. The Barthelme book, which mocks the ideals of Victorian society, is illustrated with collages made from nineteenth-century engravings and typographical specimens. It is a laconically told story and evidences a surrealistic attitude, both so typical of this author's adult books. Grifalconi's book, illustrated also with an array of memorabilia from the past, dramatizes the wrong done to women in the past, especially during the Victorian era and serves as a not too subtle supply of ammunition for those involved in the current feminist movement.

Strikingly colorful and surprise-filled collage pictures will delight the young readers of the books that Eric Carle has illustrated. Spatial and directional concepts, pattern recognition, matching shapes, following directions, and map reading are amongst the intellectual offerings in this talented author-artist's book, *The Secret Birthday Message*. The reader is introduced to numbers and number sets in Eric Carle's color-spread collages that make up the wordless book *1, 2, 3, to the Zoo. The Scarecrow Clock* consists of stunning collages which by way of ingenious and humorous graphics reveal how one can tell time.

Impressionistic Art. The impressionists emphasize the importance of color and light. They tend to tell their story through the use of "broken color." The impressionists often use dots and short dashes of pure pigment in close juxtaposition. Most often, their pictures emphasize the vibrant character of animate and inanimate things. They combine colors to produce living, palpitating shadows. In the impressionistic illustrations that are found in children's books, one quickly notices that a modern feeling of informality and detachment prevails. The impressionist does not seem to be concerned with the objects as such. He paints them as he perceives them at the moment, fleeting as that glimpse might be. The impressionistic painting must be viewed either from a distance or through squinted eyes. If one looks at it closely, he sees only the artist's dots or commalike strokes. Typical of the impressionistic paintings are some of the works of Vincent van Gogh, Claude Monet, Pablo Picasso, and Cézanne.

One need only examine the illustrations of "Looking-Glass River" or "The Cow" which appear in *A Child's Garden of Verses* by Robert Louis Stevenson to see the influence of the major impressionists on Brian Wildsmith. In these two illustrations, the lines are gone, and for the most part, form is lost in the atmosphere. Wildsmith uses fresh brilliant hues of almost every color of the spectrum to present a fresh look at a meadow filled with varied, beautiful flowers. His version is creative and visual. The spots and dashes of color that make up the floral mixture, juxtaposed on the canvas and merged by the eye, should delight his young readers.

Illustration by Brian Wildsmith for *A Child's Garden of Verses* by Robert Louis Stevenson. ©
Copyright in this edition. Oxford University Press, 1966. Reprinted with permission of Franklin
Watts, Inc.

Another artist who expresses himself in the impressionistic style is
Peter Wezel, creator of the wordless book *The Good Bird*. The fourteen
paintings that make up this story about the friendship between a red bird
and a goldfish are suggestive of Matisse. The colors used in the pictures
are stimulating in their intensity. At times the combination of hues are
surprising, clashing, or quietly harmonious. They always produce what
seems to be the perfect statement or movement or response from the book
characters *and* the reader.

44

Pointillist Technique. In pointillism, which is a form of neo-impressionism, the picture is constructed with a color technique consisting of roughly equated dots. The eye blends one color with the other, thus giving form to the subject. The pictures are thoroughly planned and carefully controlled. The works of the master artist Georges Seurat, especially "La Baignade," are examples of the pointillist technique. Pointillism depends upon the use of the original colors that make up the mixture. Examination of a picture done in this technique will usually reveal that it lacks the spontaneity and easygoing attitude that was common in the impressionists' paintings. Miroslav Sasek uses the pointillist technique occasionally in his series of guidebooks for children. In double-page spreads, he applies this technique to present many of the familiar landmarks and monuments found in the busy cities of Paris and London. The books are entitled *This Is Paris* and *This Is London*, respectively. In *This Is New York*, he also uses pointillism in the pictures that portray the sun-seekers who swarm to the beach of Coney Island on a summer Sunday, and the thousands of baseball and football fans who crowd Yankee Stadium to watch their heroes. Sasek's use of pointillism is somewhat modernized, however. The dots in his paintings are wider and longer than those in the paintings done by the originators of this technique.

Folk Art. It is probably safe to generalize that the art produced in modern times is too cosmopolitan to be labeled French art, English art, Russian art, Philippine art, and the like. The concept of "folk art" is usually associated with the culture of an agrarian society and regional boundaries; their social structure traditions and backwardness tend to be preserved by their clannishness. Folk art reflects elements of style that constitute a consolidation of artistic elements, a common mentality that was developed and inherited over a period of generations; it does not rest on achievements of individual taste. The folk artist seldom accomplishes representational or true-to-life copies of the world he sees and includes in his paintings. He tends to simplify, exaggerate, and distort that reality but he includes in his creation the artistic elements that are characteristic of his culture group—hues, style of figures, mood, philosophy of life, and the like.

Cornish folk art is suggested in the comical pictures that Margot Zemach painted for *Duffy and the Devil*, a variant of "Rumpelstiltskin" told by Harve Zemach. She uses soft tones in her ink line and wash paintings but retains the earthy verve and zest for life that is dramatized in the telling of this humorous tale.

Zemach's illustrations for Isaac Bashevis Singer's *Mazel and Shlimazel or the Milk of a Lioness* are also done in ink line and wash and present the

Illustration by Nancy Ekholm Burkert for *The Nightingale* by H. C. Andersen, translated by Eva Le Gallienne. Pictures copyright © 1965 by Nancy Ekholm Burkert. Reprinted with permission of Harper & Row, Publishers.

authentic Eastern European art. Designed in large picture-book format, this Yiddish fairy tale tells of the spirit of good fortune and the spirit of bad luck and their rivalry over the fate of a simple peasant boy. A most unique picture book is found in Lieselotte Schwarz's graphic interpretation of *The Pied Piper of Hamelin* by Robert Browning. Her paintings are strongly suggestive of Silesian peasant art. The overall effect of her use of bright primary hues and massive figures are bound to make a long-lasting impression on anyone who reads this well-known narrative poem about the Pied Piper who rid the town of rats and, when the mayor refused to pay him, took all the children away with him.

As one examines the art of the truly Eastern cultures it soon becomes apparent that there is little difference between their "folk art" and their "high art." The Eastern countries have broader regional boundaries, are less agrarian, and have a different social structure. Their art still retains common elements, but reflects a more sophisticated and rational approach to artistic expression.

In a stunning picture book entitled *The Nightingale,* by Hans Christian Andersen and translated by Eva Le Gallienne, the illustrations by Nancy Ekholm Burkert are done in a style reminiscent of early Chinese screens. This is a book of rare beauty. It was an Honor Book in the Spring Book Festival sponsored by the New York Herald Tribune in 1965 and was awarded the Gold Medal by the Society of Illustrators in 1966. The eight full-color, double-page spreads were done with brush and colored India inks. The illustrations for *Tico and the Golden Wings* are done in stylized design and colors that are suggestive of the traditional art of India. Based on a Hindu fable, this story of a bird who is different and who gives away his golden feathers in order to bring happiness to the needy, was written and illustrated by the talented graphic artist, Leo Lionni.

Naive Art. The art of the naive is a layman's art which combines the influences of the collective mentality present in the folk art and in the original. The naive painter represents the essence of things and appearance out of his own experience. Filled with his private visions and concepts, he tackles even the most difficult themes and achieves an integrity and depth of expression which distinguishes his style from all others. All this, he attempts despite the inner conflict and tension that most certainly must result between his technical ignorance and his version of inner truth, between intellectual simplicity and visual invention.[8] Wherever a genuine naivete is found in a drawing or painting the creator of that work must have a tendency toward self-sufficiency and childlike isolation. He must stand removed from artistic tradition so that he will not attempt a particular line of stylistic development or stand in opposition to one. Yet, his art often does bear some of the folklorist regional stamp, as is typical of the peasant naive artist as found among eighteenth- and nineteenth-century limners, imported slaves, Black Muslims, and Hindu revivals.

The naive artist like the child tends to present only the clearly outlined aspects of his visual world, the clearly gentle and violent aspects of his world. The "hallmarks" of naive art are perhaps its trusting openness to discovery, its vitality and awkward spontaneity, its candidness and intensity. A naive painting radiates an infectious love for life. The art of the naive is a preperspective art, characterized by the almost exclusive adherence to frontal posture or profile. There is a disregard for anatomy and perspective that suggests a less developed level of consciousness and/or lack of skill in expressing a consciousness, if indeed it exists. His style is that of simplification and only those details that comprise the essence of the reality or the experience are included in his drawings or paintings. The Crowell biographies about Grandma Moses and Pippin contain information about the major aspects of their lives as well as many full-color prints that are exemplary of these naive art works.

Raised and educated in Germany and now living in the United States Jan Balet is a recognized naive artist who illustrates books for children. Examination of *The King and the Broom Maker* and *The Fence* will bring the characteristics of naive art immediately to mind. Balet's illustrations demonstrate a meticulous detail and fine sense of composition but all this appears to be expressed in an immature childlike fashion presented through instinct-laden images and narrative simplicity.

Another naive artist is Caldecott Medal winner Leo Politi. The viewer of his illustrations, be they the illustrations in his earlier books like *Pedro, The Angel of Olvera Street* and *Song of the Swallows* or those in his latest book *The Nicest Gift*, gets a glimpse at the "wonderment of life" almost

---

8. Oto Bihalji-Merin, *Masters of Naive Art: A History and Worldwide Survey,* trans. Russell M. Stockman (New York: McGraw-Hill, 1971), p. 44.

Illustration by Jan Balet. From the book, *The Fence*, by Jan Balet. English translation, copyright ©
1969 by Macdonald & Co. (Publishers) Ltd. Originally published in Germany under the title *Der
Zaun* by Otto Maier Verlag, Ravensburg. A Seymour Lawrence Book/Delacorte Press. Used with
permission of the publisher.

as through the eyes of innocence. His love for life and all living things is
quite apparent in his illustrations. Like Balet there is present in Politi's
work a refreshing simplicity in the reality that is portrayed. The figures are
lacking in anatomy and the scenes are not done in perspective; the colors
are vivid and there is a vitality and a zest in the action.

The watercolor paintings that appear in *The Dead Bird* by Margaret
Wise Brown were done by Remy Charlip. His style is quite suggestive of
the Mexican fresco artist, Diego Rivera, especially Rivera's fresco entitled
The Night of the Poor. Emotionalism prevails in *The Dead Bird*. The illustrations so graphically portray the *feelings* of the children when they find
the dead bird and indulge in the funeral service, then soon forget about the
incident as they resume their play. Charlip eliminates unnecessary detail
and reduces shadows. His outlines are firm and clear. The delightful simplicity and naivete of children are understandingly emphasized in the
illustrations by expressionist Remy Charlip. His illustrations for *Harlequin*

and the Gift of Many Colors exemplify elements of this art style. They reflect the colors (pastel shades) and costumes worn by the French comedians and pantomimists of the 1800s and carry much of the load in telling this factual story of the origin of the harlequin costume.

Cartoon Style. Cartoon art may be classified as a form of expressionistic art. The cartoon artist, like other expressionistic artists, gives vent to his feelings and provokes an emotional response by means of his sketches, but the emotionalism is usually expressed through or in some form of humor. Two qualities are basic to cartoonism, and these qualities provoke laughter, or at least a smile, from the reader. Incongruous and incompatible characteristics or situations are depicted. Dr. Seuss (Theodore Seuss Geisel) has been successful as a cartoon artist and writer of children's humorous stories. For example, the situations which Horton, the faithful and persistent elephant, faces in *Horton Hatches the Egg* send youngsters into gales of laughter. Seuss sketched numerous wonderfully humorous and expressive pictures of this long-suffering creature. Horton, sitting on a small nest in a tree, at times looks bewildered, frightened, cold, or embarrassed. His facial expressions are indeed a delight to behold. The incongruity of such a situation as an elephant stranded on top of a tree in itself would amuse children. Scenes in which the tree, with Horton still sitting on the nest, is moved from the jungle and carried by boat across rolling and tossing ocean waters to America only to be sold to a circus and the picture of the elephant-bird bursting out of the shell of the egg that Horton sat on so long and so faithfully are other incongruities and incompatibilities in Seuss' cartoons that help to make this narrative enjoyable. Even primary-age children recognize how ridiculous these situations are.

When depicting incongruities or incompatibilities, a cartoonist employs slapstick, the absurd, exaggerations, and the like. The illustrations in *Bob Fulton's Amazing Soda-Pop Stretcher,* written by Jerome Beatty, Jr., give evidence of these qualities. Gahan Wilson, the illustrator, has captured the absolute lunacy that permeates this wonderful parody on the politics and the scientific advances of the Space Age. It is a science-fiction story of Bob Fulton's accidental invention of a non-friction-producing gook and how it gains the attention of our government as well as that of an enemy nation. The predicaments faced by Bob, the absurdities of the series of events that make up the story, and the simple sort of satire of this gay and exciting modern science-fiction novel are highlighted in Wilson's cartoon-style illustrations. Especially clever are the illustrations of the two old women, Ingrid and Annie, who knit secret messages into sweaters they send to Tierra Ninguno. Also noteworthy are those of the amazing wild

bike ride taken by Bob's sister, Jennifer, when an explosion of the Pop Stretcher causes its gooey residue to spill onto the bearings and gears of her bike wheels; and those of the number one spy of a foreign power who appears dressed in black, with even his face daubed with black coloring. The three gruesome but humorous stories of superstition that appear in George Mendoza's *The Good Luck Spider and Other Bad Luck Stories* are illustrated by Gahan Wilson, also. His grotesque cartoon-type illustrations are perfectly suited to these stories.

Steven Kellog, a cartoon artist relatively new on the scene has created some very clever illustrations for many books. The illustrations that he created for *There Was an Old Woman* are exemplary of his work.

Photographs. There is little or no doubt that a photograph can serve as an illustration. But, there is considerable debate as to whether or not a photograph should be considered a work of art. Some people consider a photograph an impersonal mechanical record, a reproduction of the visual facts of an object, scene, or document. It may be used to make a written statement more concrete, or it may be used to clarify or extend that statement. The photograph is not the personal, subjective expression of a creative mind; it is not an expression of a subjective experience of feeling. Nonetheless, photographs can be used with marked artistic sensibility to illustrate literary content, theme, or mood.

Good photographic illustration is characterized by an acceptable rendering of highlight areas and shadow detail; that is, lighting and subject matter are rather contrasting. Silhouette images usually are to be avoided, especially when it is important that the reader notice details in the subject.

Illustration for *There Was an Old Woman*. Retold and drawn by Steven Kellogg. Copyright © 1974 by Steven Kellogg. Reprinted with permission of Parents' Magazine Press.

The choice of background in a photograph is dependent upon the subject matter and upon the effect for which the illustrator is aiming. Nonetheless, the background should be even-toned and in contrast to the object that is being photographed. In general, a dark object should have a light background, and a light object should have a dark background.

When one uses photographs to illustrate a story, he usually isolates or emphasizes important picture elements. He uses lighting, for example, to make certain parts of the picture stand out. Dare Wright tends to accomplish emphasis by photographing the objects (dolls) before a background of uniform tone. Ylla often used this same technique with her illustrations of animals. When background detail is present, it must serve to establish the setting and the atmosphere. It should be subdued or, perhaps, eliminated altogether. Sometimes the technique of selective focusing is used; that is, important aspects of the subject matter are in sharp focus, and the background is out of focus. Dare Wright and Ylla have used this technique too, to accomplish emphasis.

Both of these illustrators limit the number of objects that they include within any one scene. As a result, their photographs are uncluttered and precise. The action that they illustrate is easily identifiable. This is an important characteristic of a photograph illustration.

Proportionately, there are far fewer children's books illustrated with photographs than those illustrated with other kinds of pictures. Most of the books that are illustrated with photographs are informational books rather than bona fide literary selections. There are quite a few poetry anthologies, however, especially of haiku and modern verse, that are illustrated with photographs. Numerous striking photographs (many of them scenes rather than single objects) complement or extend the poems that are included in *Reflections on a Gift of Watermelon Pickle and Other Modern Verse,* an anthology of modern verse, compiled by Stephen Dunning et al. The poems in another anthology entitled *The Wind and the Rain* and compiled by Richard Lewis reveal childlike responses to nature, and the accompanying photographs by Helen Buttfield complement these poems which were written by children from age five to thirteen.

The photographs that illustrate Thomas Matthiesen's books, *A.B.C.: An Alphabet Book* and *Things to See: A Child's World of Familiar Objects* are in color. These pictures are photographs of objects that can be identified by most children. They are reproduced in bright colors and are appealing and attractive. They are also colored photographs in *How I Feel* by June Behrens. The simple text and Vince Streano's photographs depict a gamut of emotional responses to and feelings about things fairly common to children in their day-to-day experiences and happenings.

The black-and-white photographs of the art objects that are described in Shirley Glubok's books are well-reproduced. In each case, the artifacts (ornaments, temples, jewelry, statues, etc.) are strikingly displayed. Included in her art series are *The Art of Ancient Mexico* and *The Art of the Etruscans.* The photography for each of these books was done by Alfred H. Tamarin.

White pages with two-inch-square openings cut into them alternate with full page black-and-white photographs of animals and plants in Tana Hoban's *Look Again.* As the reader looks through each small opening he is challenged to guess what the larger whole of the detail is he sees. This clever use of photographs should serve to intrigue and alert the child to the symmetry and patterns found in these as well as in other examples of nature.

National Aeronautics and Space Administration photographs were used to illustrate Gene Gurney's *Walk in Space: The Story of Project Gemini*. These photographs clarify the author's reviews of the aims and accomplishments of Project Gemini, the specific purposes and achievements of each flight, and the actions of the astronauts and the ground tracking crews.

Summary

It is in the arrangement of line and color that the style of art can be identified. The various styles of art used by graphic artists to suggest and evoke the content and other narrative elements of literature include the following: representational art, expressionistic art, cubism, surrealism, collage, impressionistic art, pointillism, folk art, naive art, cartoon-style art, and photography. Style in illustrative art is a rather elusive quality, but the author has attempted to describe some of the characteristics of each style and to cite exemplary publications in which each of these styles was used. The style of art which is used to illustrate a book may be influenced by several factors such as the content and the mood of the story, the age of the reader, the artist's concept of his anticipated audience, the basic personality of the artist, his creative talent, and the media used to make the pictures, as well as the artist's mastery of the media technique employed.

SELECTED REFERENCES

ANDERSEN, HANS CHRISTIAN. *The Nightingale*. Translated by Eva Le Gallienne. Illustrated by Nancy Ekholm Burkert. New York: Harper & Row, Publishers, 1965.

——. *Thumbelina*. Illustrated by Adrienne Adams. New York: Charles Scribner's Sons, 1961.

ASBJØRNSEN, P. C. and MOE, JORGEN E. *The Three Billy Goats Gruff*. Illustrated by Marcia Brown. New York: Harcourt Brace Jovanovich, 1957.

ASCH, FRANK. *Linda*. Illustrated by Frank Asch. New York: McGraw-Hill Book Co., 1969.

——. *Yellow, Yellow*. Illustrated by Mark Stamaty. New York: McGraw-Hill Book Co., 1971.

BALET, JAN B. *The Fence: A Mexican Tale*. Illustrated by Jan B. Balet. New York: Delacorte Press, 1969.

——. *The King and the Broom Maker*. Illustrated by Jan B. Balet. New York: Delacorte Press, 1968.

BARTHELME, DONALD. *The Slightly Irregular Fire Engine or the Hithering Thithering Djinn*. Illustrated with nineteenth-century engravings. New York: Farrar, Straus & Giroux, 1971.

BEATTY, JEROME, JR. *Bob Fulton's Amazing Soda-Pop Stretcher.* Illustrated by Gahan Wilson. New York: William R. Scott, 1963.

BEHRENS, JUNE. *How I Feel.* Illustrated with photographs by Vince Streano. Chicago: Children's Press, 1973.

BOLLIGER-SAVELLI, ANTONELLA. *The Knitted Cat.* Illustrated by Antonella Bolliger-Savelli. New York: Macmillan Co., 1972.

————. *The Mouse and the Knitted Cat.* Illustrated by Antonella Bolliger-Savelli. New York: Macmillan Co., 1972.

BROWN, MARCIA. *Cinderella.* Illustrated by Marcia Brown. New York: Charles Scribner's Sons, 1954.

————. *Once a Mouse . . . A Fable Cut in Wood.* Illustrated by Marcia Brown. New York: Charles Scribner's Sons, 1961.

BROWN, MARGARET WISE. *The Dead Bird.* Illustrated by Remy Charlip. New York: William R. Scott, 1958.

BROWNING, ROBERT. *The Pied Piper of Hamelin.* Illustrated by Lieselotte Schwarz. New York: Scroll Press, 1970.

CARLE, ERIC. *1, 2, 3 to the Zoo.* Illustrated by Eric Carle. Cleveland: World Publishing Co., 1968.

————. *The Secret Birthday Message.* Illustrated by Eric Carle. New York: Thomas Y. Crowell Co., 1972.

CULLUM, ALBERT. *The Geranium on the Window Sill Just Died but Teacher You Went Right On.* Illustrated by twenty-eight artists. New York: Harlin Quist Books, 1971.

DE LA MARE, WALTER. *Jack and the Beanstalk.* Illustrated by Joseph Low. New York: Alfred A. Knopf, 1959.

DUNNING, STEPHEN; LUEDERS, EDWARD; and SMITH, HUGH. *Reflections on a Gift of Watermelon Pickle and Other Modern Verse.* Illustrated with photographs. Glenview, Ill.: Scott Foresman & Co., 1967.

FRASCONI, ANTONIO. *See Again, Say Again.* New York: Harcourt, Brace & World, 1964.

FUCHS, ERICH. *Journey to the Moon.* Illustrated by Erich Fuchs. New York: Delacorte Press, 1970.

GLUBOK, SHIRLEY. *The Art of Ancient Mexico.* Illustrated with photographs by Alfred H. Tamarin. New York: Harper & Row, Publishers, 1968.

————. *The Art of the Etruscans.* Illustrated with photographs by Alfred H. Tamarin. New York: Harper & Row, Publishers, 1967.

GOODALL, JOHN S. *Jacko.* Illustrated by John S. Goodall. New York: Harcourt Brace Jovanovich, 1971.

————. *Paddy's Evening Out.* Illustrated by John S. Goodall. New York: Atheneum Publishers, 1973.

————. *Shrewbettina's Birthday.* Illustrated by John S. Goodall. New York: Harcourt Brace Jovanovich, 1971.

GOUDEY, ALICE E. *Butterfly Time.* Illustrated by Adrienne Adams. New York: Charles Scribner's Sons, 1964.

————. *Houses from the Sea.* Illustrated by Adrienne Adams. New York: Charles Scribner's Sons, 1959.

GRIFALCONI, ANN. *The Matter With Lucy.* Illustrated with memorabilia. New York: Bobbs-Merrill Co., 1973.

GURNEY, GENE. *Walk in Space: The Story of Project Gemini.* Illustrated with photographs. New York: Random House, 1967.

HAYS, H. R. and HAYS, DANIEL. *Charley Sang a Song.* Illustrated by Uri Schulevitz. New York: Harper & Row, Publishers, 1964.

HODGES, MARGARET. *The Wave.* Translated by Calvin K. Towle. Illustrated by Blair Lent. Boston: Houghton Mifflin Co., 1964.

IONESCO, EUGENE. *Story Number 1.* Illustrated by Etienne Delessert. New York: Harlin Quist Books, 1968.

——. *Story Number 2.* Illustrated by Etienne Delessert. New York: Harlin Quist Books, 1970.

———. *Story Number 3.* Illustrated by Philippe Corentin. New York: Harlin Quist Books, 1971.

KEATS, EZRA JACK. *The Snowy Day.* Illustrated by Ezra Jack Keats. New York: Viking Press, 1962.

KIPLING, RUDYARD. *Just So Stories.* Illustrated by Etienne Delessert. New York: Doubleday & Co., 1972.

LEWIS, RICHARD. *The Wind and the Rain.* Illustrated with photographs by Helen Buttfield. New York: Simon & Schuster, 1968.

LIONNI, LEO. *Frederick.* Illustrated by Leo Lionni. New York: Pantheon Books, 1966.

———. *Tico and the Golden Wings.* New York: Pantheon Books, 1964.

MATTHIESEN, THOMAS. *A. B. C.: An Alphabet Book.* Illustrated with photographs by Thomas Matthiesen. New York: Platt & Munk, 1966.

MCNEER, MAY. *The American Indian Story.* Illustrated by Lynd Ward. New York: Farrar, Straus & Giroux, 1963.

———. *The Canadian Story.* Illustrated by Lynd Ward. New York: Farrar, Straus & Giroux, 1950.

MENDOZA, GEORGE. *The Good Luck Spider and Other Bad Luck Stories.* Illustrated by Gahan Wilson. New York: Doubleday & Co., 1970.

———. *The Scarecrow Clock.* Illustrated by Eric Carle. New York: Holt, Rinehart & Winston, 1971.

MILES, MISKA. *The Wharf Rat.* Illustrated by John Schoenherr. Boston: Little, Brown & Co., Atlantic Monthly Press, 1972.

MOSEL, ARLENE. *The Funny Little Woman.* Illustrated by Blair Lent. New York: E. P. Dutton & Co., 1972.

POLITI, LEO, *The Nicest Gift.* Illustrated by Leo Politi. New York: Charles Scribner's Sons, 1973.

———. *Pedro, The Angel of Olvera Street.* Illustrated by Leo Politi. New York: Charles Scribner's Sons, 1946.

———. *Song of the Swallows.* Illustrated by Leo Politi. New York: Charles Scribner's Sons, 1949.

PROVENSEN, ALICE and PROVENSEN, MARTIN. *The First Noel: From the Gospel of St. Luke.* New York: Golden Press, 1954.

RAND, ANN and RAND, PAUL. *I Know a Lot of Things.* Illustrated by Paul Rand. New York: Harcourt, Brace & World, 1956.

SASEK, MIROSLAV. *This Is London.* Illustrated by Miroslav Sasek. New York: Macmillan Co., 1959.

———. *This Is New York.* Illustrated by Miroslav Sasek. New York: Macmillan Co., 1960.

———. *This Is Paris.* Illustrated by Miroslav Sasek. New York: Macmillan Co., 1959.

SCHLEIN, MIRIAM. *The Big Cheese.* Illustrated by Joseph Low. New York: William R. Scott, 1958.

SCHOENHERR, JOHN. *The Barn.* Illustrated by John Schoenherr. Boston: Little, Brown & Co., 1968.

SEIDELMAN, JAMES E. and MINTONYE, GRACE. *The 14th Dragon.* Illustrated by thirteen artists. New York: Harlin Quist Books, 1968.

SEUSS, DR. *Horton Hatches the Egg.* New York: Random House, 1940.

SINGER, ISAAC BASHEVIS. *Mazel and Schlimazel or the Milk of a Lioness.* Translated by Isaac Singer and Elizabeth Shub. Illustrated by Margot Zemach. New York: Farrar, Straus & Giroux, 1967.

SMALL, ERNEST. *Baba Yaga.* Illustrated by Blair Lent. Boston: Houghton Mifflin Co., 1966.

STEVENSON, ROBERT LOUIS. *A Child's Garden of Verses.* Illustrated by Brian Wildsmith. New York: Franklin Watts, 1966.

TENNYSON, ALFRED LORD. *The Charge of the Light Brigade.* Illustrated by Alice and Martin Provensen. New York: Golden Press, 1964.

TUDOR, TASHA. *A Is for Annabelle.* Illustrated by Tasha Tudor. New York: Henry Z. Walck, 1954.

———. *Around the Year.* Illustrated by Tasha Tudor. New York: Henry Z. Walck, 1957.

———. *Becky's Birthday.* Illustrated by Tasha Tudor. New York: Viking Press, 1960.

———. *1 Is One.* Illustrated by Tasha Tudor. New York: Henry Z. Walck, 1956.

WARD, LYND. *The Biggest Bear.* Illustrated by Lynd Ward. Boston: Houghton Mifflin Co., 1952.

———. *The Silver Pony: A Story in Pictures.* Illustrated by Lynd Ward. Boston: Houghton Mifflin Co., 1973.

WEZEL, PETER. *The Good Bird.* Illustrated by Peter Wezel. New York: Harper & Row, Publishers, 1966.

WILDSMITH, BRIAN. *Brian Wildsmith's 1, 2, 3's.* Illustrated by Brian Wildsmith. New York: Franklin Watts, 1965.

WONDRISKA, WILLIAM. *The Stop.* Illustrated by William Wondriska. New York: Holt, Rinehart & Winston, 1972.

YASHIMA, MITSU and YASHIMA, TARO. *Plenty to Watch.* Illustrated by Taro Yashima. New York: Viking Press, 1954.

YASHIMA, TARO. *Umbrella.* Illustrated by Taro Yashima. New York: Viking Press, 1958.

YOLEN, JANE. *The Girl Who Loved the Wind.* Illustrated by Ed Young. New York: Thomas Y. Crowell Co., 1972.

ZEMACH, HARVE. *Duffy and the Devil.* Illustrated by Margot Zemach. New York: Farrar, Straus & Giroux, 1973.

chapter 3
the artist's media
and techniques

A picture is a form of language. The book artist expresses his thoughts and feelings in this language through effective use of the various painterly and graphic techniques. His facility and skill at expressing himself in this language is evaluated largely in terms of the way he uses his media to reveal his understanding of the function of form, his sensitivity to the flow of line, his originality, and his mastery of the media itself. These powers are revealed in the pictures he creates for an illustrated book. There is a wide variety of media available to the book artist. The subject of the book itself is often a major determinant of the art medium that is best to use to create the illustrations for that book.

The author of an art education book for children told her young readers that the medium an artist uses changes the appearance of a picture as well as influences the way one feels about a picture.[1] The artist may use pastels, watercolors, oil paints, pencil, crayon, tempera, gouache, or ink. He may use techniques such as woodcuts, wood engravings, linoleum cuts, paper etchings, scratchboard, or stone lithograph to make his picture. The medium determines, in large measure, the lines and shapes that artist will use to make his design. It limits the extent to which he will use hatching, cross-hatching, scribbles, smudges, or washes in his drawings. It follows, then, that the materials and techniques used by the artist to create his visual images may affect the manner and extent to which the literary functions of his pictures are accomplished.

That the same story may inspire different artists in different ways is a fairly well accepted fact. Scores of studies made by students of psychology and of human growth and development substantiate the principle of individual differences and uniqueness of personality. These studies point

1. Helen Borten, *A Picture Has a Special Look* (New York: Abelard-Schuman, 1961), unpaged.

58

out the inherent differences among or between members of a group as well as differences within a given individual in capacity and performance. Research has also revealed that human variations are caused by the range of experiences and the expectations or environmental demands that are made upon individuals.

It is not at all surprising, then, that artists reading the same story will evidence through their drawings differences in perception. One artist will decide that woodcuts would be the best medium to present the message of the story, a second artist will decide that watercolors would best serve this purpose, and a third artist will think a collage technique would be best. Each artist has read the same story, and yet each will identify different aspects of importance in the story. Each will come away with different recollections and different concepts. Each will probably decide upon a different art medium to be used to make the illustrations. But even if they all agreed on the same medium, in all probability each artist would employ a markedly different style of art, and each would use a different combination of colors. The illustrations prepared by each artist would highlight the same detail of the story in an entirely different manner.

Regardless of the media used to make the pictures, the book illustrator must be able to express the individuality of his style. A woodcut print by Evaline Ness will be different from a woodcut print by Gil Miret, Ed Emberley, Antonio Frasconi, or Nonny Hogrogian. Likewise, the watercolor paintings done by Adrienne Adams will differ in elements of style from the pictures done in the same medium by Alois Carigiet, Ludwig Bemelmans, or Leo Politi. Scratchboard illustrations done by Barbara Cooney will differ from those done by Leonard Everett Fisher.

Consider the varied graphic interpretations brought to the Mother Goose rhymes. Tasha Tudor is a watercolor artist who has used her medium to create delicate and quaint interpretations of the well-known rhymes. Far more sophisticated in his treatment of these same rhymes is Brian Wildsmith, who used gouache to create his paintings. *In a Pumpkin Shell* is another Mother Goose book. It was illustrated by Joan Walsh Anglund who used pen-and-ink drawings and watercolors to make her detailed and ingenuous pictures. Philip Reed made colored wood engravings for the illustrations in *Mother Goose and Nursery Rhymes*.

Blair Lent used cardboard cutouts and overlay wash to make the illustrations that appear in *The Wave*, Margaret Hodges' version of the Japanese folktale that tells about an old man who set fire to his rice fields on the mountains to save the villagers from a tidal wave. Pastels were used by Mamoru Funai for *The Burning Rice Fields*, Sara Cone Bryant's version of this same folktale. Funai's illustrations are handsome and original as are Lent's, and yet Funai's work is far less expressionistic than Lent's is. The work by Funai is more appropriate for younger children than that of Lent. The style of the former artist has an immediate direct appeal; that of the latter is more subtle and sophisticated. The one makes use of the primary colors; the other uses subdued colors.

Some artists can work with a multiplicity of media and are not tied to any one process. The mood of the story itself will determine the medium the artist employs. The artist himself must believe that for him no other medium would be as effective as the one he chooses to tell a particular story. He must be able to exploit the qualities that make this particular medium unique. He must be able to make this medium say better what another medium could say only adequately.

Marcia Brown uses a variety of media to create her illustrations, and she uses each medium to the greatest possible advantage. She uses linoleum-block cuts, woodcuts, flat color, gouache and crayon over rubber cement, casein, ink, and watercolors. These are not all the media she uses to make the pictures for her books, but it is obvious that a single artist, like Marcia Brown, can be versatile in the media she uses and yet master the technique for each. Marcia Brown has varied the media for her many books, but in each case, she has chosen a medium (means) that will permit her to say what she has to say.

> The means will always be determined by the subject at hand, and that is why I feel that each book should look different from the others, whether or not the medium used is the same. . . . A technique learned as a formula to apply willy-nilly to any subject often knocks the life out of the subject. The vitality, the quality peculiar to the subject should dictate the method to follow.[2]

Barbara Cooney also tries to fit the medium and technique to the demands of the story. She has used pen-and-ink, pen-and-ink with wash, casein, collage, watercolors, acrylics, scratchboard, and lithographs. Evaline Ness, too, has used a wide variety of media but is better known for her work done in line-and-wash, collage, and woodcuts.

There is no doubt that before the book artist selects the art medium to make his drawings he must be able to visualize the images suggested in a manuscript. It is equally important that he have a mastery of painterly or graphic technique(s) so that he can make a meaningful and creative graphic statement of the story.

---

2. Marcia Brown, "Integrity and Intuition," in *Caldecott Medal Books: 1938-1957*, ed. Bertha M. Miller and Eleanor Field (Boston: The Horn Book, 1957), pp. 267-77.

The book artist of today is given considerable freedom in his selection of media, but Goethe once said, "It is only within limits that the master is evidenced." The book artist of today has to realize his own strengths and weaknesses as they pertain to the use of a particular art medium. Also, he has to be fully aware of the limitations, the possibilities, the advantages of the medium that he uses to deliver an author's message and his own message.

Because an artist does have the freedom to use the medium that he can handle well and that he feels will best help him interpret the text, and because most artists today are technically skilled in using varied art media, the quality of book illustration in this country is at a respectable level. In fact, the work done by many of the book artists of today is characterized by integrity and a certain self-assurance. It reflects sincere and uninhibited efforts by the artists. The practice of using a variety of media to illustrate children's books has encouraged much diversity in the styles of art employed by the illustrators of children's books. Diversity in the media, techniques, and art styles that book artists may use to make pictures for children's books tends to increase the competition in this aspect of publication of children's books. Certainly it brings forth a wider range of talents and ideas to the field of children's literature than ever before. This should help to bring more and better books to young readers.

Painterly Techniques

Paint is powder color mixed with a binding medium. One can paint with an oil medium, with watercolor, or with pastel. Each painter has his personal color sense. Each one tends to use and mix a range of colors in his own way, some artists being more timid (or aggressive) than others in the color range. Most artists do go far beyond the four process colors (red, blue, yellow, and black). Seldom are they reluctant to mix these pigments, and so they do come up with various gradations of the secondary colors.

Watercolor. Watercolor, which is powder color bound with gum arabic and glycerine, is applied in washes. It is a transparent medium, and one which is not the most popular with contemporary book artists, probably because it is not as vigorous as the other media. Artists who have used watercolor to make the original paintings for the pictures that illustrate children's books include Robert Andrew Parker, Adrienne Adams, Tasha Tudor, and Maurice Sendak. A few of the books illustrated by each of these book artists are discussed in the pages that follow.

Robert Andrew Parker, a distinguished American painter whose work is represented in collections of the Museum of Modern Art and the Whitney Museum of Modern Art in New York, used watercolor and ink for the paintings that illustrate several notable children's books. He won considerable acclaim for the illustrations in *Pop Corn and Ma Goodness* by Edna Preston, which was named a Caldecott Honor Book in 1970. Especially distinguished are the full-color watercolor paintings that illustrate two later publications *The Trees Stand Shining: Poetry of the North American Indians* compiled by Hettie Jones, and *Zeek Silver Moon* by Amy Ehrlich. The luminous paintings in these two books are reproduced as full-page illustrations and they depict and expand the text of each superbly. The respect and love for nature that is expressed in the poetry in the Jones' compilation and the mood of serenity and warmth portrayed in *Zeek Silver Moon*, which is a collection of everyday happenings in the life of a contemporary family, are dramatized tastefully by this talented watercolorist. His paintings are characterized by an understated sophisticated elegance; they evoke a deep and sincere emotional response from each one who views them. Children who experience Robert Andrew Parker's book illustrations will probably be more appreciative of contemporary art and should be more likely to derive considerable aesthetic pleasure from beautiful paintings.

Robert Andrew Parker's illustrations can be contrasted with those made by Adrienne Adams who also uses watercolor in many of her pictures. Both artists often work in full color. Ms. Adams' work was also recognized by the book critics as being outstanding for her illustrations in *Houses from the Sea* and *The Day We Saw the Sun Come Up*. Both, written by Alice E. Goudey, were runners-up for the Caldecott Medal awarded in 1960 and in 1962, respectively. Ms. Adams' paintings are representational and winsome. She uses delicate, clear colors, and her work is detailed and exact. The illustrations of seashells in *Houses from the Sea* are so authentic in each detail that they could be referred to as a quick guide for identification of the more common shells—moon shells, jingle shells, cockleshells, cowrie shells, periwinkle shells, and so on. This meticulous attention to detail is also given to her illustrations for folktales. For example, the figures in *The Shoemaker and the Elves* are clothed in authentic costumes for the period in which the Grimm brothers were collecting the folktales. The drawings in *The Shoemaker and the Elves* were executed in crayon and watercolor. The delicate and bright details found in Hans Christian Andersen's *Thumbelina* highlight the imaginary quality of this enchanting

Illustration by Robert Andrew Parker. Copyright © 1972 by Robert Andrew Parker. From the book, *Zeek Silver Moon*, by Amy Ehrlich. Reproduced with permission of The Dial Press.

fairy tale. The key drawings for this story were done in pencil and water-color wash. The pencil, which can also be a delicate instrument for art work, helps Adrienne Adams to carry out the relaxed detail that is characteristic of her watercolor paintings.

Reprinted by permission of Charles Scribner's Sons from *Thumbelina* by Hans Christian Andersen, translated by R. P. Keigwin, illustrated by Adrienne Adams. Copyright © 1961 Adrienne Adams.

Alois Carigiet uses vivid and brilliant watercolors in his book Illustrations. A recipient of the Hans Christian Andersen Award[3] in 1966, Carigiet is expressionistic in his style. His illustrations for *A Bell for Ursli* and *The Snowstorm* highlight the gaiety of the Swiss festival for which the children in the stories are preparing. Many of his illustrations in *A Bell for Ursli* and *The Snowstorm*, as well as in *Florina and the Wild Bird*, all written by Selina Chonz, are sumptuous full-color spreads. Each is suggestive of a huge mural. Carigiet's scenes of the Swiss villages and mountains por-

3. The Hans Christian Andersen Award is an international award, given every two years, by the International Board on Books for Young People. Carigiet was recognized as an artist who contributed significantly to children's literature through his illustrations.

tray Switzerland as a "paradise" that one must be certain to visit as soon as possible.

Another recognized watercolor artist is Tasha Tudor. Like Adrienne Adams, she uses pencil along with watercolors and is equally exacting and detailed in her approach. Examination of the features of her book characters, the clothing they wear, the interior settings, the landscape scenes, and her sketches of flowers and animals reveals that Tasha Tudor is a meticulous craftsman. She employs the representational style of art in her painting, and the general tenor of her work is quaint and quiet. Her approach to illustration is highly decorative. Her drawings express a make-believe quality because they include realistic and romantic excesses. This quality is seen in her illustrations for Andersen's fairy tales as well as for books classified as here-and-now stories, *Pumpkin Moonshine, Linsey Woolsey,* or the concept books, *Around the Year, 1 Is One,* and *A Is for Annabelle.* The feeling that pervades throughout Tasha Tudor's books is that of serenity and quietness, a mood quite contrary to that depicted by numerous contemporary artists who reveal their tenseness and need for activity through the use of bold colors, loose forms, and heavy lines in their paintings. Tasha Tudor's illustrations are soft and delicate. In the delightfully attractive picture book entitled *A Is for Annabelle,* she uses an old-fashioned doll with all her belongings to present the alphabet. The figures of the children who appear in the illustrations of *1 Is One,* where numbers one through twenty are presented in verse form, are clothed in old-fashioned garments typical of the nineteenth century, a not too uncommon habit with Tasha Tudor.

Another watercolor artist worthy of note is Peter Spier. He was named a runner-up for the Caldecott Medal for his illustrations in his *The Fox Went Out on a Chilly Night.* These illustrations, like those in *London Bridge Is Falling Down, Hurrah, We're Outward Bound,* and *Of Dikes and Windmills,* also by Spier, are in line-and-wash watercolors. The main features of his work include consummate skill and accurately detailed drawings. Adults and children alike are delighted with the charm and humor in his work and his wealth of authentic detail and scholarly approach to the presentation of his subject matter. He usually includes an author's note explaining his approach to the subject matter and giving the historical background of his illustrations.

Tony Chen uses watercolors, too, for the book illustrations in *Run, Zebra, Run,* which is a compilation of haiku poems that he wrote. Each detail in the illustrations in *Run, Zebra, Run* is based on fact; the perfected anatomy of the animals and attention to details throughout reflect a thorough research of all the subjects portrayed. The outline drawings are executed in many hues. This technique gives definition and provides contrast to the final paintings in transparent watercolor. The added touches of definition in pencil and various hues of opaque acrylic make the paintings even more vital and lifelike.

There are other artists who have used watercolors skillfully in their book illustrations. This art medium was used by Hardie Gramatky to create the gay cartoonlike illustrations that appear in *Little Toot* and *Bolivar*. Elmer and Berta Hader used watercolors and pencil to make the realistic drawings for *The Big Snow*, for which they were awarded the Caldecott Medal in 1949. Another Caldecott Medal book which is illustrated with watercolor paintings is *Time of Wonder* by Robert McCloskey. The illustrations in this book are done in an expressionistic style.

Pencil and watercolors were used by Marvin Bileck to create the fanciful and unbelievably detailed illustrations for the nonsense book by Julian Scheer entitled *Rain Makes Applesauce* which was a runner-up for the Caldecott Medal in 1966 and was cited by the *New York Times* in 1965 as one of the "Ten Best Illustrated Children's Books." The late Francoise (pseud. Francoise Seignobosc), author-illustrator of the Jeanne-Marie series for the nursery school audience, used watercolors to create her peasantlike drawings. The colors are cheery, and bright, and yet not brilliant. The figures are doll-like and simple. *Jeanne-Marie Counts Her Sheep, The Thank-You Book, The Things I Like,* and *Noel for Jeanne-Marie* seem to be among her most popular books.

Gouache and Poster Color.   Gouache is powder color mixed with an opaque white, usually Chinese white; poster color is a coarser version of gouache. Actually, watercolor, gouache, and poster color are the same medium, the only difference being that in the latter two media, there is an addition of the white filling. Often, a gouache painting looks like an oil painting. In the examples cited in the pages that follow, a few artists who use gouache and poster paint are identified.

Roger Duvoisin used gouache in the drawings for Alvin Tresselt's *Hide and Seek Fog*, an exquisite mood picture book. So expressionistic are these full-color paintings that one can almost feel the fog roll in from the sea, or hang wet and dripping from the articles of clothing hung on the clothesline. The use of hazy pearl gray throughout the book contributes to the effectiveness of this expressionistic art piece.

It is hard to believe that this same medium was used by Brian Wildsmith in his number and alphabet books or in the truly stunning book entitled *Brian Wildsmith's Birds*. Quite in keeping with the form of expressionistic art which he uses, namely a modern and simple sort of cubism, is the use of the wide array of brilliant and subdued colors present in all of his books. Tasha Tudor's quaint, quiet, and controlled type of illustrations were described above as being indicative of a make-believe or ideal world of the nineteenth century. One might say that Brian Wildsmith's use of form and color symbolizes the busy, uninhibited, and educated twentieth century.

Margot Zemach used gouache for the full-color paintings that illustrate *Simon Boom Gives a Wedding* by Yuri Suhl. Her illustrations reflect and extend the nonsense of the Jewish folktale. The soft colors, hues of pink, blue, and brown, seem to be in harmony with the content and mood of the story.

Full-color gouache was used in Alice and Martin Provensen's illustrations that appear in *The Charge of the Light Brigade*, a stunning expressionistic version of the well-known poem by Alfred Lord Tennyson. The double-spread colored paintings serve to justify the hostile and disgruntled feelings that permeated the ranks of the servicemen during the Crimean War after the disastrous British cavalry charge against the Russian batteries at Balaclava in 1854. The effective splashes of blue, red, and brown depict booming cannons, wounded and fallen soldiers, falling or wildly hysterical horses, as well as the arrogant, determined military leaders—all so very typical of this grim historical event. This book, by the way, exemplifies unusual book design. The text of the poem is done in Victorian script and looks like hand-lettering, thus emphasizing the fact that the servicemen carried handwritten copies of Tennyson's poem with them. The cover is a collage consisting of newspaper articles which had reported the tragic battle. The size of the book, the quality of paper used, and the physical arrangement of each page evidence careful and skillful bookmaking. The Provensens also used gouache to make the drawings for *The Golden Bible for Children: The New Testament* which was included in the American Institute of Graphic Arts Children's Book Show in 1954.

Gouache was used by Aliki (pseud. Aliki Brandenberg) in the drawings for *A Weed Is a Flower, the Life of George Washington Carver*. An understated simplicity characterizes Aliki's use of color and line. This approach is compatible with the brief, charmingly simple and dignified biography of the Negro research scientist, George Washington Carver.

Another book artist who uses gouache is the talented Leonard Weisgard who used this medium for the illustrations that appear in the 1947 Caldecott Medal book, *The Little Island* by Golden MacDonald. He painted his pictures on pressed wood that had been covered with a layer of lead white and lightly sanded. On every other page are five colorful illustrations; the alternate pages are two-color duotones. Each one is a beautiful picture.

Duvoisin and Weisgard use the same medium, and yet each has come up with strikingly different effects. Weisgard's drawings in *The Little Island* are representational in style and, in general, the colors are brilliant and sparkling. The art style used by Duvoisin in *Hide and Seek Fog* is expressionistic, and colors are muted and hazy. In *The Little Island*, Weisgard has included more decorative details than he has in more recent books. Duvoisin's book lacks the decorative quality. One would readily recognize the unique creative talents of Weisgard and Duvoisin if they compared only the mist scenes contained in *The Little Island* and in *Hide and Seek Fog*. Each artist used gouache, but the feelings each artist expresses about fog and mist are quite different; and yet each interpretation is compatible with the particular story the artist has illustrated. Weisgard also used gouache to make the pictures for Margaret Wise Brown's *The Golden Bunny* which was included in the American Institute of Graphic Arts Children's Book Show in 1954.

Celestino Piatti used poster color to make the beautiful illustrations in *The Happy Owls, Celestino Piatti's Animal ABC*, and *The Holy Night*.

The text of the latter was written by Aurel von Jüchen and translated from the German by Cornelia Schaeffer. Piatti uses a considerable amount of color in all of his paintings, and his drawings are all solid and bold. He uses thick black outlines and strong coloring in his paintings. Those in *The Holy Night* are "atmospheric." When taken individually, the pictures are strikingly handsome; collectively, these richly-colored paintings contrast with the simple and brief story, or informative text, in each of the books they illustrate.

Jacob Lawrence is one of America's foremost Negro painters. He used poster color to make the expressionistic pictures that illustrate the moving narrative verse in *Harriet and the Promised Land*. The stylized drawings, the exaggerated features of the characters, the brilliant and flat shades of color all contribute to make this artist's work beautifully artistic and noteworthy.

Tempera Tempera is a painterly technique used by numerous contemporary book artists. It is powder color ground in water and mixed with an albuminous, gelatinous, or colloidal medium. Tempera is not particularly difficult to work with. Its opacity can be increased or lessened at the will of a skillful artist, as can the brightness and shades of various colors be controlled. This medium permits carefully detailed work if the artist wishes to paint in this manner, but it also allows for loose, uninhibited brush strokes should the artist prefer that approach. Some of the major book artists who have used tempera for their medium include Leo Politi, Nicolas Sidjakov, Maurice Sendak, and Bruno Munari.

Leo Politi was awarded the Caldecott Medal in 1950 for his illustrations in *Song of the Swallows*. His medium is primarily tempera. One would probably conclude, after having examined the illustrations in *Pedro, the Angel of Olvera Street, St. Francis and the Animals,* and his most recent creation *The Nicest Gift,* that his illustrations are composed with a quiet deliberation. It seems that his style is quite stabilized as is the medium he uses in his work. His illustrations are deceptively simple. In fact, there is a naive look about many of his pictures. Particularly noticeable are the stylized lumbering figures and the oversized, stiff hands and feet, qualities so characteristic of the naive artist. Politi does not include much detail in his work. Indeed, his illustrations are characterized by an economy of detail. Nonetheless, there is considerable action depicted in his paintings, and there is enough suggestion for the child's imagination to expand. He includes enough of detail and attention to human features to give an adequate picture of people in their environment. Politi uses an assortment of tone and color in his pictures. Even when limited to two colors, he manages to produce considerable diversity in shades. His use of color to denote mood and time of day is skillful. He uses black and white or dark colors for evening scenes, for happy moods he uses brighter shades, and for sadness he uses the darker shades.

Handsome drawings are found in *Baboushka and the Three Kings*, in which Nicolas Sidjakov used tempera and felt pens in four bright colors to create his stylized woodenlike figures. Through his use of color and style, he has given a "Russian feeling" to this Russian folktale. Sidjakov uses tempera with sureness. Ruth Robbins is the author of this 1960 Caldecott Medal-winning book.

Illustration by Nicolas Sidjakov for *Baboushka and the Three Kings* by Ruth Robbins. Illustrations copyright © 1960 by Nicolas Sidjakov. Reprinted with permission of Parnassus Press.

Maurice Sendak used tempera to paint the illustrations in *Where the Wild Things Are*. The drawings for this picture book were done in cartoon style. The creatures that Max meets in his fantasy world are grotesque, but they will probably delight almost any young reader and stimulate his imagination; very likely they will humor him rather than frighten him. The playful mood and the fantasy in this picture book are fortified throughout by Sendak's brief but well-written text, his choice of colors, his style of drawing, and his use of white space.

Tempera was used for all of the illustrations that appear in the children's books that Bruno Munari created. Worthy of note are the picture books entitled *Bruno Munari's ABC*, *Bruno Munari's Zoo*, *Who's There? Open the Door!*, and *The Birthday Present*. His illustrations are very simple and are sharply drawn. Munari uses brilliant hues. Each book evidences a charming sense of humor that is certain to provoke smiles from the young reader. Each picture book reflects Munari's originality and skill as a book designer and his unique style as a tempera artist.

Martha Alexander used pencil and tempera for the expressive illustrations for her own book *Nobody Asked Me If I Wanted a Baby Sister* and for Joan Lexau's *Emily and the Klunky Baby and the Next-Door Dog.* The first book is about a brother's jealousy of his baby sister. The latter tells of a little girl whose parents are divorced and who is frustrated because her mother is too busy to play with her. She runs away from home with her baby brother in hopes of finding their father. Ms. Alexander's illustrations are pleasantly humorous and carefully executed; the colors are often subtle and delicate.

Simplicity in style and an attitude that exudes a freshness, gaiety, and verve are the characteristics of Jose and Ariane Aruego's full-color illustrations for *The Chick and the Duckling.* The illustrations are black pen-and-ink line drawings with tempera overlays. The lighthearted story about the chick who can do everything the duckling can do, except swim, and the Areugos' paintings create a delightful gem worthy of note.

An imaginative and exciting story, told only by way of monochromatic (black and shades of gray) tempera paintings, was created by Lynd Ward in *The Silver Pony.* Each reader—young and old—can tell his individual story, for each of the eighty action-filled tempera paintings that make up this lengthy wordless book stimulates creative and imaginative thinking. Each painting encourages the reader to move on to the next so he can follow each detail of the exciting and unexpected episodes that are depicted in dream sequences experienced by the lonely boy who is the major character in this unique wordless book. The paintings done in the representational style so typical of this distinguished book artist do not need full color. Lynd Ward's effective use of shading of black tempera on white paper is all that is necessary to evoke a response to each of the paintings that make up the story of *The Silver Pony.* This book was included in the 1974 Showcase exhibit and justifiably so! It is not only a graphic accomplishment but a literary accomplishment as well.

Pastel Painting.   Pastel consists of powder color mixed to the correct hue with white chalk and bound with gum tragacanth and liquids. (It is not merely white chalk stained with dye.) It is used dry, like a chalk. The artist can build up tone in delicate layers, usually on rough cardboard. Most often, the pastel is rubbed with the finger or a soft cloth. Whereas watercolor is transparent, pastel is opaque. It is also "soft" in appearance.

Some artists claim that it is easier to use than watercolors, and that they like to use pastel because its effect is immediate and its use is more rapid than most other painterly techniques.

Pastels were used by Mamoru Funai to illustrate Sara Cone Bryant's *The Burning Rice Fields,* a version of a well-known Japanese legend. The texture of this art medium is apparent in Funai's sketches; the grain of the chalk can be seen, and it looks "soft and furry." Funai used pastels to create pictures that are characterized by a pleasant simplicity and forthrightness, qualities quite consistent with the author's brief and simple version of this folktale.

Nonny Hogrogian used pastels with pen and line drawings for the 1966 Caldecott Medal award book, *Always Room for One More* by Sorche Nic Leodhas. The touches of heather color and green pastels for the fields of heather serve to convey the atmosphere and beauty of Scotland. The use of pastels to create a background of heather-covered hills adds to the elegance of Ms. Hogrogian's drawings which were done in pen-and-ink line and cross-hatching.

The same medium was used in *Helen Oxenbury's ABC of Things,* by Helen Oxenbury. Her pastel illustrations depict humorous situations and a combination of objects beginning with each respective letter of the alpha-

Illustration by Mamoru Funai for *The Burning Rice Fields* by Sara Cone Bryant. Copyright © 1963 by Holt, Rinehart and Winston, Inc. Reprinted with permission of the publisher.

bet. Her combinations are outrageously funny and imaginative (for example, "a pig and a pelican posturing and parading on a pier") and so are her handsome illustrations.

Graphic Techniques

There is a wide range of printmaking materials that are used by contemporary artists to make surface relief paintings. Traditionally, woodcuts were the main medium used. Cardboard, composition board, plastic, plywood, and paper reliefs are the media used by many contemporary relief artists. These graphic techniques are discussed in the pages that follow. Stone lithography is a planographic, or surface process of printmaking; print and nonprint surfaces are on the same level. This technique for drawing will also be discussed in this chapter.

Woodcuts. The wood that is used for woodcuts must be cut from the length of the trunk of a tree. A design is usually cut crosswise to the natural grain of the wood and can be seen after the areas to be printed white are removed by the woodcutter's gouge and knife. Various types of wood may be used, but the plank must be well-seasoned and dry and must be neither too hard nor too soft. The most popular type of wood is pear wood, but pine wood is commonly used, too. Other woods that an artist may use are cherry, lime, and beach. Nonny Hogrogian used pear wood for the block from which the prints were pulled for the keepsakes that were given to the guests attending a Caldecott Medal award dinner. Ed Emberley prefers the pine plank.

The woodcut artist traces his drawing on the planed woodblock in reverse. Thus, it will appear the right way in the print. Non-printing areas (those which will be printed white) are cut away with scoops and sharp knives; the printing areas (those which will be printed black) are the raised portions left standing. The effect of cutting a picture in wood is different from the effect of drawing a picture on canvas with a brush, a pen, or a pencil. In very general terms, the characteristic style of lines resulting from woodcutting is rather severe, powerful, and terse. Seldom can one cut lines that are delicate, supple, or fluid. These are characteristics of lines made in wood and apply when they are compared with lines made with more manipulative media such as pen or brush. Few people, however, would say that the woodcuts made by Evaline Ness, Antonio Frasconi, or Ed Emberley are lacking in delicacy, suppleness, and mobility, for their work with wood is graceful and fluid.

When the woodcut prints make use of more than one color, the artist is usually asked to make a separate woodcut drawing for each color.

The final woodcut prints are submitted to the publisher as overlays. The works of a few of the major woodcut artists are discussed briefly below.

Evaline Ness used woodcut prints for the illustrations that appear in *Tom Tit Tot, Double Discovery,* and *Josephina February.* By and large, her woodcuts are fairly sophisticated in design. She evidences remarkable skill with the tools and is able to produce graceful and delicate lines with this art medium. The woodcuts that were made to illustrate *Josephina February* are especially effective. The pictures of the charming, skinny little Josephina with very unruly hair accentuate this compassionate story of a little Haitian girl who is faced with making a choice between the baby burro which she finds and grows to love, and a pair of real leather shoes for her grandfather. The style of Ms. Ness' woodcuts and her use of color reflect the spirit of Haiti, its richness and its poverty, its beauty and its wretchedness. The woodcut prints that illustrate *Tom Tit Tot* effect a boisterously humorous mood. They are done in a far more uninhibited manner than those that were made to tell Josephina February's story. The pictures emphasize the qualities of each of the story characters—the greediness and gullibility of one, the dullness, awkwardness, and laziness of the other. Ms. Ness' illustrations are quite compatible with the style of writing that Joseph Jacobs used in "Tom Tit Tot," his version of Rumpel-stiltskin, a well-known folktale which he included in the anthology entitled *English Folk and Fairy Tales.*

Nonny Hogrogian uses free patterns in her woodcuts as she does in her line drawings. When she has an illustrating commission that calls for more than one color, making it necessary for her to use several woodblocks to build up a design, she positions one color in relation to the other by eye. She does not use guides. This is in contrast with the work done by woodcut artists Ed Emberley, Marcia Brown, and Evaline Ness whose designs are more exacting and call for a more careful use of guides in their overlays. Nonny Hogrogian studied under Antonio Frasconi at the New School for Social Research where she learned to do woodcuts.

Some of the books that Nonny Hogrogian illustrated with woodcuts include *The Kitchen Knight, Hand in Hand We'll Go,* and *Ghosts Go Haunting.* The double pages for the illustrations in Barbara Schiller's *The Kitchen Knight* are beautiful. They interpret well and with skillful simplicity the medieval chivalry and courtly love that is so much a part of the Arthurian legends. The texts and the illustrations in the other two books mentioned above could be used with great advantage to introduce Scottish dialect and lore to children from ages ten to fourteen years. Ms. Hogrogian made handsome woodcut prints for the well-chosen poems written by Robert Burns that appear in *Hand in Hand We'll Go.* The touches of brown and yellowish green that are added to the key black figures and the backgrounds of gray, brown, and mustard yellow vividly evoke the prevailing mood and scene. Complementing qualities of humor, gentleness, and strength are revealed in Burns' poetry and in Nonny Hogrogian's prints. Also in the Scottish spirit are the illustrations for *Ghosts Go Haunting* by Sorche Nic Leodhas (pseud. Alger LeClaire). The mood of the illustrations in this book is one of eeriness, although the element of humor is present, too. The collection of ghost tales (Scottish legends and ballads) is bewitching, and so are the illustrations that accompany them.

The woodcut prints by Antonio Frasconi are delightfully inventive. He is considered a master illustrator, and his work is frequently exhibited in the American Institute of Graphic Arts Children's Book Shows. He has written and illustrated several books. Some of his better-known titles are *See Again, Say Again* which can be used to introduce foreign languages to children in grades three through seven; *The Snow and the Sun,* a South American folk rhyme in English and Spanish; and *The House that Jack Built,* a nursery rhyme in English and French. Frasconi's style in woodcut is bold and spirited with just the right touch of humor. He provides lively

From *See Again, Say Again,* © 1964 by Antonio Frasconi. Reproduced by permission of Harcourt Brace Jovanovich, Inc.

variety in line and color from book to book and from page to page. He usually uses bright colors, and each of the colors has its own independent shape. This helps to give his work an exceptionally vital composition. The title pages for each of his books are usually two-page spreads and are particularly striking. Hardly any young person who glanced at one would resist its invitation to read the book. Worthy of note also is his set of woodcut prints for Doris Dana's version of *The Elephant and His Secret*. This story, told in Spanish and English, is based on a fable by the Nobel Prize-winning Chilean poet Gabriela Mistral. Frasconi's colorful woodcut prints masterfully illustrate the beauty, power, and humor that is expressed in the text.

A former student of Antonio Frasconi, Seymour Chwast is also recognized for his woodcut prints (as well as for his linoleum prints) which he created to illustrate stories for children. His illustrations are typified by an uninhibited use of wood and woodcut technique. His work suggests that he has a wonderfully comic sense of reality; he expresses an amazing range of human feeling, ranging from the bold humor to tender feeling. These characteristics will be recognized in the illustrations in *Still Another Children's Book* and *Still Another Number Book*, both written by Martin S. Moskof, and *The Pancake King*, written by Phyllis La Farge. The illustrations for the first two books named above were exhibited in the 1971-1972 American Institute of Graphic Arts Children's Book Show and the first and the last named books were included in the American Institute of Graphic Arts Fifty Books of the Year in 1971.

A Caldecott Medal winner for his illustrations in Barbara Emberley's *Drummer Hoff*, Ed Emberley handles the woodcut medium expertly. The pictures in *Drummer Hoff* were done in a thoroughly stylized manner as were the illustrations in Barbara Emberley's *One Wide River to Cross* and in his own *Green Says Go*. His lines are never careless, but he controls the wood medium with freedom and with ease. In *One Wide River to Cross*, the woodcuts are printed in black on solid-color backgrounds; the only exception is the rainbow page. Color prints are found in *Drummer Hoff* and *Green Says Go*. Although he used only three colors in these two books, he created the impression of thirteen colors by employing the overprinting technique. He made separate woodcuts for each of the three colors.

Mr. Emberley's colors are strong, bold, and flat, qualities which emphasize the simplified form that is so characteristic of this woodcut artist's work. While his woodcuts usually suit the contents and mood of the individual texts, each set of illustrations exemplifies his strong sense of design and his prolific imagination. Emberley's active sense of humor is expressed in his practice of exaggerating form and in his imaginative extension of subject matter. For example, there are the thoroughly stylized drawings of the basilisk, the unicorn, and the griffin in *One Wide River to Cross;* the charming but mammoth features of Paul Bunyan as seen in the double-page spreads in *The Story of Paul Bunyan;* and the pompous regalia worn by the military men in *Drummer Hoff.* His sense of humor, his vivid imaginative extension of the text, and his skill in handling the woodcut are very much apparent in these pictures as they are throughout any of his picture books.

Gil Miret made exquisite woodcuts for several children's books which are not children's picture books, however. His most striking woodcuts appear in Barbara C. Smucker's realistic fiction novel for children entitled *Wigwam in the City.* His lines are powerfully expressive, tending to choppy linear effects and to broad planes in bold black-and-white contrast. The tone of the drawings is as serious and real as the story itself.

Miret's work is different from Emberley's. When his work is compared with Emberley's illustrations, particularly those in *Drummer Hoff* and *One Wide River to Cross,* it is hard to believe that the same art medium was used by these two artists. The differences serve once again to remind us that each artist has his own unique style of drawing and of handling his art medium, and that each story will influence the mood expressed by use of line, detail, and tones.

Other woodcut artists abound, but space does not permit elaboration on their work. Two accomplished artists who cannot go unmentioned and who have contributed significantly to the field of children's literature are Ann Grifalconi, who illustrated Mary Hays Weik's *The Jazz Man* and Elizbeth Bishop's *The Ballad of the Burglar of Babylon,* and Clement Hurd, who made the unique illustrations that appear in *Wildfire* and *Wingfin and Topple,* both written by Evans G. Valens, Jr.

Cardboard Cutouts. Blair Lent uses laminated cardboard cutouts with watercolor overlays. His cutting tool is a single-edged razor blade. He has also used safety pins to create a particular effect in his prints. Lent used the cardboard cutouts to make the pictures for Margaret Hodges' *The Wave,* Ernest Small's *Baba Yaga,* and his own *Why the Sun and the Moon Are in the Sky* and *John Tabor's Ride.*

Most of the stories he illustrated are folktales and legends and Blair Lent's pictures literally demand that the reader believe each highly fantastic tale. His art work matches the tone of each text. Through control of blade and brush, Lent leaves no doubt in the mind of the reader that a tidal wave can lift houses from the soil and carry them away, as was portrayed in *The Wave.* The pictures in *John Tabor's Ride* emphasize that the

man who came to the whaler's rescue was spry and eccentric and that he wore an unruly beard that was speckled with seaweed and tobacco. The reader is reassured by Lent's graphics in *Baba Yaga* that the witch is an old hag, frightening in appearance, but essentially harmless.

Lent uses free-flowing swirls in almost all of his books. His representations of wind, smoke, clouds, steam, or bodies of water are expressively moving and are drawn with grace and ease. Although all of his work is done with the blade and brush, he is able to depict a humorous overtone when and where it is the main mood, as it is in *John Tabor's Ride, Why the Sun and Moon Are in the Sky*, and *Baba Yaga*. When the mood is one of seriousness and the feeling is one of tenseness, he can portray that, as he did so well in *The Wave* and *Oasis of the Stars*, the latter written by Olga Economakis.

Linocut.   An artist may select linoleum instead of wood to make a surface painting. Linoleum is more yielding than wood and, thus, is an easier medium to handle. Because of its softness, gracefully curved lines can be cut, but the lines cannot be fine lines. Two types of linoleum may be used for linocuts, namely the kind which contains cork filler and permits clean-edged cuts, and the cork-free variety, the edge of which tends to crumble, thus causing the lines in a print to be slightly rough.

A skillfully contrived picture book illustrated by Marcia Brown with two-color linoleum cuts is *Dick Whittington and His Cat*. Her handling of this medium is vigorous and is nicely integrated with the concise and brief text (prose). The linocut prints in this book are suited to the period and the nature of this old favorite folktale. Much more dramatic are the handsome linocuts that illustrate the Hawaiian legend entitled *Backbone of the King: The Story of Paka'a and His Son Ku*. Once again, Marcia Brown vividly retains the authentic quality of the legend she has illustrated. In *Backbone of the King*, the exact features, the strong lines, and the effective use of color depict the fundamental struggles and powers of the ancient Hawaiians as well as their frailties.

Striking linoleum cuts made by Eric Carle illustrate the refreshing verses by the well-known poet and nature writer Aileen Fisher in *Feathered Ones and Furry*. The linocuts, printed in black on tan and white pages,

Illustrations by Blair Lent for *The Wave* by Margaret Hodges, adapted from Lafcadio Hearn's *Gleanings in Buddha-Fields*. Pictures copyright © 1964 by Blair Lent. Reprinted with permission of Houghton Mifflin Company.

are masterfully expressive and reflect a genuine and great appreciation, wonderment, and respect for birds and animals. The book as a graphic production is superb. The illustrations in and of themselves, the style of type and placement of text and illustrations, the quality and shade of paper, the binding, the quality of reproduction, and so on combine to make this book an exemplary, one well worth including in a home or school library. The simple poems are excellent for reading aloud in a family or classroom setting.

Wood Engraving. Wood engraving is a modification of the woodcut. For engraving, the wood must be cut across the trunk to obtain an end grain. (In woodcuts, the side grain is used.) The most suitable wood is

From *Feathered Ones and Furry* by Aileen Fisher. Illustrations Copyright © 1971 by Eric Carle, with permission of Thomas Y. Crowell Company, Inc., publisher.

boxwood, for it is the hardest, and it permits the engraver to cut fine curved lines in depth. The tool of the wood engraver is a burin similar to that used by a metal engraver. In contrast to a woodcut design, the wood engraving can carry considerable detail. It may also carry hatching in any direction and produce halftones.

The wood engravings that Philip Reed made for *Mother Goose and Nursery Rhymes* are done with considerable care and attention to detail, which is made possible and even encouraged by wood engraving as an illustrating technique. *Mother Goose and Nursery Rhymes* is a charming book, done in beautiful format, and Philip Reed has brought a refreshing interpretation to the popular as well as to the not-so-well-known rhymes. The human figures in his drawings appear to be rustic, and the animals are quite spirited. This wood engraver has revealed a delightfully droll sense of humor in his drawings. He uses a great deal of color in his work. *Mother Goose and Nursery Rhymes* was done in six colors.

Scratchboard.   Scratchboard, also called scraperboard, is comparable to an etching. Scratchboard consists of a drawing board covered with layers of chalk. Most commonly, the scraperboards are smooth-surfaced white or black boards, but there is actually a wide range in various surface textures obtainable. The chalk surface of the board is indented with different grains and varies in degrees of fineness. The smooth-surfaced board allows the artist more scope for where shading is required; to show contours he can use pen dots, ticks, or thin lines, according to the texture of the subject. There is no limit to the effect that can be obtained on the plain surfaced board. It often entails the tedious task of the placing of the dots or thin line, but it permits sharp, clear-cut lines for detail work. The grain boards offer a shortcut to many shaded effects, though some of them are restricted in their uses. Regardless of the texture of the board surface, the chalk layers are scraped with a sharp instrument (needle, graver, or blade), as is done when making an etching, in order to expose the underneath layer. The result is a precise, sharp line. Shading may be accomplished by parallel lines, cross-hatching, or strippling. As with a wood engraving, the artist usually makes his drawing on tracing paper in the exact size that the illustration will be in the book. Then he transfers this onto the scratchboard "face up," and the drawing is inked in. After the ink has dried, he proceeds to scrape in or scratch in his design. Scratchboard is primarily a black-and-white medium. When an artist uses this medium for illustrations in more than one color, he must employ the preseparated technique and make a separate scratchboard drawing for each color. Barbara Cooney is commonly associated with the scratchboard technique. Two other scratchboard artists worthy of attention are Leonard Everett Fisher and Anthony Ravielli. A brief discussion of their work follows.

Most notable of Barbara Cooney's illustrations are those that appear in *Chanticleer and the Fox.* Her work in this book and in others is recognized by her attention to minute detail. Each setting is authentically and faithfully presented, even to the carefully delineated thatch-roofed cottage and the variety of flowers that appear in the countryside scenes. The flowers and grasses in her drawings are typical of those that grew in the England of Chaucer's time. Ms. Cooney even includes the magpie, which the people of Chaucer's day regarded as an evil omen, to warn the reader of the disaster that is to befall Chanticleer. The delicacy of the lines and the meticulous attention to detail highlight the medieval flavor of this fable, yet it is as fresh and contemporary as one would want it to be. Barbara Cooney also expresses a sophisticated wit in her drawings for this adaptation of *The Canterbury Tales,* a spirit that prevails throughout her other picture books, also.

From *Casey at the Bat* by Ernest L. Thayer. Introduction by Casey Stengel. Illustrated by Leonard Everett Fisher. Copyright © by Franklin Watts, Inc. Reprinted with permission of the publisher.

Leonard Everett Fisher used the scratchboard technique to make the pictures for Ernest L. Thayer's *Casey at the Bat,* the famous poem which first appeared in the *San Francisco Examiner* on June 3, 1888. Fisher's pictorial version of this poem was selected in 1964 as one of that year's "Ten Best Illustrated Children's Books." The illustrations are bold black-and-white drawings, and are done in a style that is especially well-disciplined.

Fisher also used scratchboard for the art work in the Colonial American Craftsman series, which includes *The Silversmiths, The Papermakers, The Hatters,* and *The Wigmakers.* The books in this series are factual, and Leonard Everett Fisher's illustrations are filled with considerable detail. They reinforce the content of the text, but they also extend it and help the reader to gain understanding and appreciation for the work and workers indigenous to colonial life. The illustrations, which are strong and handsome black-and-white drawings, are an integral part of the books in this series. They are compatible with the brief, but interesting, descriptions of the techniques used by each colonial craftsman.

Fisher used scratchboards to make the dramatic illustrations for Gerald W. Johnson's *America Is Born*. These drawings, which are fairly representational in style, vividly recreate the incidents involving the purchase of Manhattan Island by the colonial Dutch people from the American Indians.

Fisher's strikingly forceful scratchboard drawings illustrate a book containing Abraham Lincoln's two most famous speeches, *The First Book Edition of the Gettysburg Address and The Second Inaugural*. These drawings emphasize Lincoln's most salient phrases. Leonard Everett Fisher has profusely illustrated other books in The First Book Edition series with very fine scratchboard drawings. Included are those in which the complete text for each of the following documents or pieces of literature is given: "The Declaration of Independence," "John F. Kennedy's Inaugural Address," "A Man Without a Country," "A Message to Garcia," and the aforementioned "Casey at the Bat."

Anthony Ravielli used the scratchboard technique to make drawings for a science book series. The first book in this series is entitled *Wonders of the Human Body*. Another book in the series, *The World Is Round*, is also illustrated with scratchboard drawings. Ravielli's illustrations are detailed and instructive. They are representational, and yet delightfully imaginative. Each set of illustrations is in perfect unity with the text, and each brings greater depth of understanding to the subject being considered.

Stone Lithography.   Stone lithography is a planographic technique for making a print. Few contemporary artists use this process, but among those who do are Lynd Ward, the D'Aulaires, and Felix Hoffmann.

The stone lithographer uses slabs of fine-grained Bavarian limestone which are ground down and polished with Carborundum to produce a smooth and level surface. The artist then draws his design (laterally reversed) in litho drawing ink, using pen or brush. He may also use litho chalk or crayon to draw his design onto the stone slab. Whatever drawing material he uses to develop his subject on the stone, that material must be a compound of grease, wax, and lampblack. The grease mixture makes it possible to produce the printed image, and many copies of this image can be reproduced. The drawing must be the exact size as it will appear on the page in the book.

Having finished the drawing, the artist then proves the stone. The stone is treated with chemicals, gum arabic, and nitric acid, then a solution of asphalt in fatty oils. The oil sinks into the stone in the image areas or drawn parts; this area repels water. The undrawn areas protected by the gum arabic are water-sensitive and grease-resistant. At this point, the stone is dampened with water which soaks into the nonprinting parts of the stone only. Next, a greasy ink is rolled over the stone. This ink is absorbed by the printing parts, but repelled by the damp parts. Paper is pressed against the stone, and an impression is made from the inked (greased) areas. Upon close examination, the fine grain of the limestone can be discerned in the image that is impressed on the paper.

When more than one color is used, the artist must draw a separate design on another slab of stone. Only the part of the design that is to appear in a specific color is drawn on the stone. Thus, whatever elements in the picture that are to appear in red are drawn on another stone, and so on, for each additional color. Eventually, the designs that appear on various stones are printed one after another on a single sheet of paper, and a multicolored lithoprint is created.

Examples of children's picture books illustrated in this technique are found in the classics that were written and illustrated by Edgar and Ingri D'Aulaire, specifically, *George Washington, Buffalo Bill, Pocahontas,* and *Abraham Lincoln.* Recently, the D'Aulaires remade the illustrations for *Abraham Lincoln,* using acetates instead of the stone lithography technique, because the offset printers objected to handling the stone. The colors used in their books are cheerful and bright. The full-page lithographs that appear in each of these books portray the greatness of each of the famous personages and help the reader to appreciate the contributions they made to America's history. The D'Aulaires have paid particular attention to details in their drawings, and each detail reflects the authenticity of their brief biographies. The interiors of the buildings, the clothing of the various periods, and the actual appearance of the people about whom the biographies deal were depicted as authentically as the artists could possibly determine through careful research.

When illustrating fairy tales, Felix Hoffmann uses a considerable amount of color. *The Seven Ravens* was done in seven colors, and five colors were used in the lithographs in *Rapunzel, The Sleeping Beauty,* and *The Wolf and the Seven Little Kids.* The illustrations for each of these fairy tales contribute much toward making each publication a handsome picture book. Each book will undoubtedly offer the young reader much

pleasure, for the illustrations are works of art which are completely harmonious interpretations of the stories.

Hoffmann's figures are uniquely stylized. This artist gives careful
attention to the features and facial expressions of each story character as
well as to the articles of clothing worn by each. He pays particular attention to the settings and landscapes that surround the action so that the
mood of each story is highlighted and sustained. It is through these interesting details that the young reader gets an exciting new look at his
favorite old fairy tales.

Few artists have created such attractive interpretations of the traditional tales as has Felix Hoffmann. Considering that the medium Hoffmann used to create his colorful pictures was lithostone, his accomplishments are even more astonishing. He has also illustrated another book by
using the prints made from stone lithograph. *Picture Bible* is done in black-
and-white stone lithographs.

Lynd Ward is another important stone lithographic artist. He used
this medium to make the drawings for May McNeer's *The Mexican Story*
and *The Canadian Story*. Ward's work is characterized by its unique vitality, masculinity and his approach to drawing, which appears to be one of
sincerity and thoughtfulness. His lithographs evidence a disposition toward
thoroughness and exactness. The scenes of Mexico and the wilds of
Canada are detailed and are factually accurate, and yet they are not
photographic. They are imaginative and are indigenous to the locale and
the personalities he has portrayed. None of his illustrations are ever condescending. Instead, he tends to raise the viewer of his prints to greater
heights of understanding and appreciation for the graphic arts, for good
reading, and for the contents of the books they illustrate. Each book is
filled with drawings that highlight the dramatic episodes and pageantry
that are so typical of May McNeer's stories. The realistic and detailed
drawings are perfectly compatible with the texts they illustrate.

Color Separations (Acetate, Vellum, or Bourges). Many times, an
artist will prepare his own color separations for his illustrations. Color separations are done with "overlays" of vellum, acetate, or Bourges.

Vellum is a heavy, translucent tracing paper that accepts all media—
ink, pencil, paint, and crayon. Since it has a tendency to buckle if large
areas are painted, and also because it stretches with changes in humidity,
vellum may not be used were tight register is called for.

Acetate is more permanent than vellum; it is transparent and is available in several thicknesses. It will accept pencil, ink, or paint only if it is
specially treated. When using acetate, the artist must make a separate

drawing for each color. Regardless of the colors that will be included in the picture when it is printed, the artist uses black for each drawing.

Bourges is a series of transparent sheets which are coated with removable printing ink colors. To execute a color separation with Bourges, the artist removes, builds up, or cuts out sections of the color overlays. In fact, these colors can be used as color guides for the printer. This is not the case when acetates and vellum are used for copy, because the copy made with these media is in black. Color is achieved with ink on the press instead of in the preparation of the art work. The printer must use color swatches as his guide.

Following are the steps that are used to make color separations. The key drawing, which contains the plotting for the dominant color as well as for the major forms in the picture, is made first. Register marks, a cross drawn with the ruling pen, the T-square, and the triangle, are placed on the key drawing and each overlay sheet. One edge of the overlay is taped to the illustration board and is placed on top of the key drawing. The overlay is positioned so that each registration mark is perfectly aligned. The parts of the picture that are to be printed in the second color are drawn in black. This procedure is used with each additional color. The platemaker makes a separate plate for each color in the composition. The printer mixes his inks to match the color swatches that the artist has provided for each color in the combination.

This process is used by many contemporary book artists. Joan Walsh Anglund used pen-and-ink drawings with two-color overlays done on frosted acetate for the illustrations that appear in *A Friend Is Someone Who Likes You*. The D'Aulaires used acetates for their latest edition of *Abraham Lincoln*. They tried to make the prints look as though they had been done with stone lithography, the medium used to make the illustrations that appear in their biography series. They were successful, for only the keenest eye would notice that stone was not used to make these prints. Roger Duvoisin used acetate for the color separations in *Veronica* and *Petunia, Beware!*, two wonderfully humorous picture books for young readers.

H. A. Rey also does his own color separations. His key drawings are made with wash, india ink, and black crayon on drawing paper. The overlays are done in black and gray crayon, gray gouache, and flat Bourges grays on acetate.

Process Printing for Continuous Art Work. Continuous art work in full color, such as paintings and color montage, are reproduced by process color printing. The plates for process printing are made by the photomechanical separation of the primary colors—red, yellow, and blue. Black is added to reinforce the details and to facilitate the reproduction of neutral colors. Each plate is a complete halftone plate of one of the primary colors. The exact proportion and distribution of the color as it exists in the original subject is duplicated.

To make the color separation negatives for a set of four-color process plates, the full-color painting is photographed—once for each of the four component colors of the final full-color reproduction. Each photograph is made through a different filter which separates the particular color to be recorded. These color-separated negatives are in continuous tone. To make a halftone negative, the continuous tone negatives have to be rephotographed to produce continuous tone positives. Any color inaccuracies are corrected at this point. Then, the retouched positives are photographed through a halftone screen to create the four-color process halftone negatives. A separate printing plate is made for each color. Photomechanical separations are costly but are used occasionally. The camera was used to separate the colors that appear in the illustrations by Barbara Cooney in *A White Heron: A Story of Maine* and all of Brian Wildsmith's brilliant multicolored picture books. The color separations of Robert Andrew Parker's award-winning watercolor illustrations that appear in *Zeek Silver Moon* and *The Trees Stand Shining* were done by camera. This same mechanical process was used to prepare the paintings that illustrate John Burningham's *Mr. Grumpy's Outing*, a 1972 Showcase title, and Blair Lent's pen drawings and acrylic paintings in the Caldecott Medal book, *The Funny Little Woman*.

Summary

Various painterly and graphic techniques are used by contemporary book artists. The artist may use pastels, watercolors, oil paints, pencil, crayon, tempera, gouache, or ink. He may make prints with woodcuts, wood engravings, linoleum cuts, scratchboard, stone lithography, and color separation media. The technique for reproducing continuous art work has been described. The artists' media and techniques have been discussed briefly, and some children's books which contain pictures made with one or more of these media or techniques have been identified.

SELECTED REFERENCES

ALEXANDER, MARTHA. *Nobody Asked Me If I Wanted a Baby Sister*. Illustrated by Martha Alexander. New York: Dial Press, 1971.

ALIKI (pseud. ALIKI BRANDENBERG). *A Weed is a Flower: the Life of George Washington Carver.* Englewood Cliffs, N. J.: Prentice-Hall, 1965.

ANDERSEN, HANS CHRISTIAN. *Thumbelina.* Illustrated by Adrienne Adams. New York: Charles Scribner's Sons, 1961.

ANGLUND, JOAN WALSH. *A Friend Is Someone Who Likes You.* Illustrated by Joan Walsh Anglund. New York: Harcourt, Brace & World, 1958.

———. *In a Pumpkin Shell.* New York: Harcourt, Brace & World, 1960.

BISHOP, ELIZABETH. *The Ballad of the Burglar of Babylon.* Illustrated by Ann Grifalconi. New York: Farrar, Straus & Giroux, 1968.

BROWN, MARCIA. *Backbone of the King: The Story of Paka'a and His Son Ku.* New York: Charles Scribner's Sons, 1966.

———. *Dick Whittington and His Cat.* Illustrated by Marcia Brown. New York: Charles Scribner's Sons, 1950.

BROWN, MARGARET WISE. *The Golden Bunny.* Illustrated by Leonard Weisgard. New York: Golden Press, 1953.

BRYANT, SARA CONE. *The Burning Rice Fields.* Illustrated by Mamoru Funai. New York: Holt, Rinehart & Winston, 1963.

BURNINGHAM, JOHN. *Mr. Grumpy's Outing.* Illustrated by John Burningham. New York: Holt, Rinehart & Winston, 1971.

BURNS, ROBERT. *Hand in Hand We'll Go: Ten Poems.* Illustrated by Nonny Hogrogian. New York: Thomas Y. Crowell Co., 1965.

CHEN, TONY. *Run, Zebra, Run.* Illustrated by Tony Chen. New York: Lothrop, Lee and Shepard Co., 1972.

CHONZ, SELINA. *A Bell for Ursli.* Illustrated by Alois Carigiet. New York: Henry Z. Walck, 1953.

———. *Florina and the Wild Bird.* Illustrated by Alois Carigiet. New York: Henry Z. Walck, 1953.

———. *The Snowstorm.* Illustrated by Alois Carigiet. New York: Henry Z. Walck, 1958.

CHWAST, SEYMOUR and MOSKOF, MARTIN STEPHEN. *Still Another Children's Book.* Illustrated by Seymour Chwast. New York: McGraw-Hill Book Co., 1972.

———. *Still Another Number Book.* Illustrated by Seymour Chwast. New York: McGraw-Hill Book Co., 1971.

COONEY, BARBARA. *Chanticleer and the Fox.* New York: Thomas Y. Crowell Co., 1958.

DANA, DORIS. *The Elephant and His Secret.* Illustrated by Antonio Frasconi. New York: A Margaret McElderry Book/Atheneum Publishers, 1974.

D'AULAIRE, EDGAR and D'AULAIRE, INGRI. *Abraham Lincoln.* Illustrated by Edgar and Ingri D'Aulaire. Garden City, N.Y.: Doubleday & Co., 1957.

———. *Buffalo Bill.* Illustrated by Edgar and Ingri D'Aulaire. New York: Doubleday & Co., 1952.

———. *George Washington.* Illustrated by Edgar and Ingri D'Aulaire. New York: Doubleday & Co., 1936.

———. *Pocahontas.* Illustrated by Edgar and Ingri D'Aulaire. New York: Doubleday & Co., 1946.

ECONAMAKIS, OLGA. *Oasis of Stars.* Illustrated by Blair Lent. New York: Coward-McCann, 1965.

EHRLICH, AMY. *Zeek Silver Moon.* Illustrated by Robert Andrew Parker. New York: Dial Press, 1972.

FRASCONI, ANTONIO. *The House That Jack Built*. Illustrated by Antonio Frasconi. New York: Harcourt, Brace & World, 1958.

———. *See Again, Say Again*. Illustrated by Antonio Frasconi. New York: Harcourt, Brace & World, 1964.

———. *The Snow and the Sun*. Illustrated by Antonio Frasconi. New York: Harcourt, Brace & World, 1961.

GINSBURG, MIRRA. *The Chick and the Duckling*. Translated from the Russian by V. Suteyev. Illustrated by Jose and Ariane Aruego. New York: Macmillan Co., 1972.

GOUDEY, ALICE E. *The Day We Saw the Sun Come Up*. Illustrated by Adrienne Adams. New York: Charles Scribner's Sons, 1961.

———. *Houses from the Sea*. Illustrated by Adrienne Adams. New York: Charles Scribner's Sons, 1959.

GRAMATKY, HARDIE. *Bolivar*. Illustrated by Hardie Gramatky. New York: G. P. Putnam's Sons, 1961.

———. *Little Toot*. Illustrated by Hardie Gramatky. New York: G. P. Putnam's Sons, 1939.

GRIMM, JACOB and GRIMM, WILHELM. *Rapunzel*. Illustrated by Felix Hoffmann. New York: Harcourt, Brace & World, 1961.

———. *The Seven Ravens*. Illustrated by Felix Hoffmann. New York: Harcourt, Brace & World, 1963.

———. *The Shoemaker and the Elves*. Illustrated by Adrienne Adams. New York: Charles Scribner's Sons, 1960.

———. *The Wolf and the Seven Little Kids*. Illustrated by Felix Hoffmann. New York: Harcourt, Brace & World, n.d.

HADER, BERTA and HADER, ELMER. *The Big Snow*. Illustrated by Berta and Elmer Hader. New York: Macmillan Co., 1948.

EMBERLEY, BARBARA. *Drummer Hoff*. Illustrated by Ed Emberley. Englewood Cliffs, N.J.: Prentice-Hall, 1967.

———. *One Wide River to Cross*. Illustrated by Ed Emberley. Englewood Cliffs, N. J.: Prentice-Hall, 1966.

———. *The Story of Paul Bunyan*. Illustrated by Ed Emberley. Englewood Cliffs, N. J.: Prentice-Hall, 1963.

EMBERLEY, ED. *Green Says Go*. Illustrated by Ed Emberley. Boston: Little, Brown & Co., 1968.

The First Book Edition of the Declaration of Independence. Illustrated by Leonard Everett Fisher. New York: Franklin Watts, 1968.

FISHER, AILEEN. *Feathered Ones and Furry*. Illustrated by Eric Carle. New York: Thomas Y. Crowell Co., 1971.

FISHER, LEONARD EVERETT. *The Hatters*. Illustrated by Leonard Everett Fisher. New York: Franklin Watts, 1965.

———. *The Papermakers*. Illustrated by Leonard Everett Fisher. New York: Franklin Watts, 1965.

———. *The Silversmiths*. Illustrated by Leonard Everett Fisher. New York: Franklin Watts, 1965.

———. *The Wigmakers*. Illustrated by Leonard Everett Fisher. New York: Franklin Watts, 1965.

FRANCOISE (pseud. FRANCOISE SEIGNOBOSC). *Jeanne-Marie Counts Her Sheep*. Illustrated by Francoise. New York: Charles Scribner's Sons, 1957.

————. *Noel for Jeanne-Marie*. Illustrated by Francoise. New York: Charles Scribner's Sons, 1953.

————. *The Thank-You Book*. Illustrated by Francoise. New York: Charles Scribner's Sons, 1947.

————. *The Things I Like*. Illustrated by Francoise. New York: Charles Scribner's Sons, 1960.

HALE, EDWARD EVERETT. *The First Book Edition of a Man Without a Country*. Illustrated by Leonard Everett Fisher. New York: Franklin Watts, 1968.

HODGES, MARGARET. *The Wave*. Illustrated by Blair Lent. Boston: Houghton Mifflin Co., 1964.

HUBBARD, ELBERT. *The First Book Edition of a Message to Garcia*. Illustrated by Leonard Everett Fisher. New York: Franklin Watts, 1967.

JACOBS, JOSEPH, ed. "Tom Tit Tot," In *English Folk and Fairy Tales*. New York: G. P. Putnam's Sons, n.d.

JEWETT, SARAH ORNE. *A White Heron: A Story of Maine*. Illustrated by Barbara Cooney. New York: Thomas Y. Crowell Co., 1963.

JOHNSON, GERALD W. *America is Born*. Illustrated by Leonard Everett Fisher. New York: William Morrow & Co., 1958.

JONES, HETTIE. *The Trees Stand Shining: The Poetry of the North American Indians*. Illustrated by Robert Andrew Parker. New York: Dial Press, 1971.

KENNEDY, JOHN F. *The First Book Edition of John F. Kennedy's Inaugural Address; Proclamation by Lyndon B. Johnson*. Illustrated by Leonard Everett Fisher. New York: Franklin Watts, 1964.

LA FARGE, PHYLLIS. *The Pancake King*. Illustrated by Seymour Chwast. New York: Delacorte Press, 1971.

LAWRENCE, JACOB. *Harriet and the Promised Land*. Illustrated by Jacob Lawrence. New York: Windmill Books/Simon & Schuster, 1968.

LENT, BLAIR. *John Tabor's Ride*. Illustrated by Blair Lent. Boston: Little, Brown & Co., Atlantic Monthly Press, 1966.

————. *Why the Sun and the Moon Are in the Sky*. Illustrated by Blair Lent. Boston: Houghton Mifflin Co., 1968.

LEXAU, JOAN M. *Emily and the Klunky Baby and the Next-Door Dog*. Illustrated by Martha Alexander. New York: Dial Press, 1972.

LINCOLN, ABRAHAM. *The First Book Edition of the Gettysburg Address and the Second Inaugural*. Illustrated by Leonard Everett Fisher. New York: Franklin Watts, 1963.

McCLOSKEY, ROBERT. *Time of Wonder*. Illustrated by Robert McCloskey. New York: Viking Press, 1957.

MacDONALD, GOLDEN. *The Little Island*. Illustrated by Leonard Weisgard. New York: Doubleday & Co., 1946.

McNEER, MAY. *The Canadian Story*. Illustrated by Lynd Ward. New York: Farrar, Straus & Giroux, 1958.

————. *The Mexican Story*. Illustrated by Lynd Ward. New York: Farrar, Straus & Giroux, 1953.

MOSEL, ARLENE. *The Funny Little Woman*. Illustrated by Blair Lent. New York: E. P. Dutton & Co., 1972.

MUNARI, BRUNO. *The Birthday Present*. Illustrated by Bruno Munari. Cleveland: World Publishing Co., 1959.

————. *Bruno Munari's ABC*. Illustrated by Bruno Munari. Cleveland: World Publishing Co., 1960.

――. *Bruno Munari's Zoo.* Illustrated by Bruno Munari. Cleveland: World Publishing Co., 1963.

――. *Who's There? Open the Door!* Illustrated by Bruno Munari. Cleveland: World Publishing Co., 1957.

NESS, EVALINE. *Double Discovery.* Illustrated by Evaline Ness. New York: Charles Scribner's Sons, 1965.

――. *Josephina February.* Illustrated by Evaline Ness. New York: Charles Scribner's Sons, 1963.

――. *Tom Tit Tot.* Illustrated by Evaline Ness. New York: Charles Scribner's Sons, 1965.

NIC LEODHAS, SORCHE (pseud. ALGER LeCLAIRE). *Always Room For One More.* Illustrated by Nonny Hogrogian. New York: Holt, Rinehart & Winston, 1965.

――. *Ghosts Go Haunting.* Illustrated by Nonny Hogrogian. New York: Holt, Rinehart & Winston, 1965.

OXENBURY, HELEN. *Helen Oxenbury's ABC of Things.* Illustrated by Helen Oxenbury. New York: Franklin Watts, 1972.

PERRAULT, CHARLES. *The Sleeping Beauty.* Illustrated by Felix Hoffmann. New York: Harcourt, Brace & World, 1959.

PIATTI, CELESTINO. *Celestino Piatti's Animal ABC.* Illustrated by Celestino Piatti. New York: Atheneum Publishers, 1966.

――. *The Happy Owls.* Illustrated by Celestino Piatti. New York: Atheneum Publishers, 1964.

POLITI, LEO. *The Nicest Gift.* Illustrated by Leo Politi. New York: Charles Scribner's Sons, 1973.

――. *Pedro, the Angel of Olvera Street.* Illustrated by Leo Politi. New York: Charles Scribner's Sons, 1946.

――. *Saint Francis and the Animals.* Illustrated by Leo Politi. New York: Charles Scribner's Sons, 1959.

――. *Song of the Swallows.* Illustrated by Leo Politi. New York: Charles Scribner's Sons, 1949.

PRESTON, EDNA M. *Pop Corn and Ma Goodness.* Illustrated by Robert Andrew Parker. New York: Viking Press, 1969.

RAVIELLI, ANTHONY. *Wonders of the Human Body.* Illustrated by Anthony Ravielli. New York: Viking Press, 1954.

――. *The World is Round.* Illustrated by Anthony Ravielli. New York: Viking Press, 1963.

REED, PHILIP, ed. *Mother Goose and Nursery Rhymes.* Illustrated by Philip Reed. New York: Atheneum Publishers, 1963.

ROBBINS, RUTH. *Baboushka and the Three Kings.* Illustrated by Nicolas Sidjakov. Berkeley: Parnassus Press, 1960.

SCHEER, JULIAN. *Rain Makes Applesauce.* Illustrated by Marvin Bileck. New York: Holiday House, 1964.

SCHILLER, BARBARA. *The Kitchen Knight.* Illustrated by Nonny Hogrogian. New York: Holt, Rinehart & Winston, 1965.

SENDAK, MAURICE. *Where the Wild Things Are.* Illustrated by Maurice Sendak. New York: Harper & Row, Publishers, 1963.

SMALL, ERNEST. *Baba Yaga.* Illustrated by Blair Lent. Boston: Houghton Mifflin Co., 1966.

SMUCKER, BARBARA C. *Wigwam in the City.* Illustrated by Gil Miret. New York: E. P. Dutton & Co., 1966.

SPIER, PETER. *The Fox Went Out on a Chilly Night.* Illustrated by Peter Spier. New York: Doubleday & Co., n.d.

————. *Hurrah, We're Outward Bound.* Illustrated by Peter Spier. New York: Doubleday & Co., 1968.

————. *London Bridge Is Falling Down.* Illustrated by Peter Spier. New York: Doubleday & Co., 1967.

————. *Of Dikes and Windmills.* Illustrated by Peter Spier. New York: Doubleday & Co., 1969.

SUHL, YURI. *Simon Boom Gives a Wedding.* Illustrated by Margot Zemach. New York: Four Winds Press, 1972.

TENNYSON, ALFRED LORD. *The Charge of the Light Brigade.* Illustrated by Alice and Martin Provensen. New York: Golden Press, 1964.

THAYER, ERNEST L. *The First Book Edition of Casey at the Bat.* Illustrated by Leonard Everett Fisher. New York: Franklin Watts, 1965.

THURBER, JAMES. *Many Moons.* Illustrated by Louis Slobodkin. New York: Harcourt, Brace & World, 1943.

TRESSELT, ALVIN. *Hide and Seek Fog.* Illustrated by Roger Duvoisin. New York: Lothrop, Lee & Shepard & Co., 1965.

TUDOR, TASHA. *A Is for Annabelle.* Illustrated by Tasha Tudor. New York: Henry Z. Walck, 1954.

————. *Around the Year.* Illustrated by Tasha Tudor. New York: Henry Z. Walck, 1957.

————. *Linsey Woolsey.* Illustrated by Tasha Tudor. New York: Henry Z. Walck, 1946.

————. *1 Is One.* Illustrated by Tasha Tudor. New York: Henry Z. Walck, 1956.

————. *Pumpkin Moonshine.* Illustrated by Tasha Tudor. New York: Henry Z. Walck, 1962.

VALENS, EVANS G., JR. *Wildfire.* Illustrated by Clement Hurd. Cleveland: World Publishing Co., 1963.

————. *Wingfin and Topple.* Illustrated by Clement Hurd. Cleveland: World Publishing Co., 1962.

VON JÜCHEN, AUREL. *The Holy Night.* Illustrated by Celestino Piatti. New York: Atheneum Publishers, 1968.

WARD, LYND. *The Silver Pony: A Story in Pictures.* Illustrated by Lynd Ward. Boston: Houghton Mifflin Co., 1973.

WEIK, MARY HAYS. *The Jazz Man.* Illustrated by Ann Grifalconi. New York: Atheneum Publishers, 1966.

WERNER, ELSA JANE, ed. *The Golden Bible for Children: The New Testament.* Illustrated by Alice and Martin Provensen. New York: Golden Press, 1953.

WILDSMITH, BRIAN. *Brian Wildsmith's Birds.* Illustrated by Brian Wildsmith. New York: Franklin Watts, 1967.

chapter 4
using illustrations
in the school

One of the most effective ways to stimulate learning is to surround children with attractive books about things of interest to them. They should be exposed to these books during their preschool years and throughout their entire school careers. A balanced collection in a school library includes many books that satisfy varied reading interests and that span a wide range of reading difficulties. Chances are very good that students will acquire habits of independent reading, study, and learning that will endure throughout their lifetime when they are encouraged to explore the book collection, to pursue their own interests, and to read as widely and deeply as they will.[1] When these books are well written and are illustrated in a fashion that permits the reader's imagination to roam and create, he will also develop a sense of criticism and love of beauty.[2]

Illustrated books are much preferred by children. An astute and ambitious book selector will be able to find quantities of illustrated books that would be appropriate for the varied reading interests and reading achievement levels of most children in any one classroom. Picture books are not written only for the preschoolers or for kindergarten and primary-school children. There are numerous picture books that would delight students in the upper grades and high school, and even the adult. That picture books are not solely for the preschooler and the child of primary-school age is demonstrated with the recently published *Picture Books for Children.*[3] In it almost 400 titles of picture books that would be of interest and would appeal to children from ages four through fourteen and even

1. James Cass, ed., *Books in the Schools* (New York: American Book Publishers Council, 1961), p. iii.

2. Artemis Nicolaidis, "Illustrating Children's Books," *Bookbird* 8 (15 December 1970):71-72.

3. Patricia Cianciolo, ed., *Picture Books for Children* (Chicago: American Library Association, 1973), 159 pp.

older are annotated and categorized according to subject categories that reflect the basic concerns of all children. This bibliography is not comprehensive; it represents only the type of picture books that children within this broad age range will probably enjoy and derive some benefit from.

One can find very fine picture books about a wide variety of topics addressed to readers of all ages and of various levels of reading achievement. Examination of the books which have been included in the Children's Book Council's Showcase and the American Institute of Graphic Arts Children's Book Shows will reveal the many topics on which picture books are focused. The American Indian, animals of all kinds, history of the United States, explorers, biographies of interesting and important people, modes of transportation of the present and of the past, religion, wars, number books and alphabet books, the circus, environment and pollution, atoms, astronomy, and space travel are a mere sampling of the topics about which picture books are written. The list is unending. Think of the wonderful variety of books that one can offer readers both young and old when one considers the *illustrated books,* the broader classification of books which contain pictures and text. A reader of any age could be given beautifully illustrated books about almost any subject; he could use illustrated books to learn or to escape, and to have fun and pleasure from his reading.

Reading is a process which demands that the reader understand the printed word. It is a process which encourages the reader to identify with the book characters and with the action of the story. It is a process which can provide the reader with a wealth of vicarious experiences. Illustrations in books can help the reader to create visual images and can help him to go beyond the printed word. Illustrations in books can facilitate the reader's comprehension, identification, and experiencing.

The youngest as well as the oldest child can gain considerable fun and pleasure from reading an attractively illustrated and well-written book. He can use reading as a wholesome means of escape from life that, for him, may be humdrum and provincial or which may be filled with pressures and grimness. He can use books as a source from which to gain increased knowledge and understanding of himself and others and of the world in which he lives. Acquiring knowledge and understanding often brings considerable pleasure and stimulation to the reader. To some degree, certain developmental needs can be satisfied through reading because the reader identifies with the book characters and the action of the story. Thus he can experience life vicariously and satisfy basic and developmental needs.

Since illustrations help to make the printed word more concrete and to extend the text, it follows that an illustrated book could help the reader to realize fun, pleasure, and varied worthwhile experiences more completely. Picture books and other illustrated books can help educators to accomplish even more, however. In the pages that follow, some specific objectives will be identified, objectives that can be realized when illustrated books (especially picture books) are chosen with care and are used "the right way with the right child at the right time."

A Source of Pleasure. Reading just for the enjoyment it brings should be encouraged at all levels in the educational program. It should be recognized as a perfectly respectable and rewarding activity. When a book is well-chosen in terms of content and style of illustrations, the reader is likely to become thoroughly involved in it and to get a feeling of exhilaration and well-being. This gift of pleasure-filled hours can come from selective reading of beautifully illustrated books of fiction or non-fiction, prose or poetry, classical literary selections or contemporary works, fantasy or realistic stories, humorous tales or serious narratives.

Occasionally, the child will want to read and examine a factual picture book like *Houses from the Sea* and *Butterfly Time,* semi-narratives by Alice E. Goudey. Both of these books are simple texts with attractive representational pictures in exquisite colors done by Adrienne Adams. Each of these picture books should alert the reader to the wonder and beauty that surround him. In *Houses from the Sea,* the rhythmic text, which contains the common names of a variety of seashells, and the carefully detailed full-color illustrations would fascinate many young readers. The accurately colored drawings of twelve common butterflies and the explanation of the life cycle of butterflies would also bring considerable pleasure to the young reader of *Butterfly Time.* An attractive treat is in store for the reader of *Of Dikes and Windmills* by Peter Spier. Textually interesting and scholarly and a graphic arts feat, this "biography of a country" presents interesting historical and contemporary facts about the topography, geography, archeology, architecture, and people of Holland.

Children like to read factual books that are profusely and attractively illustrated. There is no question that they can gain much pleasure from books that have a factual slant. One need only watch the expressions on the faces of children of any age as they sit in the school library or in their own classrooms, reading or just looking at factual picture books. Their expressions are those of awe and engrossed attention when the factual books deal with topics of interest to them. There is much pleasure to be had, indeed, a great feeling of well-being and accomplishment is experienced when one finishes reading or examining an interesting factual book or storybook.

Individuals vary in their reading interests. What brings pleasure and enjoyment to one reader may not bring pleasure and enjoyment to another. Individuals vary considerably, too, in their responses to the illustrations that accompany stories. One child may be delighted with *The Nightingale*, translated by Eva Le Gallienne and illustrated by Nancy Ekholm Burkert with stunning double-page color paintings and decorations that are suggestive of early Chinese screens. This same child may also enjoy the well-told story and the lovely detailed, soft-colored pictures that are offered in *Snow-White and the Seven Dwarfs: A Tale of the Brothers Grimm*, translated by Randall Jarrell and illustrated by Nancy Burkert. Another child, of the same age, may get far more enjoyment from the more sophisticated fantasy by Randall Jarrell entitled *The Bat-Poet*, which is sparsely illustrated with Maurice Sendak's exquisite black-and-white line drawings that look like fine etchings. A young reader may find that the realistic illustrations in Lynd Ward's *The Biggest Bear* and the main character's repeatedly unsuccessful attempts to get rid of his beloved pet constitute a thoroughly enjoyable book. This same child might be unable to appreciate either Alice Dalgliesh's lengthy and tension-filled adventure story, *The Bears on Hemlock Mountain*, or Helen Sewell's highly stylized illustrations that accompany it, whereas both the story and the illustrations of *The Bears on Hemlock Mountain* might delight another child in his class.

Some picture books are fairly universal in their appeal and will bring many pleasure-filled hours to almost any reader. An example is the picture book entitled *Alexander and the Terrible, Horrible, No Good, Very Bad Day* by Judith Viorst. The expressive black-and-white crosshatch drawings by Ray Cruz expand so well upon the meaningful, yet brief, text. Few children will fail to identify or empathize with Alexander's mishaps. We all have bad days, but Alexander's day was disastrous and started when he got up in the morning and lasted through to the moment he went to bed.

Most children will appreciate the efforts of Peter as he struggles in his attempt to learn to whistle, as depicted in Ezra Jack Keats' picture book *Whistle for Willie*, another book with general appeal. The illustrations are done in collage and paint, and they stress the universality of a child's struggle to accomplish the adult feat of whistling.

Narrative verse is the form of literature that Aileen Fisher used in her picture book *In the Middle of the Night* to report what happens at nighttime to the small creatures that inhabit the woods, grass, and sky. Adrienne

Adams' illustrations add considerable charm to this book and serve to emphasize Ms. Fisher's reassuring message that the wonder and beauty which fills the night leaves little room for fears.

Joyous hours will be given the child who has a chance to hear the story and see the illustrations in *One Morning in Maine*. Robert McCloskey's text and illustrations almost demand repeated perusal by five- or-six-year-olds, who will most certainly agree with Sal that it is a wonderfully important occasion when one loses his first tooth. Both the story line and the realistic illustrations in *One Morning in Maine* serve as a comforting reminder to the young reader that he is growing up, just like Sal.

A Source for Fun and Laughter.   Picture books and other illustrated books can be used to bring smiles and laughter to youngsters. The capacity for enjoying humor and nonsense can be fostered through stories and through the illustrations that accompany them. Much of the child's world —in school and out—is filled with pressures and grimness, or at least, with serious and matter-of-fact realities. It is important that he have fun and laughter in order to relieve tensions caused by these pressures and realities. It is important that he be allowed to forget his problems, even temporarily, so that he can view them in proper perspective, perhaps, or reinforce himself with sufficient emotion fortitude so that he can cope with his problems or, hopefully, resolve them eventually.

Humor for young children must be simple and spontaneous. Most children chuckle at Don Freeman's *Dandelion,* the story of a lion who dresses up so much for a party that his hostess fails to recognize him and refuses to let him in. The story and the cartoon-style illustrations are indeed humorous, and yet the theme, that one should be true to one's nature, comes out "loud and clear." Since it is presented in this delightfully humorous manner rather than in a didactic manner, the young reader is more likely to accept this message as being a worthy one.

Many times laughter is provoked when the unexpected happens especially if it occurs as a surprise ending. Thought-provoking humor is offered in the picture book entitled *The World's Greatest Freak Show* written and illustrated by Ellen Raskin. The way Alastair Pflug gets his comeuppance when he takes an assortment of individuals to the country of Tizwthee and presents them as "the world's greatest freaks" not only surprises the protagonist in the story but will undoubtedly surprise and delight the reading audience. This author-artist employed very clever wordplay throughout her sophisticated story and created strikingly beautiful, color-filled illustrations. These factors, along with the situations portrayed in the story, should provide the reader a source for fun and laughter, be it bittersweet.

The surprise ending, as well as the peddler's frustration at his inability to get his caps back from the monkeys, provide the bases for the humor in the old favorite, *Caps for Sale*, written and illustrated by Esphyr Slobodkina. This story was written in traditional folktale style and was appropriately illustrated with simple line drawings and bold opaque colors. A newer version of this classic tale is found in Suzanne Suba's *The Monkeys and the Peddler*. She too tells this humorous story about the peddler and the mimicking monkeys but she illustrates it with striking, colorful watercolor painting. Both versions should please the young reader. Children enjoy dramatizing this simple tale. They have no difficulty playing the role of the angry peddler who vainly tries to convince the monkeys that his caps must be returned, and they have much fun portraying the mimicking, mischievous monkeys.

The impact that Dr. Seuss (pseud. Theodore S. Geisel) has had on helping children to appreciate simple satirical humor is well-known. Exaggeration, incongruity, and the discomfiture of others are depicted in text and cartoon-style illustrations in the story, *Horton Hatches the Egg*. The situations, plus wonderful play on words, provide the humor for this narrative poem about Horton, the elephant who kept his word—one hundred percent! As a humorist (satirist perhaps is a better word for his brand of humor), Dr. Seuss has written and illustrated several other narratives that have provoked gales of laughter from young readers. His means of creating highly amusing situations are usually the same. Among his fantastic tales in picture book format that children find humorous are *And to Think That I Saw It on Mulberry Street*, *The 500 Hats of Bartholomew Cubbins*, *The King's Stilts*, and *The Cat in the Hat*. Children will readily see some humor in his stories, especially if they can view the illustrations while the text is being read to them. Nonetheless, a five- or six-year-old child who is fairly immature, or who is lacking in a rich background of experience, may miss Dr. Seuss' clever verbal wit and will likely fail to appreciate fully the humor and satire of the situations portrayed in each narrative.

Like Dr. Seuss, Tomi Ungerer presents a rather sophisticated humor in his writing and illustrating of children's picture books. Especially worthy of note are *Moon Man* and *Zeralda's Ogre*. *Moon Man* is a cleverly imaginative tale which relates the series of events that happen to the Moon Man after he descends to Earth on the fiery tail of a comet. He is thought to be an invader and is captured and thrown into prison. By means of unique lunar powers, he escapes and has a gay time for a short while but eventually returns to the moon by way of a spacecraft. *Zeralda's Ogre* is about a child-eating ogre whose food preferences undergo change during the course of the story. The conversations about such culinary creations as roast turkey à la Cinderella and chocolate sauce Rasputin provoke much of the humor in this picture book. Both stories are illustrated with bold cartoon-type illustrations that effectively capture their humorous qualities. Vivid colors are used in both books. If a child has sufficient background of knowledge and experience (phases of the moon, spacecraft, and common folktales), these imaginative stories will bring him many moments of fun and laughter.

The fun derived from reading *The Loudest Noise in the World* by Benjamin Elkin comes partly from the closeness to real life situations and the humorous exaggeration of these situations portrayed by the author, but James Daugherty's vigorous illustrations make this story of a little boy's reaction to his grandfather's snoring even funnier.

The nonsense depicted in the text and illustrations of the Jewish folktale entitled *Simon Boom Gives a Wedding* results in quite a jewel. Children will be amazed when witnessing Simon Boom's ludicrous gullibility and his misinterpretation of the colorful idioms in the comical surprise text. Margot Zemach's gouache paintings in soft pinks, blues, beiges, and browns greatly increase the humor of the story about this not-so-wise and silly peasant.

The reader of *The Scroobious Pip* must have an active imagination in order to respond to the brand of nonsense characterized in that story. The reader must go far beyond his "real" world to find humor in the absolutely nonexistent, "way-out" creatures and situations that are described in this nonsense poem which was begun by Edward Lear and finished by Ogden Nash. If the reader is a creative thinker, he probably could appreciate the nonsensical quality of this poem without really needing the illustrations that accompany the text. On the other hand, Nancy Burkert's detailed illustrations would be especially helpful to those readers who have not as yet been introduced to Lear's brand of humor and who have not learned to be free and imaginative in their response to his literary masterpieces.

Four- and five-year-olds are thrilled with the loveable, but horribly ugly, monsters that Max meets in his dreams as portrayed by Maurice Sendak in *Where the Wild Things Are*. The appearance of the monsters and their "wild rumpus" create an eerie atmosphere, and yet the monsters' happy expressions and Max's power over the animals can't help but cause the reader to chuckle. Most children thoroughly enjoy having *Where the Wild Things Are* read to them, and they spend much time examining each fantastic creature created by Sendak's active imagination. The author has used an interesting technique to involve the reader in Max's fantasies. As Max moves into his fanciful world, the pages become increasingly filled with color. As he moves back again into his real world, more white space fills the pages. In all probability, young readers will not be conscious of the manipulative use of color. Nonetheless, the impact of the technique will be felt. The readers, like Max, will move into the fanciful world and then back again to reality.

Seeing Oneself as a Functioning, Growing Individual. Literature may be used to help children realize that growing up is a universal human experience. This very process of growing up is not an easy one, and contemporary literature does depict this truism. Books permit a young reader to view and to experience vicariously many of the realities of growing up; they permit the reader to "try out" various roles and acts of living so that he may eventually select the ones that are most suitable to his unique needs and personality makeup. Perhaps the picture books which are discussed in the following paragraphs serve to justify a growing conviction that books can be used to help children understand that they are growing, functioning individuals, similar to other people in some ways and also different from people in other ways.

A long time favorite with four-, five-, and six-year-olds is *The Growing Story* which was written by Ruth Krauss. The text, and the precise but simple line drawings by Phyllis Rowand, depict a little boy watching many things grow—grass, flowers, chickens, and a puppy, among other things. He doesn't realize until he puts on his warm clothes in late autumn that he, too, has grown. Identification with the book character who is involved in a situation as common as this will be easy for the young reader. He will appreciate more fully that he, too, is growing up. *The Growing Story* can be used to help the young reader accept with ease and grace the physical changes that are taking place within him.

An Anteater Named Arthur by Bernard Waber is a fantasy. Nonetheless, the young reader will easily see himself in this endearing and exasperating creature. The read of *An Anteater Named Arthur* will find comfort in learning that other children, even a young anteater, can be forgetful, messy, inquisitive, choosy, and loveable. The humor in the text is simple and obvious. Bernard Waber's droll cartoon-style illustrations are, for the most part, in pink and brown, and they help to make this a thoroughly engaging picture book. They also help the child to laugh at himself and perhaps even to view life in a more related and wholesome manner.

The brief text and cartoon drawings in Ellen Raskin's *Spectacles* amusingly and imaginatively demonstrate what it is like to be nearsighted and have to wear glasses. Likewise, the pangs one might feel when he is the tallest child are aptly portrayed in *Tall Tina* written by Muriel Stanek and illustrated by Lucy Hawkinson. Books such as these help children come to grips with their feelings about themselves and also serve to alert those who do not have to cope with situations such as these to the feelings of others.

Sometime in the process of growing up children will experience the death of a beloved pet or a relative or a friend. Recently several books dealing with death have been published for the young reading audience. Worthy of note are *A Taste of Blackberries* by Doris B. Smith and *The Tenth Good Thing About Barney* by Judith Viorst. Neither of these stories is depressing or maudlin; both stories are touching and in both, people's reaction to the death of a person or pet is treated candidly, realistically, and acceptingly. In *A Taste of Blackberries*, the boy's death is the result of an allergic reaction to a bee sting; in *The Tenth Good Thing About Barney*, a small boy's beloved cat has just died. These stories and others done with equally good taste could help a child come to grips, to some extent at least, with the fact of death as a reality of life.

From his first junior book on, the young reader can use books to find out something of what people, including himself, are really like. Whether or not he has observed family strife and quarreling, picture books like *Striped Ice Cream* by Joan Lexau and *The Jazz Man* by Mary Hays Weik will help him to have a better understanding of basic human emotions and human frailties. The free pencil sketches that John Wilson made to illustrate *Striped Ice Cream* emphasize the genuine family situations that are portrayed in this engaging story. The problems of poverty experienecd by this self-reliant, fatherless black family are a major part of Joan Lexau's realistic story. An equally important aspect of the story is the believable behavior of the five children in the family. Young readers from every social and cultural group will recognize the universal human traits that are delineated in *Striped Ice Cream*. There is little doubt that they will identify with the ups and downs, the quarreling, and subsequent making up of this interesting family. The story of *The Jazz Man* is direct and true, strong and honest. The hunger and the family conflict, as well as the family's closeness to each other, are included because they are all a part of life the author writes about. *The Jazz Man* may be a grim story, but it is not depressing or fatalistic. The text is full of beautiful imagery, and the superb woodcut illustrations by Ann Grifalconi open windows to the world. Through these windows, children will see more and more each time they read *The Jazz Man*.

Another book which highlights aspects of family life is *Every Day a Dragon*, written by Joan Lexau. This mirthful story about a daily game of make-believe between a little boy and his father will add to the reader's feeling of well-being. Ben Shecter's sketches are very appropriate for this amusing picture book.

These are only a few of the books which exemplify the fact that picture books and illustrated books can be used to help children of all ages realize that their wishes, feelings, and actions may be very normal, that oftentimes they are merely a part of the process of growing up. Books such as these may also be used to help children recognize that people differ in their needs, wishes, and feelings, and that these differences should be cherished.

Vocabulary and Concept Builders. An illustrated book, especially a picture book, is a construction in language and in art, both of which are modes of symbolic representation of the concrete world and of human experiences. When the writer and the illustrator express these representations in ways that permit the reader to create accurate and detailed images of his own, and to relate new or extended meanings to old associations, the result is that the reader will grow in language power; he will form more mature and more adequate concepts about himself and his gradually increasing world.

Actually, wide reading and close reading of all forms of literature will help the child grow in word power and will help him to view his world more adequately. However, if a child comes to school with limited language facility and with an impoverished experiential background, it is best that he read many picture storybooks about his here-and-now world, as well as "concept" books, both of which will help him learn to make generalizations and to extend his vocabulary.

Some of the books included in the series entitled Let's-Read-and-Find-Out are excellent for this purpose. The titles are self-explanatory, but it might be well to say that in each case the child is alerted to his immediate surroundings and is encouraged to look, feel, smell, and listen carefully. His curiosity is aroused, and he is helped to be more responsive to all kinds of experiences. Some of the titles in this series are *Follow Your Nose* and *Look at Your Eyes,* both of which were written by Paul Showers and illustrated by Paul Galdone; and *My Five Senses* and *My Hands,* which were written and illustrated by Aliki.

Other picture books that are effective vocabulary and concept builders include the Noisy Books, written by Margaret Wise Brown. *The Country Noisy Book,* exemplary of the books in this series, is illustrated by Leonard Weisgard and portrays the sounds made by country animals. A book which explains nighttime happenings is *While Susie Sleeps,* a matter-of-fact interpretation by Nina Schneider, the author, and Dagmar Wilson, the illustrator.

Other picture books that are effective vocabulary and concept builders include those created by Eric Carle. His collage illustrations are colorful, attractive, and pleasing and will serve to help the young preschooler acquire some very basic concepts and verbalize about size, number, life cycles of plants and animals, and the like. Some concept books by this talented author-artist are *The Tiny Seed* (life cycle of a flowering plant), *The Very Hungry Caterpillar* and *1, 2, 3 to the Zoo* (counting and number sets), *The Secret Birthday Message* (spatial and directional concepts, pattern and shape recognition, following directions, etc.), and *The Scarecrow Clock* (telling time).

Brian Wildsmith's books on groupings of birds, wild animals, and fishes appeal to the more sophisticated children; his fantasy-colored creatures would certainly stimulate their imaginations. The combination of these unusual pictures and the terms which are used to assemble each of the groups are excellent vocabulary builders. When grouping the birds, captions like the following are used: "a sedge of herons," "a nye of pheasants," and "a stare of owls." The groupings of wild animals include "a skulk of foxes" and "a pride of lions." To mention a few of the groupings of fishes, there are "a cluster of porcupine fish," "a flock of dolphins," "a battery of barracuda," and "a flotilla of swordfish." Brian Wildsmith's nimble brush and his choice of words should contribute much toward enriching the reading, speaking, and writing vocabularies of those who read and examine his books carefully.

Extending Background of Experiences. It is important that the child's world extend beyond himself and his home. He must be introduced to a greater world, a more varied world. This can be done, of course, through real and actual experiences, but picture books may be used to extend the child's world, too. Rich experiences, be they real or vicarious, will permit the child to function as an effective citizen in a cosmopolitan and vital world. A rich background of experiences is essential if the child is to realize success and is to attain more realistically his actual potential in the academic world. Children have an inner drive, desire for knowledge, and intellectual stimulation. Numerous carefully chosen books can provide the young learners with enriching vicarious experiences. Books that are adequately illustrated can be an excellent source from which to obtain a wealth of information in a clear and meaningful way.

Alert, inquisitive young minds will find some interesting and satisfying answers about the wondrous world of nature that are provided in

Betty Jean Lifton's picture book, *The Secret Seller*. An effective combination of black-and-white photographs and stylized illustrations in four colors is used to tell the story of Ken, a little boy who lives in an apartment building in New York City. The youngster has everything he wants except a secret. In his encounters with several other children, it develops that each child has a secret that he will not share with Ken. This portion of the narrative is told by means of black-and-white photographs. The many secrets that Ken finds in Central Park, with the aid of the secret seller, are portrayed with four-color illustrations. Where squirrels store their nuts, how bees gather nectar from the flowers, and where ants store their food and raise their young, are a few of the many secrets that are brought to Ken's attention. *The Secret Seller* is an irresistible story, told with the intent to make children more curious about their surroundings.

Something about color that children would like to know—the names of colors, what happens when colors are mixed, and how colors "talk" or affect moods and feelings—may be learned from *Green Says Go*, a simple picture book, written and illustrated by Ed Emberley. The illustrations are woodcut prints in bright, bold colors and are imaginative and witty. This brief and simple concept book is noteworthy in that it stimulates the average child to be more sensitive to the varied uses of color and encourages him to experiment with painting so that he can make his own unusual colors and shades.

Much about the life patterns of wild animals, especially their struggle for survival, can be learned from *The Barn*, a picture book that was written and illustrated by John Schoenherr. The black-and-white illustrations are "subjectively representational." Along with the text, they portray with sympathetic realism the stark terror experienced by the skunk when he becomes the prey of a great horned owl during a severe summer drought. John Schoenherr tells with expressive words and illustrations a grim and moving story that is sure to enlighten many young readers. Of equal worth and interest is Miska Miles' *Wharf Rat* which Schoenherr illustrated with drawings quite as beautiful and awesome as those which appear in *The Barn*. *Wharf Rat* is a straightforward narrative in which the reader is told what happens to a wharf rat when a disastrous oil slick fouls the waterfront. It should serve to further an interest in the need for a cleaner environment, even the "world" in which the wharf rat lives.

Ranked among the most beautiful books ever published are the long-time favorites created by Holling C. Holling. Each of these books follows the same design and format. Numerous large, strikingly dramatic colored illustrations done by Holling are found in each book. Marginal drawings and diagrams elaborate on significant details mentioned or implied in the brief, but highly informative, texts. A wealth of knowledge can be obtained from these superb books. In *Minn of the Mississippi* and *Pagoo*, the life histories of a turtle and hermit crab, respectively, are traced. A map is provided for the reader's use in following the travels of a small canoe in *Paddle-to-the-Sea*. The reader will learn much about geography, particularly about the regions of the Great Lakes, Niagara Falls, the St. Lawrence River, and the Grand Banks off the coast of Newfoundland. A reference map is also included in *Tree in the Trail* to help bring the reader a greater insight into the various aspects of the westward movement. This story, which tells of the incidents that happened under and around one particular tree that stood on the westward trail, reveals facts that relate directly to subject disciplines such as anthropology, history, and geography. *Seabird* is a story about the triumphs in navigation. More specifically, it is an exciting adventure story revolving around Seabird, an ivory gull, through whose eyes the reader learns about whaling ships, clipper ships, steamships, and aircraft. The author took three or four years to write each book, because his narratives, paintings, and sketches were based upon the findings of his painstaking and conscientious research. Each book would make a fine contribution to any child's personal library.

Information about and an appreciation of people of various cultural groups may be obtained from picture books, be they factual or fictional books. Two very attractive factual picture books are identified below. A wealth of information about how the prehistoric American Southwest Indians prepared and used their pottery can be found in *When Clay Sings* by Byrd Baylor. The attractive illustrations which were prepared by Tom Bahti and caused this book to be named among the 1973 Caldecott Medal Honor Books, are derived from original works done by ancient potters of the Anasazi, Mogollan, Hohokan, and Membres cultures. Another picture book that offers information about the ways of people of another culture, but along a different vein, is Muriel Feelings' *Moja Means One: Swahili Counting Book*, illustrated by Tom Feelings and also named a Caldecott Medal Honor Book (1972). One can indeed learn his numbers by using this really stunning book; but more importantly, perhaps he will acquire some basic facts about the ways of the people who live in East Africa today.

The course of a forest fire caused by a flash of lightning is depicted with fascinating imagery and suspense in *Wildfire*, which was written by Evans G. Valens, Jr. and illustrated by Clement Hurd. How the birds and animals of the forest react to the raging fire, and how the cycle of life is resumed in the burned-out area are told in prose that reads like exquisite verse. The striking illustrations in this large picture book were made with a print-on-print technique. That is, Clement Hurd, the illustrator, placed linoleum block prints on a background of print made from the grain of weathered wood, after which the prints were made on wet rice paper.

In some elementary schools sex education is included in the curriculum. There are now available several picture books on the topic designed to be read by children. Each of the following should demonstrate the variety of attitudes and approaches which are present in the literature for children if one chooses to use picture books as a way to inform children about aspects of sex. The cartoon-style illustrations by Arthur Robins and the light tone of the text in *Where Did I Come From? The Facts of Life Without Any Nonsense and With Illustrations* by Peter Mayle contrasts with the softly colored paintings by Sheila Bewley and the serious forthright style of the text in *Where Do Babies Come From?* by Margaret Sheffield. Still another style used to present information about sex is Eleanor Hamilton's *What Made Me?* which is illustrated with fine-line drawings the style of which is compatible with the brief and candid text. All three picture books present information including practically all of the facts and with the use of correct terminology. Yet each is so different from the other. Each offers an appeal to some readers.

The house that Virginia Lee Burton created in *The Little House* comes alive and over the years experiences the inevitable changes that are the result of progress. These books and numerous others present, through appropriate language and illustrations, meaningful commentaries upon experiences common to most children. Reading about these experiences brings satisfaction to children for it permits them to look back at experiences which they have had, or to share and look back at experiences which they have not had but which the writers or other people have had.[4]

Providing a Literary and Cultural Heritage. Several popular imaginative literary selections that have been enjoyed by children for generations have recently been illustrated by some of the most outstanding contemporary book artists. Among them are Margot Zemach, Uri Shulevitz, Ezra Jack Keats, Adrienne Adams, Evaline Ness, and Paul Nussbaumer.

Margot Zemach has illustrated a number of folk classics that are representative of several national or regional groups. She made the line drawings for *Mommy, Buy Me a China Doll* (retold by Harve Zemach), a picture-book version of an Ozark Mountain-area folk song. She has also illustrated several Russian folk pieces. Among these are *Salt* (retold by Harve Zemach), the story of Ivan, the foolish son of a Russian merchant,

---

4. James R. Squire, ed., *Response to Literature* (Champaign, Ill.: National Council of Teachers of English, 1968), p. 3.

who brings salt to his homeland when his older and supposedly wiser brothers fail in this task, and *The Speckled Hen* (retold by Harve Zemach), an amusing Russian nursery rhyme that tells of the disturbances caused by a hen that lays a speckled egg. Margot Zemach also illustrated *Nail Soup* (retold by Harve Zemach), the somewhat altered Swedish version of the tale about soldiers who make soup with nails. In each of the books mentioned here, Margot Zemach's illustrations are strong, rustic line drawings and are in full-color wash. She illustrated the 1974 Caldecott Medal-winning book *Duffy and the Devil,* which was retold by Harve Zemach and is a Cornish variant of Rumpelstiltskin.

Uri Shulevitz won the 1969 Caldecott Medal for his illustrations of a Russian folktale entitled *The Fool of the World and the Flying Ship,* by Arthur Ransome. He also illustrated the Hebrew legend, *The Carpet of*

From *Nail Soup* by Harve Zemach. Illustrated by Margot Zemach. Copyright © 1964 by Margot Zemach. Published by Follet Publishing Company. Reprinted with permission of Margot Zemach.

Solomon, retold by Sulamith Ish-Kishor. The pictures in this book match so well the dramatic account of the proud King Solomon and how he learns the wisdom of humility. Shulevitz's line-and-wash drawings are quite different from those done by Margot Zemach. Yet, they seem equally appropriate for the tales they interpret.

Another folktale in picture-book form and worthy of note is *John Henry,* retold and illustrated by Ezra Jack Keats. This American legend is illustrated in the modern art style associated with Keats. Nonetheless, the large, bold figures reflect the spirit of the powerful legendary figure who was "born with a hammer in his hand."

Adrienne Adams illustrated the Grimm Brothers' fairy tale *The Shoemaker and the Elves* with soft watercolors. Evaline Ness used woodcuts to make the brown, blue, and black prints for *Tom Tit Tot,* a variant of the well-known tale Rumpelstiltskin. Paul Nussbaumer created with poster paint the colorful pictures that illustrate *Away in a Manger,* a Christmas story told by Mares Nussbaumer. Beautifully illustrated versions of familiar and unfamiliar folktales abound. This is fortunate, for it makes it so much easier and more enjoyable to introduce universal literature to today's children. Folktales are a traditional form of expression. Each tale has been handed down through the ages, and each tale links the young readers of today with a cultural heritage of the past. Many of the folktales portray the dreams of all mankind; many depict the frailties of humanity. Some folktales depict the basic emotions and strengths of people. Some identify the absurdities of life and help children to learn to laugh *at* themselves and to laugh *with* others. Reading and thinking about the themes of folktales will help to develop appreciation for and enjoyment of one's own literary and cultural heritage, as well as the heritage of others. The many picture-book versions of these folktales will help, perhaps, to accomplish these goals more quickly and more easily.

Also of particular worth are the picture-book versions of folktales cited and described briefly below. Each is illustrated by an outstanding artist foreign to the United States. Each constitutes a significant contribution in helping English-speaking children to be exposed to and benefit from literary selections that for many generations have been important to their literary and cultural heritage or to the heritage of other social groups (religious, racial or ethnic). The unique graphic interpretation of Robert Browning's *The Pied Piper of Hamelin* by the well-known German artist Lieselotte Schwarz, as well as her exciting, bold, childlike pictures done in strong clear colors for the new translation of *Sleeping Beauty,* should certainly favorably impress and influence young readers. Impressionistic paintings in full vivid color made by Toma Bogdanovic to illustrate Naomi

Illustration by Lieselotte Schwarz for *The Sleeping Beauty* written by Jacob and Wilhelm Grimm.
Pictures by Lieselotte Schwarz. Copyright © 1967 by Verlag Heinrich Ellerman, Munich, Germany.
First U.S. publication by Scroll Press, Inc. Reprinted with permission of Scroll Press, Inc.

Lewis' adaptation of Andersen's *The Snow Queen* are masterpieces each
in and of themselves and as a total entity in a storytelling effort. In *The
Magic Hat*, ethereal watercolor paintings and a text presented in Japanese
characters as well as in English are combined and become one beautiful
interpretation of the story. The plot concerns a poor woodcutter whose
magic hat makes it possible for him to understand what the creatures of
the forest and the trees are saying and to save a beautiful girl from death.
Wakana Kei is the author and illustrator of this version of the Japanese
folktale.

Two fables by Gabriela Mistral, recipient of the Nobel Prize for Literature in 1945, were translated and adapted by Doris Dana in two picture
books, namely *The Elephant and His Secret* and *Crickets and Frogs*. Both

books contain Spanish and English versions of the stories; both are illustrated with the super woodcut print illustrations by Antonio Frasconi. Both stories should delight English- and Spanish-speaking children in North America as well as those in Latin America. All will be richer for having experienced the literature created by Gabriela Mistral, as interpreted by Doris Dana and Antonio Frasconi.

Developing Appreciation and Understanding of the Graphic Arts. A child's taste for the beautiful in visual arts starts as he looks at the illustrations. He should have an opportunity to see a wide variety of art styles and should read many picture books and illustrated books wherein these varieties in style are employed. Also, it is necessary that he do some close reading and some careful looking at these illustrations.[5] This latter approach to using a picture book is usually taken to mean direct instruction about characteristics of the various styles of art as well as attention to the possible media artists might use to illustrate a story. It means careful appraisal of an illustrated or picture book in terms of specific criteria. The first response one should get from reading literature should be that of enjoyment. Critical reading skills which call for evaluation of the quality of writing used to tell the story and appraisal of the illustrations that accompany the text may well help the reader to be more discriminating in his reading and will bring more enjoyment to the act of reading itself. Some attention, then, should be given to a book as being of the graphic arts.

Wide and careful reading of books that are illustrated with beautiful paintings and designs will help the reader to acquire an appreciation for and an understanding of fine art. Careful reading of many books that exemplify quality writing will lead him to be more discriminating in his selection of quality literary selections. There are numerous picture books and other illustrated books that have excellent illustrations in them and that are written well.

Exposure to excellence alone will not develop attitudes of appreciation or discrimination for quality literature or art. Children must be given numerous opportunities to make comparisons with the mediocre as well as with the beautiful selections. They should be asked to compare the work of one book artist with another. They should compare and contrast the ways in which artists have illustrated the same or similar stories. They should compare and contrast the manner in which artists have used the same media; they should be aware of the major characteristics of the various media and of the styles of art available to book artists.

5. *Ibid.,* p. 8.

When children write and illustrate their own picture books they learn to appreciate the effort, the talent, and the skills that are necessary to create a fine book. Children of all ages can engage in this sort of activity. Four and five year olds, twelve year olds, and even adults learn much and find enjoyment in this sort of creative effort.

Four- and five-year-old kindergarteners in a Milwaukee (Wisconsin) public school were involved in a "storymaking" project. Throughout the year, the children dictated their stories and then used a variety of media to illustrate them. Their teacher read many excellent picture books to them. They talked about the stories themselves, identifying and evaluating (on the young child's level, of course) plot, setting, characterization, and theme. They talked about the pictures in the books. Whenever the teacher knew what medium an artist had used to make the pictures, she would share this information with the pupils. If she had any biographical information or knew anecdotes about the author or illustrator, this also was shared with the children. By the end of the year, the children had grown in language power (oral expression), in creative thinking ability, and in drawing and painting ability. They were extremely sensitive and alert to various techniques used by book artists; they noticed that the illustrations were done in different styles of art. They were fully cognizant of the individual authors and illustrators of the picture books that were included in their school and library collections.

A sixth-grade classroom of children attending a public school in Bloomfield Hills (Michigan) carefully studied the styles of art and the media used by book artists who illustrated the picture books in their school library collection. These pupils were not the least bit hesitant to get picture books from their library. They read the stories—and enjoyed them. Then they studied the aspects of illustrating which have been mentioned here previously. They read articles in *The Horn Book, Elementary English,* and *Publishers' Weekly* that were written about or by book artists. Some of these periodicals were brought in by their teacher, but the children also went to their public library to get the necessary information about the artists they chose to study. Some children, in order to have a more direct source for their information, wrote to artists Ezra Jack Keats, Maurice Sendak, Robert McCloskey, and H. A. Rey. Excitement and delight ran rampant when their letters were answered by these important and talented book artists. Several of the pupils wrote their own stories and tried to illustrate them in the same style, or with the same medium as the artists each had studied. The enthusiasm that this group of sixth graders developed and the wealth of knowledge for the graphic arts and literature that they acquired were rewarding to say the least—rewarding for them, and for their teacher, too.

Identified below are some specific activities that teachers might ask children to participate in. These same activities are quite appropriate for university students of children's literature, be they at the graduate or undergraduate level of study. When the teacher or adult student of children's literature needs a better grasp of information in order to satisfactorily complete the activities, professional resources are cited. (When children need this information to participate in the activities it is understood that the teacher will read the professional material and share with her pupils the information that she gleaned from her reading.)

ACTIVITIES PERTAINING TO AND INVOLVING ILLUSTRATED BOOKS

1. Examine numerous wordless picture books addressed to children within several age ranges. Identify how they may be used to teach reading, visual literacy, and to study literature as a subject in itself. Read the article: Cianciolo, Patricia J., "Use Wordless Picture Books to Teach Reading, Visual Literacy and to Study Literature," *Top of the News.* 29 (April 1973): 226-34.
2. Compare and contrast illustrations in children's books made with woodcuts and wood etchings. Identify quality examples of each kind of illustration. Appraise the artist's effective use of each media in terms of the story illustrated.
3. Examine some of the illustrations in Caldecott Medal-winning books and runners-up. Note the varied styles of art that have been declared appropriate for use in illustrating children's books over a period of years. What conclusions do you draw?
4. Examine several "concept books." Create a series of original *illustrations* for a concept which you might wish to present to children. Some examples of "concept books" are: *1, 2, 3 to the Zoo* by Eric Carle; *The Secret Birthday Message* by Eric Carle; *Seasons* by John Burningham; *Elephant Buttons* by Noriko Ueno; *First Delights: A Book* by Tasha Tudor and *Look Again* by Tana Hoban.
5. Compare various editions of ABC books. Identify artist, medium used, uniqueness of ideas, and quality of art work.
6. Read several Lionni titles noting strong and different themes in each book. Read the article: Lionni, Leo, "Lionni's Artichokes: An Interview," *Wilson Library Bulletin* 44 (May 1970): 947-50.
7. Select at least five "easy-to-read," controlled-vocabulary books. Evaluate them using the general criteria for picture books. Note the advantages and disadvantages of this type of literature. Read the article:

Newman, Robert, "What the Cat in the Hat Begat, Begat," *Elementary English* 40 (November 1963): 751-52. Some authors known for their writing of controlled-vocabulary picture books are Dr. Seuss, P. D. Eastman, Sid Hoff, and Elsa Minarik.

8. Examine editions of Mother Goose. English and American editions as well as traditional and modern versions should be perused.

9. View kinescope "The Illustrator: Louis Slobodkin" (University of Michigan Television Center) and film "The Lively Art of Picture Books" (Weston Woods). Note the procedures Louis Slobodkin follows to illustrate a story for children. Compare his views about the role(s) of illustrating for children with those expressed by Barbara Cooney, Maurice Sendak, and Robert McCloskey, the three book artists interviewed in "The Lively Art of Picture Books." Examine and read the picture books created by these four illustrators.

10. Read the article: Brown, Marcia, "My Goals as an Illustrator," *The Horn Book* 43 (June 1967): 304-16. Read and examine at least five of the picture books created by this author-artist. Evaluate them in terms of her stated goals and the general criteria for picture books. Can you make any generalizations about how subject matter and mood of a story may influence the media and style a book illustrator uses to illustrate that story?

11. Read at least one picture book. Evaluate the selection in terms of how well it exemplifies each of the characteristics of picture books as a broad type of literature.

12. Select several outstanding picture books (you might choose from those designated as Showcase Books, Caldecott Medal and Honor Award Books, or ALA Notable Books). Note the styles of art exemplified and note the artists and titles of the picture books that have been identified as the award committees' pace setters or noteworthy publications. What conclusions can you make regarding book selectors' attitudes about the styles of art that are "appropriate" for illustrating books for children?

13. Select picture books in which the action is set in a foreign country. Note the techniques used by the authors and artists to portray the "spirit" of the culture group.

14. View the film "The Lively Art of Picture Books" (Weston Woods). Note how differently each artist views his task of illustrating books for children. Note the influence the artist's background of experience, apparent personality traits, and attitude about his contribution to the field of children's literature tend to have on the kind of art he produces.

15. View film interpretations of picture books. Appraise the extent to which each film version is harmonious with the content, style, and mood of the book itself. What would be the advantages or disadvantages of using this film with children before or after they read the book upon which it is based? Some films on literary themes: "The Magic Tree" (Texture films), "Little Blue and Little Yellow" (Con-

temporary/McGraw-Hill Films), "Three Stone Blades" (International Film Bureau) based upon the book *Three Stone Woman* by Glo Coalson, "The Snowy Day" (Weston Woods), "This is New York" (Weston Woods), "Paddle-to-the-Sea" (National Film Board of Canada), and "Swimmy" (Connecticut Films).

16. Examine numerous picture books. In each case try to identify the style of art used by the artist. Appraise the selection of that style of art as an appropriate means to reflect the theme, action, and/or mood of the story, and appraise the effectiveness of the artist's use of the style of art.

17. Examine numerous picture books—at least ten to twenty-five. In each case try to identify the art media used by the artist. Appraise the selection of the medium as an appropriate means to reflect the theme, action, and/or mood of the story, and appraise the effectiveness of the artist's use of medium.

18. Create a series of original illustrations for a story not yet illustrated (an original story, a recording, or story that has been told by someone else). Use such media as charcoal, colored chalk, pastels, crayon, fabric, ink, pencil, oil, water paint, or acrylics.

19. Compare the use of collage by different artists (Lionni, Carle, Keats, etc.). Note the differences as to how each artist has used this technique to illustrate stories. How appropriately has each artist used this technique to illustrate the stories?

20. Compare and contrast the following picture books as designated:[6]
    a. *Wilson's World* by Edith Hurd, Harper & Row, 1971; *The Last Free Bird* by A. Harris Stone, Prentice-Hall, 1967; *The Mountain* by Peter Parnall, Doubleday, 1971; *Noah's Ark* by Gail Haley, Atheneum, 1971; *The Wump World* by Bill Peet, Houghton Mifflin, 1970.
       (1) How are these books alike? Different?
       (2) Which book moralizes the most? The least?
       (3) Which book offers the best solution(s)?
    b. *Uptown* by John Steptoe, Harper & Row; *When I Grow Up* by Lois Lenski, Walck.
       (1) How are these books alike? Different?
       (2) What are the implications about one's adulthood in each of these books?
       (3) Contrast the illustrations.
       (4) Estimate the copyright date on both of these.
       (5) How effective is the language in each book?
    c. *William's Doll* by Charlotte Zolotow, Harper & Row; *I'm Glad I'm a Boy, I'm Glad I'm a Girl!* by Robert Kraus, Simon & Schuster; *Let's Play House* by Lois Lenski, Walck.
       (1) Estimate the copyright date on each of these books.

---

6. Format suggested by Charlotte S. Huck at the National Conference on the Language Arts in the Elementary School, Chicago, Illinois, April 7, 1973.

(2) Do the covers of each of these books reflect the "new" notion of sexism?

d. *Wildfire* by Evans G. Valens, Jr., World, 1963; *The Death of a Wombat* by Ivan Smith, Scribner's, 1973.
  (1) How are these books alike? Different?
  (2) Contrast the illustrations.
  (3) How effective is the style of writing in each book, especially in relation to the style of art of the illustrations in each book?

e. *Baby* by Fran Manushkin, Harper & Row, 1972; *Wonderful Story of How You Were Born* by Sidone M. Gruenberg, Doubleday, 1970; *What Made Me?* by Eleanor Hamilton, Hawthorne Booke, 1970; *Where Did I Come From?* by Peter Mayle, Lyle Stuart, 1973; *Where Do Babies Come From?* by Margaret Sheffield, Knopf, 1973.
  (1) How are these books alike? Different?
  (2) How does the writing style and the style of illustrations influence the reader's attitude toward the content of the books?
  (3) Which book(s) presents the "right" or "best" attitude and array of facts about the subject?

f. *Noah's Ark* by Judy Brook, Watts, 1973; *One Wide River to Cross* by Barbara Emberley, Prentice-Hall, 1966; *The Ark* by Marie Angel, Harper & Row, 1973; *Why Noah Chose the Dove* by Isaac Bashevis Singer, Farrar, Straus & Giroux, 1974; *The Elephant and His Secret* by Doris Dana, Atheneum, 1974; and *Noah's Ark* by Gail Haley, Atheneum, 1971.
  (1) How do the interpretations of this story vary? How are they similar?
  (2) Identify the theme of each publication.

g. *Let's Be Enemies* by Janice Udry, Harper & Row, 1961; *I'll Fix Anthony* by Judith Viorst, Harper & Row, 1969; *Billy and Milly* by Miriam Young, Lothrop, Lee & Shepard, 1968; *The Hating Book* by Charlotte Zolotow, Harper & Row, 1969.
  (1) How are these books alike? Different?
  (2) Which book moralizes the most? The least?
  (3) Which book offers the most realistic and believable solution? The most "acceptable"?

h. *The Holy Night* by Aurel von Jüchen and Celestino Piatti, Atheneum, 1968; *A New Day* by Don Bolognese, Delacorte, 1970.
  (1) What is the theme of these books?
  (2) Contrast the setting and time. How is this revealed?

i. *The Burning Rice Fields* by Sara Cone Bryant, Holt, Rinehart & Winston, 1963; *The Wave* by Margaret Hodges, Houghton Mifflin, 1964.
  (1) How are these books alike? Different?
  (2) What is the theme of these books?
  (3) Contrast the illustrations.

j. *The Funny Little Woman* by Arlene Mosel, Dutton, 1972; *Snow-White and the Seven Dwarfs* by Bros. Grimm. Translated by Randall Jarrell, Farrar, Straus & Giroux, 1972.
   (1) How are these stories similar? Different?
   (2) Contrast the illustrations—do they give you a clue as to the country where this version of the folktale originated?

k. *Annie and the Old One* by Miska Miles, Atlantic, Little, Brown, 1971; *Across the Meadow* by Ben Shecter, Doubleday, 1973; *The Tenth Good Thing About Barney* by Judith Viorst, Harper & Row, 1971; *Growing Time* by Sandol S. Warburg, Houghton Mifflin, 1969; *Taste of Blackberries* by Doris Smith, Crowell, 1973.
   (1) How are these books alike? Different?
   (2) Which interpretation do you find most "acceptable" for children?
   (3) Which book would children like most?

l. *Hide and Seek Fog* by Alvin Tresselt, Lothrop, Lee & Shepard, 1965; *White Snow, Bright Snow* by Alvin Tresselt, Lothrop, Lee & Shepard, 1967; *Emilio's Summer Day* by Miriam Bourne, Harper & Row, 1966; *Staying Home Alone on a Rainy Day* by Chihiro Iwasaki, McGraw-Hill, 1969.
   (1) How have the authors described the weather? Have they made you feel the cold? The moisture or rain?
   (2) Identify the expressions and phrases that you might highlight with the children *after* the story is read in order to alert them to the "power of words."

m. *Nothing Ever Happens on My Block* by Ellen Raskin, Atheneum, 1966; *And to Think That I Saw It on Mulberry Street* by Dr. Seuss, Vanguard, 1937.
   (1) From whose point of view are these stories being told?
   (2) For what age level is each of these books?
   (3) How many different things *really* did occur in each story?

n. *Through the Window* by Charles Keeping, Watts, 1970.
   (1) Who is telling the story?
   (2) Do both of the boys see the same things?
   (3) What is the significance of the extent to which the curtains are opened? Of the end papers?
   (4) How many times is the shadow of the cross shown? What does it symbolize?
   (5) What is the significance of the child's drawing at the end of this story?

o. Compare sound filmstrip version (from Children's Literature series, McGraw-Hill, 1973) and the book of any one of the following titles. How are they similar? Different? Which edition most effectively depicts the theme, the mood, and/or the action of the story?

A *Pair of Red Clogs* by Masako Matsuno, World, 1960; *The Dead Bird* by Margaret Wise Brown, Young Scott, 1958; *The Big Pile of Dirt* by Eleanor Clymer, Holt Rinehart & Winston, 1968; *Staying Home Alone on a Rainy Day* by Chihiro Iwasaki, McGraw-Hill, 1969; *Many Moons* by James Thurber, Harcourt Brace Jovanovich, 1943; *Veronica* by Roger Duvoisin, Knopf, 1961; *A Little House of Your Own* by Beatrice S. de Regniers, Harcourt Brace Jovanovich, 1955; *George's Store* by Frank Asch, McGraw-Hill, 1969; *My Mother Is the Most Beautiful Woman in the World* by Becky Reyher, Lothrop, Lee & Shepard, 1945; *Fog Is Secret* by Theresa K. Smith, Prentice-Hall, 1966; *Yellow, Yellow* by Frank Asch, McGraw-Hill, 1971; *I Like a Whole One* by Marguerita Rudolph, McGraw-Hill, 1968; *Peter's Long Walk* by Lee Kingman, Doubleday, 1953.

Summary

A reader of any age may be given beautifully illustrated books about almost any subject. He may use these books to help him to realize diversified personal or educational objectives. Some of the specific objectives have been discussed in this chapter. Illustrated books can serve as an excellent source from which children can view and experience (vicariously) many of the realities of growing up. They can be used to help the young reader form more mature and more adequate concepts of himself and of his ever-expanding world. They can be used to provide the background of experiences and understanding that will help the learner grow in language power. Illustrated books may be used to help the reader acquire a literary and cultural heritage, and they may be used to help the student to understand and appreciate the graphic arts and the fine arts. A few titles of illustrated books that might be used to help children realize these goals have been presented.

SELECTED REFERENCES

ALIKI (pseud. ALIKI BRANDENBERG). *My Five Senses.* Illustrated by Aliki. New York: Thomas Y. Crowell Co., 1962.
———. *My Hands.* Illustrated by Aliki. New York: Thomas Y. Crowell Co., 1962.
ANDERSEN, HANS CHRISTIAN. *The Nightingale.* Translated by Eva Le Gallienne. Illustrated by Nancy Ekholm Burkert. New York: Harper & Row, Publishers, 1965.
———. *The Snow Queen.* Adapted by Naomi Lewis. Illustrated by Toma Bogdanovic. New York: Scroll Press, 1967.
ASCH, FRANK. *George's Store.* Illustrated by Frank Asch. New York: McGraw-Hill Book Co., 1969.

———. *Yellow, Yellow*. Illustrated by Mark Stamaty. New York: McGraw-Hill Book Co., 1971.

BAYLOR, BYRD. *When Clay Sings*. Illustrated by Tom Bahti. New York: Charles Scribner's Sons, 1972.

BOLOGNESE, DON. *A New Day*. Illustrated by Don Bolognese. New York: Delacorte Press, 1970.

BOURNE, MIRIAM ANNE. *Emilio's Summer Day*. Illustrated by Ben Shecter. New York: Harper & Row, Publishers, 1966.

BROWN, MARGARET WISE. *The Country Noisy Book*. Illustrated by Leonard Weisgard. New York: Harper & Row, Publishers, 1940.

———. *The Dead Bird*. Illustrated by Remy Charlip. New York: William R. Scott, 1958.

BROWNING, ROBERT. *The Pied Piper of Hamelin*. Illustrated by Lieselotte Schwarz. New York: Scroll Press, 1970.

BRYANT, SARA CONE. *The Burning Rice Fields*. Illustrated by Mamoru Funai. New York: Holt, Rinehart & Winston, 1963.

BURTON, VIRGINIA LEE. *The Little House*. Illustrated by Virginia Lee Burton. Boston: Houghton Mifflin Co., 1942.

CARLE, ERIC. *The Secret Birthday Message*. Illustrated by Eric Carle. New York: Thomas Y. Crowell Co., 1972.

———. *The Tiny Seed*. Illustrated by Eric Carle. New York: Thomas Y. Crowell Co., 1970.

———. *The Very Hungry Caterpillar*. Illustrated by Eric Carle. New York: World Publishing Co., 1970.

CHONZ, SELINA. *A Bell for Ursli*. Illustrated by Alois Carigiet. New York: Henry Z. Walck, 1953.

CLYMER, ELEANOR. *The Big Pile of Dirt*. Illustrated by Robert Shore. New York: Holt, Rinehart & Winston, 1968.

COALSON, GLO. *Three Stone Woman*. Illustrated by Glo Coalson. New York: Atheneum Publishers, 1971.

DALGLIESH, ALICE. *The Bears on Hemlock Mountain*. Illustrated by Helen Sewell. New York: Charles Scribner's Sons, 1952.

DANA, DORIS. *Crickets and Frogs: A Fable by Gabriela Mistral*. Illustrated by Antonio Frasconi. New York: A Margaret McElderry Book/Atheneum Publishers, 1972.

———. *The Elephant and His Secret*. Illustrated by Antonio Frasconi. New York: A Margaret McElderry/Atheneum Publishers, 1974.

DE REGNIERS, BEATRICE SCHENK. *May I Bring a Friend?* Illustrated by Beni Montresor. New York: Atheneum Publishers, 1964.

DUVOISIN, ROGER. *Veronica*. Illustrated by Roger Duvoisin. New York: Alfred A. Knopf, 1961.

ELKIN, BENJAMIN. *The Loudest Noise in the World*. Illustrated by James Daugherty. New York: Viking Press, 1954.

EMBERLEY, ED. *Green Says Go*. Illustrated by Ed Emberley. Boston: Little, Brown & Co., 1968.

FEELINGS, MURIEL. *Moja Means One: Swahili Counting Book*. Illustrated by Tom Feelings. New York: Dial Press, 1971.

FISHER, AILEEN. *In the Middle of the Night*. Illustrated by Adrienne Adams. New York: Thomas Y. Crowell Co., 1965.

FREEMAN, DON. *Dandelion*. Illustrated by Don Freeman. New York: Harper & Row, Publishers, 1965.

GOUDEY, ALICE E. *Butterfly Time.* Illustrated by Adrienne Adams. New York: Charles Scribner's Sons, 1964.

———. *Houses from the Sea.* Illustrated by Adrienne Adams. New York: Charles Scribner's Sons, 1964.

GRIMM, JACOB and GRIMM, WILHELM. *The Shoemaker and the Elves.* Illustrated by Adrienne Adams. New York: Charles Scribner's Sons, 1960.

———. *The Sleeping Beauty.* Illustrated by Lieselotte Schwarz. New York: Scroll Press, 1967.

———. *Snow-White and the Seven Dwarfs.* Translated by Randall Jarrell. Illustrated by Nancy Ekholm Burkert. New York: Farrar, Straus & Giroux, 1972.

GRUENBERG, SIDONIE M. *The Wonderful Story of How You Were Born.* Illustrated by Hildegard Woodward. New York: Doubleday & Co., 1970.

HALEY, GAIL E. *Noah's Ark.* Illustrated by Gail E. Haley. New York: Atheneum Publishers, 1971.

HAMILTON, ELEANOR VIRGINIA. *What Made Me?* New York: Hawthorn Books, 1970.

HODGES, MARGARET. *The Wave.* Illustrated by Blair Lent. Boston: Houghton Mifflin Co., 1964.

HOLLING, HOLLING C. *Minn of the Mississippi.* Illustrated by Holling C. Holling. Boston: Houghton Mifflin Co., 1951.

———. *Paddle-to-the-Sea.* Illustrated by Holling C. Holling. Boston: Houghton Mifflin Co., 1941.

———. *Pagoo.* Illustrated by Holling C. Holling. Boston: Houghton Mifflin Co., 1957.

———. *Seabird.* Illustrated by Holling C. Holling. Boston: Houghton Mifflin Co., 1947.

———. *Tree in the Trail.* Illustrated by Holling C. Holling. Boston: Houghton Mifflin Co., 1942.

HURD, EDITH THATCHER. *Wilson's World.* Illustrated by Clement Hurd. New York: Harper & Row, Publishers, 1971.

ISH-KISHOR, SULAMITH. *The Carpet of Solomon.* Illustrated by Uri Shulevitz. New York: Pantheon Books, 1966.

IWASAKI, CHIHIRO. *Staying Home Alone on a Rainy Day.* Illustrated by Chihiro Iwasaki. New York: McGraw-Hill Book Co., 1969.

JARRELL, RANDALL. *The Bat-Poet.* Illustrated by Maurice Sendak. New York: Macmillan Co., 1964.

KEATS, EZRA JACK. *Whistle for Willie.* Illustrated by Ezra Jack Keats. New York: Viking Press, 1964.

KINGMAN, LEE. *Peter's Long Walk.* Illustrated by Barbara Cooney. Garden City, N.Y.: Doubleday & Co., 1953.

KLEIN, NORMA. *Girls Can Be Anything.* Illustrated by Roy Doty. New York: E. P. Dutton Co., 1973.

KRAUSS, RUTH. *The Growing Story.* Illustrated by Phyllis Rowand. New York: Harper & Row, Publishers, 1947.

LEAR, EDWARD and NASH, OGDEN. *The Scroobious Pip.* Illustrated by Nancy Ekholm Burkert. New York: Harper & Row, Publishers, 1968.

LENSKI, LOIS. *When I Grow Up.* Illustrated by Lois Lenski. New York: Henry Z. Walck, 1960.

LEXAU, JOAN M. *Every Day a Dragon*. Illustrated by Ben Shecter. New York: Harper & Row, Publishers, 1967.

———. *Striped Ice Cream*. Illustrated by John Wilson. Philadelphia: J. B. Lippincott Co., 1968.

LIFTON, BETTY JEAN. *The Secret Seller*. Illustrated by Etienne Delessert. Photographs by Norma Holt. New York: W. W. Norton & Co., 1968.

LIONNI, LEO. *Little Blue and Little Yellow*. Illustrated by Leo Lionni. New York: Ivan Obolensky, 1959.

MANUSHKIN, FRAN. *Baby*. Illustrated by Ronald Himler. New York: Harper & Row Publishers, 1972.

MATSUNO, MASAKO. *A Pair of Red Clogs*. Illustrated by Kazue Mizumura. Cleveland: World Publishing Co., 1960.

MAYLE, PETER. *Where Did I Come From? The Facts of Life Without Any Nonsense and With Illustrations*. Illustrated by Arthur Robins. London: Lyle Stuart, 1973.

MCCLOSKEY, ROBERT. *One Morning in Maine*. Illustrated by Robert McCloskey. New York: Viking Press, 1952.

———. *Time of Wonder*. Illustrated by Robert McCloskey. New York: Viking Press, 1957.

MCDERMOTT, GERALD. *The Magic Tree*. Illustrated by Gerald McDermott. New York: Holt, Rinehart & Winston, 1973.

MENDOZA, GEORGE. *The Good Luck Spider and Other Bad Luck Stories*. Illustrated by Gahan Wilson. New York: Doubleday & Co., 1970.

———. *The Scarecrow Clock*. Illustrated by Eric Carle. New York: Holt, Rinehart & Winston, 1971.

MILES, MISKA. *Annie and the Old One*. Illustrated by Peter Parnall. Boston: Little, Brown & Co., 1971.

———. *Wharf Rat*. Illustrated by John Schoenherr. Boston: Little, Brown & Co., Atlantic Monthly Press, 1972.

MOSEL, ARLENE. *The Funny Little Woman*. Illustrated by Blair Lent. New York: E. P. Dutton & Co., 1972.

NESS, EVALINE. *Tom Tit Tot*. Illustrated by Evaline Ness. New York: Charles Scribner's Sons, 1965.

NUSSBAUMER, MARES. *Away in a Manger: A Story of the Nativity*. Illustrated by Paul Nussbaumer. New York: Harcourt, Brace & World, 1965.

PARNALL, PETER. *The Mountain*. Illustrated by Peter Parnall. New York: Doubleday & Co., 1971.

PEET, BILL. *The Wump World*. Illustrated by Bill Peet. Boston: Houghton Mifflin Co., 1970.

RANSOME, ARTHUR. *The Fool of the World and the Flying Ship*. Illustrated by Uri Shulevitz. New York: Farrar, Straus & Giroux, 1968.

RASKIN, ELLEN. *Nothing Ever Happens on My Block*. Illustrated by Ellen Raskin. New York: Atheneum Publishers, 1966.

———. *Spectacles*. Illustrated by Ellen Raskin. New York: Atheneum Publishers, 1968.

———. *The World's Greatest Freak Show*. Illustrated by Ellen Raskin. New York: Atheneum Publishers, 1971.

REYER, BECKY. *My Mother Is the Most Beautiful Woman in the World*. Illustrated by Ruth Gannett. New York: Lothrop, Lee & Shepard Co., 1945.

RUDOLPH, MARGUERITA. *I Like a Whole One.* Illustrated by John C. Johnson. New York: McGraw-Hill Book Co., 1968.

SASEK, MIROSLAV. *This Is New York.* Illustrated by Miroslav Sasek. New York: Macmillan Co., 1960.

SCHNEIDER, NINA. *While Susie Sleeps.* Illustrated by Dagmar Wilson. New York: William R. Scott, 1948.

SCHOENHERR, JOHN. *The Barn.* Illustrated by John Schoenherr. New York: Little, Brown & Co., Atlantic Monthly Press, 1968.

SENDAK, MAURICE. *Where the Wild Things Are.* Illustrated by Maurice Sendak. New York: Harper & Row, Publishers, 1963.

SEUSS, DR. (pseud. THEODORE S. GEISEL). *And to Think That I Saw It on Mulberry Street.* Illustrated by Dr. Seuss. New York: Vanguard Press, 1937.

————. *The Cat in the Hat.* Illustrated by Dr. Seuss. New York: Random House, 1957.

————. *The 500 Hats of Bartholomew Cubbins.* Illustrated by Dr. Seuss. New York: Vanguard Press, 1937.

————. *Horton Hatches the Egg.* Illustrated by Dr. Seuss. New York: Random House, 1940.

————. *The King's Stilts.* Illustrated by Dr. Seuss. New York: Random House, 1939.

SHECTER, BEN. *Across the Meadow.* Illustrated by Ben Shecter. New York: Doubleday & Co., 1973.

SHEFFIELD, MARGARET. *Where Do Babies Come From?* Illustrated by Sheila Bewley. New York: Alfred A. Knopf, 1973.

SHOWERS, PAUL. *Follow Your Nose.* Illustrated by Paul Galdone. New York: Thomas Y. Crowell Co., 1963.

————. *Look at Your Eyes.* Illustrated by Paul Galdone. New York: Thomas Y. Crowell Co., 1962.

SLOBODKINA, ESPHYR. *Caps for Sale.* Illustrated by Esphyr Slobodkina. New York: William R. Scott, 1947.

SMITH, DORIS. *A Taste of Blackberries.* Illustrated by Charles Robinson. New York: Thomas Y. Crowell Co., 1973.

SMITH, IVAN. *The Death of a Wombat.* Illustrated by Clifton Pugh. New York: Charles Scribner's Sons, 1973.

SMITH, TERESA. *Fog Is Secret.* Illustrated by Teresa Smith. Englewood Cliffs, N.J.: Prentice-Hall, 1966.

SPIER, PETER. *Of Dikes and Windmills.* Illustrated by Peter Spier. New York: Doubleday & Co., 1969.

STANEK, MURIEL. *Tall Tina.* Illustrated by Lucy Hawkins. Racine, Wis.: Albert Whitman Co., 1970.

STEPTOE, JOHN. *Uptown.* Illustrated by John Steptoe. New York: Harper & Row, Publishers, 1970.

STONE, A. HARRIS. *The Last Free Bird.* Illustrated by Sheila Heins. Englewood Cliffs, N. J.: Prentice-Hall, 1967.

SUBA, SUZANNE. *The Monkeys and the Peddler.* Illustrated by Suzanne Suba. New York: Viking Press, 1970.

SUHL, YURI. *Simon Boom Gives a Wedding.* Illustrated by Margot Zemach. New York: Four Winds Press, 1972.

THURBER, JAMES. *Many Moons.* Illustrated by Louis Slobodkin. New York: Harcourt, Brace & World, 1943.

TRESSELT, ALVIN. *Hide and Seek Fog.* Illustrated by Roger Duvoisin. New York: Lothrop, Lee & Shepard Co., 1965.

——. *White Snow, Bright Snow.* Illustrated by Roger Duvoisin. New York: Lothrop, Lee & Shepard Co., 1947.

UDRY, JANICE. *Let's Be Enemies.* Illustrated by Maurice Sendak. New York: Harper & Row, Publishers, 1961.

UNGERER, TOMI. *Moon Man.* Illustrated by Tomi Ungerer. New York: Harper & Row, Publishers, 1967.

——. *Zeralda's Ogre.* Illustrated by Tomi Ungerer. New York: Harper & Row, Publishers, 1967.

VALENS, EVANS G. JR. *Wildfire* Illustrated by Clement Hurd. Cleveland: World Publishing Co., 1963.

VIORST, JUDITH. *Alexander and the Terrible, Horrible, No Good, Very Bad Day.* Illustrated by Ray Cruz. New York: Atheneum Publishers, 1972.

——. *I'll Fix Anthony.* Illustrated by Arnold Lobel. New York: Harper & Row, Publishers, 1969.

——. *The Tenth Good Thing About Barney.* Illustrated by Erik Blegvad. New York: Atheneum Publishers, 1971.

VON JÜCHEN, AUREL. *The Holy Night.* Illustrated by Celestino Piatti. New York: Atheneum Publishers, 1968.

WABER, BERNARD. *An Anteater Named Arthur.* Illustrated by Bernard Waber. Boston: Houghton Mifflin Co., 1967.

WAKANA, KEI. *The Magic Hat.* Illustrated by Kei Wakana. New York: Scroll Press, 1970.

WARBURG, SANDOL. *Growing Time.* Illustrated by Leonard Weisgard. Boston: Houghton Mifflin Co., 1969.

WARD, LYND. *The Biggest Bear.* Illustrated by Lynd Ward. Boston: Houghton Mifflin Co., 1952.

WILDSMITH, BRIAN. *Brian Wildsmith's Birds.* Illustrated by Brian Wildsmith. New York: Franklin Watts, 1967.

——. *Brian Wildsmith's Fishes.* Illustrated by Brian Wildsmith. New York: Franklin Watts, 1968.

——. *Brian Wildsmith's Wild Animals.* Illustrated by Brian Wildsmith. New York: Franklin Watts, 1967.

YOUNG, MIRIAM. *Billy and Milly.* Illustrated by Robert Quackenbush. New York: Lothrop, Lee & Shepard Co., 1968.

ZEMACH, HARVE. *Duffy and the Devil.* Illustrated by Margot Zemach. New York: Farrar, Straus & Giroux, 1973.

——. *Nail Soup.* Illustrated by Margot Zemach. Chicago: Follett Publishing Co., 1964.

——. *Salt.* Illustrated by Margot Zemach. Chicago: Follett Publishing Co., 1965.

——. *The Speckled Hen: A Russian Nursery Rhyme.* Illustrated by Margot Zemach. New York: Holt, Rinehart & Winston, 1966.

——. *Mommy, Buy Me A China Doll.* Illustrated by Margot Zemach. Chicago: Follett Publishing Co., 1966.

ZOLOTOW, CHARLOTTE. *The Hating Book.* Illustrated by Ben Shecter. New York: Harper & Row, Publishers, 1969.

——. *William's Doll.* Illustrated by William Pène du Bois. New York: Harper & Row, Publishers, 1972.

introduction to bibliography of illustrated books

The bibliography that follows constitutes a compilation of books that contain pictures which effectively illustrate the accompanying texts. Some of the books have only a few pictures; others are profusely illustrated. The illustrations in each book are a significant part of the book. Each entry serves to exemplify the qualities that were elaborated upon in the chapter entitled "Appraising Illustrations in Children's Books":

Something of significance is said.

Audience is understood and respected.

Artistic talent prevails.

Illustrations go beyond the text.

Color (and shading) is used to serve an expressive goal.

Sizes and shapes of the illustrated books vary.

An attempt was made to include illustrated books that are a representative sampling of the various styles of art as well as of the various media and techniques used by the artists. Illustrated books and picture books for children of from four to sixteen years of age are included in the bibliography and should lead young readers on their way to satisfying, informative, and discriminating reading experiences.

bibliography of illustrated books

ABRAHAM, JEAN-PIERRE. *The Pigeon Man.* Illustrated by Alan E. Cober. New York: Harlin Quist Books, 1971.

Barnaby, who raises pigeons and uses them as messengers of goodwill, is rejected and abused by his neighbors. Pen-and-ink drawings are as macabre as the story. Ages 9-16.

ADDAMS, CHARLES. *The Chas. Addams Mother Goose.* Illustrated by Charles Addams. New York: Harper & Row, Publishers, 1967.

Traditional Mother Goose rhymes illustrated in a sophisticated and satirical manner. Ages 9-12.

Illustration for *The Chas. Addams Mother Goose* written and illustrated by Charles Addams. Copyright © 1967 by Charles Addams. Reprinted with permission of Harper & Row, Publishers.

ADOFF, ARNOLD. *Black Is Brown Is Tan.* Illustrated by Emily A. McCully. New York: Harper & Row, Publishers, 1973.

Line-and-wash illustrations combined with verse tell this warm and affectionate story about the vivacious activities and feelings of an interracial family. Ages 4-8.

AIKEN, CONRAD POTTER. *Cats and Bats and Things with Wings.* Illustrated by Milton Glaser. New York: Atheneum Publishers, 1965.

A compilation of sixty witty poems about animals. Illustrations are brilliantly colored paintings done in a unique and expressive style. Ages 5-11.

ALEXANDER, MARTHA. *I'll Protect You from the Jungle Beasts.* Illustrated by Martha Alexander. New York: Dial Press, 1973.

A delightful dream sequence about a little boy who bravely protects his teddy bear from the strange noises until the noises get too loud and then the teddy bear, because he has a special kind of stuffing, protects the little boy. Ages 3-7.

————. *Nobody Asked Me If I Wanted a Baby Sister.* Illustrated by Martha Alexander. New York: Dial Press, 1971.

Pencil with tempera paintings in subtle and delicate colors illustrate this believable story about a brother's jealousy of his baby sister. Ages 4-7.

————. *Sabrina.* Illustrated by Martha Alexander. New York: Dial Press, 1971.

Amusing, two-color drawings tell the story of Sabrina who is embarrassed by her unusual name until she discovers that her classmates like it. Ages 3-6.

ALLARD, HARRY. *The Stupids Step Out.* Illustrated by James Marshall. Boston: Houghton-Mifflin Co., 1974.

This is a whimsical spoof depicting hilarious episodes had by the Stupids on their family outing. Cartoon-styled, line-and-wash illustrations complement this original story, the humor of which is at times very obvious and at others cleverly subtle. Ages 5-10.

AMBRUS, VICTOR G. *A Country Wedding.* Illustrated by Victor G. Ambrus. Reading, Mass.: Addison-Wesley Publishing Co., 1975.

The fox and wolf get their comeuppance when they crash a village wedding to steal food and wine from the wedding feast. Bold and colorful cartoon-styled illustrations add much to the telling of this whimsical tale. Ages 5-9.

————. *The Sultan's Bath.* Illustrated by Victor G. Ambrus. New York: Harcourt Brace Jovanovich, 1972.

This is a story of how a Sultan who ruled over a dry country and the Gardener, Gul-Baba, resolved the problem of the water crisis. Vividly colorful and detailed illustrations and simple text are combined to depict this retelling of an old Hungarian folktale. Ages 5-9.

ANDERSEN, HANS CHRISTIAN. *Hans Clodhopper.* Illustrated by Leon Shtainmets. Philadelphia: J. B. Lippincott Co., 1975.

Pen and wash paintings in antic cartoon style expand the wry humor of this story of how Hans Clodhopper wed a princess and became the king. Ages 5-9.

————. *The Little Match Girl.* Illustrated by Blair Lent. Boston: Houghton Mifflin Co., 1968.

Expressionistic paintings in muted shades result in a superb graphic interpretation of this classic tale. Ages 6-12.

——. *The Nightingale.* Translated by Eva Le Gallienne. Illustrated by Nancy Ekholm Burkert. New York: Harper & Row, Publishers, 1965.
A familiar Andersen fairy tale illustrated with carefully detailed paintings in a style suggestive of early Chinese screens. Ages 6-10.

——. *The Snow Queen.* Adapted by Naomi Lewis. Illustrated by Toma Bogdanovic. New York: Scroll Press, 1967.
Vivid and colorful impressionistic painting make this version of the classic fairy tale a memorable one. Ages 6-11.

——. *Thumbelina.* Illustrated by Adrienne Adams. New York: Charles Scribner's Sons, 1961.
Classic fairy tale illustrated with realistically styled and carefully detailed watercolor paintings. Ages 5-8.

ANGLUND, JOAN WALSH. *In a Pumpkin Shell.* Illustrated by Joan Walsh Anglund. New York: Harcourt, Brace & World, 1960.
A nursery rhyme and alphabet book illustrated with colored and pen-and-ink drawings. Ages 3-7.

——. *Nibble, Nibble Mousekin.* Illustrated by John Walsh Anglund. New York: Harcourt, Brace & World, 1962.
A picture-book and simplified version of Grimms' *Hansel and Gretel.* Illustrations are in the detailed and ingenuous style typical of Anglund's work. They are done in full-color and line technique. Ages 5-8.

ANNO, MITSUMASA. *Anno's Alphabet.* Illustrated by Mitsumasa Anno. New York: Thomas Y. Crowell Co., 1975.
A stunning, sophisticated, and challenging wordless alphabet book! Each letter is formed with solid pieces of rough-grained wood. Objects beginning with that letter are placed on the facing page. Each double-page spread is framed with drawings of flowers and animal forms the names of which begin with the letter being highlighted. Ages 6-9.

ARDIZZONE, EDWARD and ARDIZZONE, AINGELDA. *The Little Girl and the Tiny Doll.* Illustrated by Edward Ardizzone. New York: Delacorte Press, 1967.
A miniature doll, cold and frightened because she was abandoned in the self-service freezer in a grocery store, is found by a little girl who brings it warm handmade clothing and eventually assumes ownership of the doll. Illustrations are line-and-wash drawings, alternating in mustard and lavender colors. Ages 4-7.

ARUEGO, JOSE. *Look What I Can Do.* Illustrated by Jose Aruego. New York: Charles Scribner's Sons, 1971.
Black line drawings with tints of various hues assumes the major responsibility for telling this nonsensical story about two caribou in a series of follow-the-leader antics. *Almost* a wordless book. Ages 3-6.

ASBJØRNSEN, P. C. *The Squire's Bride.* Illustrated by Marcia Sewall. New York: Atheneum Publishers, 1975.
Black-and-white pencil sketches and a forthright text in the style of a competent storyteller are effectively combined to tell this Norwegian folk-

tale about an elderly and wealthy squire whose marriage proposal was rejected by the daughter of a neighboring and poor farmer. Ages 5-9.

ASCH, FRANK. *George's Store*. Illustrated by Frank Asch. New York: McGraw-Hill Book Co., 1969.

Spontaneous, surprise-filled cartoon-styled sketches in black and white tell so much more than the text about the many things that George sells in his store and his many customers. Ages 7-12.

ATWOOD, ANN. *Haiku: The Mood of Earth*. Illustrated with photographs by Ann Atwood. New York: Charles Scribner's Sons, 1971.

A truly artistic piece combining expressive haiku and photographs in full color. Ages 8-16.

BALET, JAN B. *The Fence: A Mexican Tale*. Illustrated by Jan B. Balet. New York: Delacorte Press, 1969.

Illustrations suggestive of naive art add considerable vitality to this clever tale about a tiff between neighbors. Ages 4-8.

———. *The Gift: A Portuguese Christmas Tale*. Illustrated by Jan B. Balet. New York: Delacorte Press, 1967.

Joanjo gives the Christ Child his appreciation of a sunbeam, a moonbeam, and the twinkle of the evening star, whereas others bring lovely gifts of flowers, food, and music. Illustrations are doll-like figures dressed in traditional peasant costumes, all of which are gaily colored. Ages 4-6.

———. *Joanjo, a Portuguese Tale*. Illustrated by Jan B. Balet. New York: Delacorte Press, 1967.

Joanjo, a small boy in a Portuguese fishing village dreams he travels and becomes rich and important and greedy, then awakens convinced that a fisherman's life is for him. Illustrations are in full color and reflect the spirit of the tale. Ages 5-8.

BARRETT, JUDI. *Benjamin's 365 Birthdays*. Illustrated by Ron Barrett. New York: Atheneum Publishers, 1974.

Benjamin had a birthday (every April 6), but because he enjoyed having extra birthdays he wrapped up something in his house every night of every month all year long and gave it to himself the next morning. It added up to 365 birthdays until the next April 6 which he celebrated with his friends on his rooftop. Ages 4-7.

BARRY, ROBERT. *Mr. Willowby's Christmas Tree*. Illustrated by Robert Barry. New York: McGraw-Hill Book Co., 1963.

This is an amusing little fantasy about how the forest animals shared Mr. Willowby's Christmas tree which was too big to fit in his parlor. Children will enjoy the pen-and-ink sketches that depict this refreshing cumulative tale. Ages 4-8.

BASKIN, HOSEA; BASKIN, TOBIAS; and BASKIN, LISA. *Hosie's Alphabet*. Illustrated by Leonard Baskin. New York: Viking Press, 1972.

In this masterpiece of graphic art, stunning expressionistic paintings are integrated with imaginary-building, poetic captions. Ages 6-10.

BEATTY, JEROME, JR., *Bob Fulton's Amazing Soda-Pop Stretcher*. Illustrated by Gahan Wilson. New York: William R. Scott, 1963.

A parody on the politics and the scientific advances of the Space Age, this is a story about the events that occur after a boy accidently invents a non-friction-producing gook. Illustrated with clever cartoon-style sketches. Ages 9-14.

BEHRENS, JUNE. *How I Feel.* Photographs by Vince Streano. Chicago: Children's Press, 1973.

Colored photographs and simple, easy-to-read text depict a gamut of emotional responses to and feelings about everyday experiences and happenings common to most young children. Ages 4-7.

BELKNAP, JODI PARRY. *Felisa and the Magic Talking Bird.* Illustrated by Martin Charlot. Honolulu: Island Heritage Books, 1973.

Full-color representational drawings on double-page spreads illustrate this story about the colorful rural life of a Filipino family and stresses the importance of giving one's full effort to everything one does. Ages 5-10.

BEMELMANS, LUDWIG. *Madeline.* Illustrated by Ludwig Bemelmans. New York: Viking Press, 1939.

A humorous account in rhymed couplets which tells what happens when Madeline, one of twelve girls attending a French boarding school in Paris, is taken to a hospital for an appendectomy. Illustrations are in the expressionistic style and are colored. Ages 5-8.

BERSON, HAROLD. *Balarin's Goat.* Illustrated by Harold Berson. New York: Crown Publishers, 1972.

A humorous French folktale about how Marinette gets her husband to treat her as well as he treats his goat. Illustrations in three-color preseparated ink and wash drawings with wash overlays complement this pleasant action-filled story. Ages 5-8.

——. *The Boy, the Baker, the Miller and More.* Illustrated by Harold Berson. New York: Crown Publishers, 1974.

This adaptation of a French folktale called *Un Morceau de Pain,* charmingly illustrated with four-color preseparated ink and wash drawings with wash overlays, is a refreshing cumulative tale about a very hungry boy who had to go through more than he bargained to get a mere piece of bread. Ages 6-10.

——. *A Moose Is Not a Mouse.* Illustrated by Harold Berson. New York: Crown Publishers, 1975.

A great play with words for the beginning reader: mouse/moose, victor/ Victor, cow/sow. Impressionistic illustrations are four-color preseparated ink and wash drawings with wash overlays produced in halftone. Ages 5-8.

BISHOP, ELIZABETH. *The Ballad of the Burglar of Babylon.* Illustrated by Ann Grifalconi. New York: Farrar, Straus & Giroux, 1968.

Micucu, an escaped convict and murderer, no longer treated as human by society, is chased through the hills like a dangerous animal and finally killed. Exquisitely styled woodcuts emphasize the message of this ballad— Micucu's death on Babylon is "an immortal archetypal myth of the scapegoat." Ages 12-16.

BLAINE, MARY. *The Terrible Thing That Happened at Our House.* Illustrated by John C. Wallner. New York: Parent's Magazine Press, 1975.

Surrealistic paintings and a first-person statement are effectively combined to tell what happens to a family when the mother is employed. Ages 4-9.

BLAKE, QUENTIN. *Snuff*. Illustrated by Quentin Blake. Philadelphia: J. B. Lippincott Co., 1973.

Snuff, who is a young page being taught how to be a knight by his master, proves that he will be an intelligent and brave knight when he frightens away four boot thieves. The animated line-and-wash sketches add to the delightful action and humor of this pleasant story. Ages 5-8.

BODECKER, N. M., trans. *It's Raining Said John Twaining*. Illustrated by N. M. Bodecker. New York: A Margaret McElderry Book/Atheneum Publishers, 1973.

This is a unique compilation of nonsense nursery rhymes translated from the Danish. Illustrated with humorous paintings in full, rich color, some cartoon styled. Ages 3-7.

BODECKER, N. M. *The Mushroom Center Disaster*. Illustrated by Erik Blegvad. New York: A Margaret McElderry Book/Atheneum Publishers, 1974.

Intricate line drawings enhance this delightful and fascinating fantasy of how a beetle, a ladybug, a snail, a spider, a moth, and a cricket use to advantage rubbish tossed away by thoughtless and careless picnickers. Ages 5-8.

BOLLIGER, MAX. *The Wooden Man*. Illustrated by Fred Bauer. New York: Seabury Press, 1974.

Full-color, double-page, expressionistic paintings and a brief and simple text are artistically united to present this story about what happened when a family of birds noticed the sudden appearance and subsequent disintegration of the wooden man (a scarecrow) in a wheat field. Ages 5-8.

BOLLIGER-SAVELLI, ANTONELLA. *The Knitted Cat*. Illustrated by Antonella Bolliger-Savelli. New York: Macmillan Co., 1972.

The adventure-prone, knitted, striped cat's mistress forgot to finish off his tail and a mouse pulls at the thread and unravels it. All turns out well when the owl ties it into a bow until the little girl can finish her job. Illustrations consist of objects created by clever arrangements of bright and bold colored paper cut in various shapes and patterns. A wordless book. Ages 4-7.

———. *The Mouse and the Knitted Cat*. Illustrated by Antonella Bolliger-Savelli. New York: Macmillan Co., 1974.

In this palatable story, the loveable knitted, striped cat goes on a lady-bug hunt, jumps into the lake by mistake but is rescued by a duck and a mouse. Illustrations are made by using flat, deep, and brightly colored paper cutouts. Ages 4-7.

BONSALL, CROSBY. *I'll Show You Cats*. Illustrated by Ylla (pseud. Camilla Koffler). New York: Harper & Row, Publishers, 1964.

A compilation of action-filled photographs of cats and kittens, accompanied by a brief but imaginative text. Ages 4-8.

BONTEMPS, ARNA. *Lonesome Boy*. Illustrated by Feliks Topolski. Boston: Houghton Mifflin Co., 1955 and 1967.

A symbolic account of events involving Bubber, a New Orleans boy who loves his trumpet, and falls under the spell of jazz. Exquisite expressionistic line drawings interpret this mood story. Ages 12 and up.

BORACK, BARBARA. *Grandpa.* Illustrated by Ben Shecter. New York: Harper & Row, Publishers, 1967.

A little girl guilelessly tells about the fun she has with her grandfather. Illustrated with simple drawings done in color. Ages 4-7.

BRANDENBERG, ALIKI. *Go Tell Aunt Rhody.* Illustrated by Aliki. New York: Macmillan Co., 1974.

Double-page gouache paintings in vivid full color depict this early American song about the demise of an old gray goose in a millpond. Ages 5-8.

———. *Three Gold Pieces: A Greek Folktale.* Illustrated by Aliki. New York: Pantheon Books, 1967.

A peasant who has worked far from home for ten years, exchanges his total earnings of three pieces of gold for three pieces of advice, avoids death twice, and returns home with pockets and a bundle filled with gold. Illustrations consist of full-color paintings alternating with black-and-white drawings. Ages 5-8.

BRANDENBERG, FRANZ. *Fresh Cider and Pie.* Illustrated by Aliki. New York: Macmillan Co., 1973.

Marvelously detailed, full-color illustrations (pen-and-ink line drawings with halftone overlays for yellow, blue, and red) depict this story about two friendly enemies—a spider who is outwitted by a fly. Ages 3-7.

BREINBURG, PETRONELLA. *Shawn Goes to School.* Illustrated by Erroll Lloyd. New York: Thomas Y. Crowell Co., 1974.

A convincing account of a little boy's reaction to his first day at nursery school. Stunning acrylic paintings in warm, full colors add great depth of feeling to this simply told, heartwarming story. Ages 4-6.

BRENNER, ANITA. *The Timid Ghost, or What Would You Do with a Sackful of Gold?* Illustrated by Jean Charlot. New York: William R. Scott, 1966.

A retelling of a Mexican folktale about a ghost who wanders around seeking a right answer to his question, "What would you do with a sackful of gold?" Three-color line drawings illustrate this ironic tale. Ages 9-12.

BRENNER, BARBARA. *If You Were An Ant* . . . Illustrated by Fred Brenner. New York: Harper & Row, Publishers, 1973.

By way of simple written text and detailed pen-and-ink, line-and-wash representational drawings, this picture book serves as a unique storehouse of information about ants. Much of it is presented from the perspective of an ant. Ages 5-8.

———. *Mr. Tall and Mr. Small.* Illustrated by Tomi Ungerer. New York: William R. Scott, 1966.

A giraffe and a mouse are almost trapped by a forest fire as they argue about which one is the better size. They realize that each size has its unique advantages as they find their way to safety by combining what the mouse hears when he puts his ear to the ground and what the giraffe sees when he looks over the treetops. Humorous cartoon-type drawings in four colors illustrate the story. Ages 4-7.

BROWN, MARCIA. *Backbone of the King: The Story of Paka'a and His Son Ku.* Illustrated by Marcia Brown. New York: Charles Scribner's Sons, 1966.

A retelling of a Hawaiian legend concerning the events that brought about the exiled Paka'a's restoration of his rightful place as personal attendant or "backbone of the king." The author has used authentic Hawaiian names and chants to portray effectively the ancient Hawaiian culture. Exquisite linoleum-block prints illustrate this legend. Ages 10-14.

Reprinted by permission of Charles Scribner's Sons from *Backbone of the King: The Story of Paka'a and His Son Ku,* written and illustrated by Marcia Brown. Copyright © 1966 Marcia Brown.

————. *Cinderella.* Illustrated by Marcia Brown. New York: Charles Scribner's Sons, 1954.

A picture-book version of a favorite fairy tale, illustrated with delicate drawings in pen line and colored crayon in a style suggestive of period French art. Ages 5-8.

————. *Stone Soup.* Illustrated by Marcia Brown. New York: Charles Scribner's Sons, 1947.

An old folktale which tells how the soldiers tricked the villagers into providing them with all of the ingredients for a soup "fit for a king." Illustrated with humorous red and black drawings in a style suggestive of peasant art. Ages 6-9.

————. *Once a Mouse . . . A Fable Cut in Wood.* Illustrated by Marcia Brown. New York: Charles Scribner's Sons, 1961.

An Indian fable about a mouse that is changed into a cat, then a dog, and a tiger, and back again into a timid mouse. Illustrated with colored woodcut prints. Ages 5-9.

BROWN, MARGARET WISE. *The Dead Bird*. Illustrated by Remy Charlip. New York: William R. Scott, 1958.

Children find a dead bird, conduct a funeral service for it, and soon forget about it as they play. Firm and clear naive paintings illustrate this brief and simple story. Ages 4-6.

BROWNING, ROBERT. *The Pied Piper of Hamelin*. Illustrated by Lieselotte Schwarz. New York: Scroll Press, 1970.

Paintings in a style suggestive of Silesian peasant art expressively depict this classic narrative poem. Ages 6-10.

BRYANT, SARA CONE. *The Burning Rice Fields*. Illustrated by Mamoru Funai. New York: Holt, Rinehart & Winston, 1963.

A brief and simplified version of the Japanese folktale about a man who burned the rice fields on top of a mountain to save the lives of the villagers who were threatened by a tidal wave. Illustrated with double-spread pictures done with pastels. Ages 5-8.

BRYSON, BERNARDA. *Gilgamesh*. Illustrated by Bernarda Bryson. New York: Holt, Rinehart & Winston, 1967.

A retelling of a myth about the Sumerian god-king Gilgamesh. Stunning watercolor paintings and pastel drawings illustrate this large picture book. Ages 10-14.

BUDBILL, DAVID. *Christmas Tree Farm*. Illustrated by Donald Carrick. New York: Macmillan Co., 1974.

Impressionistic paintings in black pencil and wash drawings with overlays in red, yellow, and blue detail this informative statement of how Christmas trees are grown, harvested, and replaced. Ages 6-10.

BULLA, CLYDE ROBERT. *Jonah and the Great Fish*. Illustrated by Helga Aichinger. New York: Thomas Y. Crowell Co., 1970.

Expressionistic paintings in beautiful color composition illustrate this version of the familiar Bible story. Ages 6-10.

BURCH, ROBERT. *The Hunting Trip*. Illustrated by Suzanne Suba. New York: Charles Scribner's Sons, 1971.

Stylized watercolors portray and expand upon the humor and serious message offered in this well-written story about the beauty of nature and the importance of the preservation of wildlife. Ages 6-9.

———. *Joey's Cat*. Illustrated by Don Freeman. New York: Viking Press, 1969.

Joey's cat has kittens but almost loses them to a possum. Illustrations are blue and black sketches done in a free representational style. Ages 5-8.

BURNINGHAM, JOHN. *John Burningham's ABC*. Illustrated by John Burningham. London: Jonathan Cape, 1964.

Colorful watercolor paintings and pen-and-ink drawings reflecting this artist's master draftsmanship provide a humorous interpretation of the letters of the alphabet. Ages 3-6.

———. *Mr. Grumpy's Outing.* Illustrated by John Burningham. New York: Holt, Rinehart and Winston, 1971.

The impressionistic watercolor paintings alternating with cross hatch drawings integrated with brief text produce a memorable story about an outing that unruly children and animals have on Mr. Grumpy's boat. Ages 3-6.

———. *Seasons.* Illustrated by John Burningham. New York: Bobbs-Merrill Co., 1970.

The beauties of nature each season of the year are highlighted in colorful posterlike paintings. Ages 5-8.

BURNS, ROBERT. *Hand in Hand We'll Go: Ten Poems.* Illustrated by Nonny Hogrogian. New York: Thomas Y. Crowell Co., 1965.

An inviting compilation of ten poems composed by the Scottish poet, Robert Burns. Illustrated with colored woodcuts which aptly evoke moods and scenes of the poems. Included is a glossary of the Scottish words. Ages 12 and up.

BURTON, VIRGINIA LEE. *The Little House.* Illustrated by Virginia Lee Burton. Boston: Houghton Mifflin Co., 1942.

A picture-book account of a little house in the country that gradually finds itself surrounded by skyscrapers and the busy traffic and human activities typical of a city. Illustrated with appropriate realistic and detailed watercolor paintings. Ages 5-8.

BYARS, BETSY. *Go and Hush the Baby.* Illustrated by Emily A. McCully. New York: Viking Press, 1971.

A believable and humorous story of how a boy attempts to quiet his crying baby brother. Illustrated with line-and-wash drawings in two colors. Ages 3-5.

CARIGIET, ALOIS. *Anton the Goatherd.* Illustrated by Alois Carigiet. New York: Henry Z. Walck, 1966.

A young Alpine goatherd searches for three runaway goats. Distinctive and colorful illustrations portray the Swiss village and the meadow in which this story is set. Ages 6-10.

CARLE, ERIC. *Do You Want to be My Friend?* Illustrated by Eric Carle. New York: Thomas Y. Crowell Co., 1971.

The pictorial accompaniments, Eric Carle's stunning collages in striking hues, keep the reader intrigued until the very end when he finds that another little mouse and none of the large creatures whose tails the mouse approaches says "yes" to his proposition. Ages 3-6.

———. *1, 2, 3, to the Zoo.* Illustrated by Eric Carle. Cleveland: World Publishing Co., 1968.

An imaginative number book without text. Illustrations consist of double-page spreads, each of which contains a number and a corresponding number of zoo animals in a train car. A little mouse travels along throughout, chatting with each "set" of animals. Illustrations are done in the collage and poster paint technique. Ages 2-7.

———. *The Secret Birthday Message.* Illustrated by Eric Carle. New York: Thomas Y. Crowell Co., 1972.

Tim has to follow the directions included in a message written in rebus in order to find his birthday present. This suspenseful story is illustrated with colorful collages. Ages 6-9.

———. *The Very Hungry Caterpillar.* Illustrated by Eric Carle. Cleveland: World Publishing Co., 1970.

As the caterpillar eats his way through various foods the reader learns to count and to identify the days of the week and learns about the life cycle of this creature. Collage illustrations and clever die cuts are appealing highlights of this beautiful picture book. Ages 4-7.

CARRICK, CAROL. *Lost in the Storm.* Illustrated by Donald Carrick. New York: Seabury Press, 1974.

Stunning expressionistic seascapes, storm scenes, and well-written text tell the believable story about a boy's visit with his new friend and the long restless night when his dog is lost in a storm. Illustrations are crayon and watercolor paintings. Ages 5-8.

CARRICK, DONALD. *Drip, Drop.* Illustrated by Donald Carrick. New York: Macmillan Co., 1973.

Wordless book in which the black-and-white, pencil and wash drawings, with a wash overlay for the blue and gray, depict the "adventures" experienced by a family during a rain storm. Ages 3-7.

CARROLL, RUTH and CARROLL, LATROBE. *Tough Enough.* Illustrated by Ruth Carroll. New York: Oxford University Press, 1954.

An exciting story set in the Great Smoky Mountains of North Carolina deals with a mischievous puppy who is thought to have killed chickens, is exonerated, and becomes a hero when he saves the children from a flash flood. Illustrated with realistic action-filled pencil drawings. Ages 7-10.

CAUDILL, REBECCA. *Did You Carry the Flag Today, Charley?* Illustrated by Nancy Grossman. New York: Holt, Rinehart & Winston, 1966.

Charley, an independent and curious five year old, meets with some exciting circumstances during a summer school for four and five year olds in the Appalachian Mountain area. Appropriate line drawings highlight his experiences. Ages 5-8.

CHARLOT, MARTIN. *Sunnyside Up.* Illustrated by Martin Charlot. Honolulu: Island Heritage Books, 1973.

Line-and-wash illustrations in this oversized wordless book constitute an urging of man to communicate and be compatible with nature. Ages 6-9.

CHASEK, JUDITH. *Have You Seen Wilhelmina Krumpf?* Illustrated by Sal Murdocca. New York: Lothrop, Lee & Shepard Co., 1973.

An excellent example of effective black-and-white illustrations is seen in the many and detailed pen-and-ink wash drawings that appear in this story about a forty-six-year-old Dutch housewife who dared to be different. Ages 6-10.

CHAUCER, GEOFFREY. *The Franklin's Tale.* Retold by Ian Serrailier. Illustrated by Philip Gough. New York: Frederick Warne and Co., 1972.

Full-color paintings reflecting the Middle Ages in England extend this modern English version of the witty and humorous classic tale. Ages 8-12.

CHEN, TONY. *Run, Zebra, Run.* Illustrated by Tony Chen. New York: Lothrop, Lee & Shepard Co., 1972.

Marvelously detailed watercolor paintings (with definition in pencil and some acrylic) effectively interpret this author-artist's own haiku poetry. Ages 6-12.

CHONZ, SELINA. *A Bell for Ursli.* Illustrated by Alois Carigiet. New York: Henry Z. Walck, 1953.

Ursli finds a bell to use during the festival celebrating the arrival of spring. Exquisite colorful paintings depicting Swiss mountain villages add much to this story. Ages 5-8.

CLEAVER, ELIZABETH. *The Miraculous Hind.* Illustrated by Elizabeth Cleaver. Toronto: Holt, Rinehart & Winston, 1973.

Full-color, double-page collage illustrations and precise prose are effectively united to present an artistic rendition of this well-known Hungarian folktale. Ages 8-11.

CLIFTON, LUCILLE. *All Us Come Cross the Water.* Illustrated by John Steptoe. New York: Holt, Rinehart & Winston, 1973.

A thought-provoking graphic and verbal statement emphasizing that all black Americans "crossed the water." Vibrant, full-color paintings illustrate this story that stresses the unity of black Americans. Ages 5-9.

COALSON, GLO. *Three Stone Woman.* Illustrated by Glo Coalson. New York: Atheneum Publishers, 1971.

Strong, simple words and stunning, bold stylized drawings done in the tradition of the Eskimo are combined to tell this Eskimo folktale about how the good-hearted widow Ana finds happiness and her selfish, hard-hearted sister-in-law is punished for her evil ways. Ages 6-10.

COATSWORTH, ELIZABETH JANE. *Troll Weather.* Illustrated by Ursula Arndt. New York: Macmillan Co., 1967.

Selma gathers information about trolls and learns that different people have different ideas about them. Black-and-white drawings highlight sprightly moods of the tale and the various aspects of life in the Norwegian mountains. Ages 7-10.

COLE, WILLIAM, ed. *Oh, What Nonsense.* Illustrated by Tomi Ungerer. New York: Viking Press, 1966.

An anthology of fifty nonsense verses composed by well-known poets, Laura E. Richards, John Ciardi, David McCord, and Spike Milligan. Black-and-white drawings very effectively reflect the gaiety and the nonsensical spirit of the poems. Ages 6-11.

COONEY, BARBARA. *Chanticleer and the Fox.* Illustrated by Barbara Cooney. New York: Thomas Y. Crowell Co., 1958.

An adaptation of one of *The Canterbury Tales,* this fable emphasizes the dangers of accepting flattery. Illustrated in a style reminiscent of illuminated manuscripts and includes numerous detailed scenes and settings typical of the England of Chaucer's time. Ages 7-10.

CULLUM, ALBERT. *The Geranium on the Window Sill Just Died but Teacher You Went Right On.* Illustrated by twenty-eight artists. New York: Harlin Quist Books, 1971.

Surrealistic poetry interpreted by twenty-eight sardonic illustrations comment about life in the classroom. Ages 10-18.

DALGLIESH, ALICE. *The Bears on Hemlock Mountain.* Illustrated by Helen Sewell. New York: Charles Scribner's Sons, 1952.

A tension-filled story telling what happens to Jonathan when he meets two bears on Hemlock Mountain while returning with a big kettle that he has borrowed from his aunt. Ages 5-9.

DANA, DORIS. *Crickets and Frogs: A Fable by Gabriela Mistral.* Illustrated by Antonio Frasconi. New York: A Margaret McElderry Book/Atheneum Publishers, 1972.

A beautifully poetic account of the "musical" battle between the crickets and the frogs, who both try to sing the loudest. Told in Spanish as well as in English. Illustrated with woodcut prints. Ages 6-10.

———. *The Elephant and His Secret.* Illustrated by Antonio Frasconi. New York: A Margaret McElderry Book/Atheneum Publishers, 1974.

This story, told in Spanish and in English, is based on a fable by the Nobel Prize-winning Chilean poet, Gabriela Mistral. When the Second Deluge (40 days of rain) occurs, the elephant saves his friends from the rising flood by taking them to Ararat, that high mountain where Noah's Ark landed during the First Deluge. The beauty, power and humor expressed in this story are dramatized and masterfully illustrated with colorful, double-spread woodcut prints. Ages 5-8.

DAUGHERTY, JAMES. *Daniel Boone*. Illustrated by James Daugherty. New York: Viking Press, 1939.

A narrative biography in which Daniel Boone is zestfully portrayed as a hero, and aspects of his exploits and personality are depicted accurately within the setting of America's westward expansion. Illustrations are bold and realistic line drawings in brown, green, and black. Ages 10-14.

D'AULAIRE, EDGAR and D'AULAIRE, INGRID. *Abraham Lincoln*. Illustrated by Edgar and Ingri D'Aulaire. Garden City, N.Y.: Doubleday & Co., 1939, 1957.

A brief biography of Lincoln presented in picture-book format. Illustrations for first edition were large stone lithograph prints in full-color alternating with large black-and-white drawings; those for the revised edition were made with acetates. Ages 8-12.

DE LA MARE, WALTER. *Jack and the Beanstalk*. Illustrated by Joseph Low. New York: Alfred A. Knopf, 1959.

A picture-book (long and thin in shape) version of the well-known tale. Illustrated with bold and heavy, but whimsical, line drawings. Ages 4-9.

DELAUNAY, SONIA. *Sonia Delaunay's Alphabet*. Illustrated by Sonia Delaunay. New York: Thomas Y. Crowell Co., 1972.

Abstract paintings in brilliant, clear colors are created around each letter of the alphabet. Each letter is accompanied by a rhyme that begins with that letter. Ages 6-12.

DE REGNIERS, BEATRICE SCHENK. *May I Bring a Friend?* Illustrated by Beni Montresor. New York: Atheneum Publishers, 1964.

A childlike and humorous story of a small boy who brings his friends (giraffe, hippopotamus, and lions) with him when the King and Queen invite him to tea, dinner, lunch, breakfast, Halloween, and Apple Pie Day. Illustrations, which resemble stage settings, are basic line drawings in three colors. Ages 5-8.

DICKENS, CHARLES. *A Christmas Carol in Prose: Being a Ghost Story of Christmas*. Illustrated by Philip Reed. New York: Atheneum Publishers, 1966.

Numerous colored woodcuts aptly convey the mood and events of this familiar story. Ages 12-16.

DOMANSKA, JANINA. *If All the Seas Were One Sea*. Illustrated by Janina Domanska. New York: Macmillan Co., 1971.

Intricate geometric figures and clear bright colors are combined to interpret this well-known nursery rhyme. Ages 4-6.

———. *Little Red Hen*. Illustrated by Janina Domanska. New York: Macmillan Co., 1973.

Clip, almost terse text and stylized illustrations typical of Domanska's geometric designs and fresh bright colors are combined to present a unique and humorous version of this classic favorite of young children. Ages 4-8.

———. *The Turnip*. Illustrated by Janina Domanska. New York: Macmillan Co., 1969.

Tapestrylike paintings in soft shades and earth hues add a "new" look to this version of the Slavic cumulative folktale about the tug-of-war between

Illustration for *If All the Seas Were One Sea* written and illustrated by Janina Domanska. Copyright © 1971 by Janina Domanska. Reprinted with permission of Macmillan Publishing Company, Inc.

a giant-sized turnip and the grandmother, grandfather, animals, and birds. Ages 5-9.

———. *What Do You See?* Illustrated by Janina Domanska. New York: Macmillan Co., 1974.

Aniline colors on scratchboard illustrate this lively story which demonstrates dramatically and whimsically that we know the world in terms of our own orientation and background of experience. The bat, the frog, the fern, and the lark each sees the world's beauty but each in its own way. Ages 4-7.

DU BOIS, WILLIAM PÈNE. *Bear Circus.* Illustrated by William Pène du Bois. New York: Viking Press, 1971.

The illustrations for this happy fanciful tale are transparent watercolors and opaque watercolors. It is a refreshing story about a friendship between koala bears and kangaroos. Ages 5-8.

DU BOIS, WILLIAM PÈNE and PO, LU. *The Hare and the Tortoise and the Tortoise and the Hare/La Liebre y la Tortuga y la Tortuga y la Liebre.* Illustrated by William Pène du Bois. New York: Doubleday and Co., 1972.

Cartoon-styled drawings tell these two versions of the well-known fable. The one retold by du Bois is an Aesop's fable wherein the Tortoise wins; that retold by Po is the Oriental version and the winner is the Hare. Ages 6-9.

DUNN, JUDY. *Things.* Photographs by Phoebe and Tris Dunn. Garden City, N.Y.: Doubleday & Co., 1968.

Colored photographs effectively illustrate a variety of "things" children can do, hold, taste, and wonder about. Text is brief and appropriate. Ages 4-10.

From *Things* by Judy Dunn. Illustrated by Phoebe and Tris Dunn. Copyright © 1968 by Doubleday & Company, Inc. Reprinted with permission of the publisher.

DUNNING, STEPHEN; LUEDERS, EDWARD; and SMITH, HUGH, eds. *Reflections on a Gift of Watermelon Pickle and Other Modern Verse.* Illustrated with photographs. Glenview, Ill.: Scott Foresman & Co., 1966.

A compilation of 114 selections of modern verse, illustrated with striking photographs that complement, interpret, or extend the poems. Ages 10 and up.

EHRLICH, AMY. *Zeek Silver Moon.* Illustrated by Robert Andrew Parker. New York: Dial Press, 1972.

This is a story about the everyday activities of a loving family. Full-color watercolor paintings in the expressionistic style effectively portray and extend the mood and action of the text. Ages 5-8.

EINSEL, WALTER. *Did You Ever See?* Illustrated by Walter Einsel. New York: William R. Scott, 1962.

A compilation of imaginative and humorous rhymes. Illustrations and heavy line drawings in bold bright colors. Ages 4-6.

ELKIN, BENJAMIN. *Why the Sun Was Late.* Illustrated by Jerome Snyde. New York: Parents' Magazine Press, 1966.

A cumulative African folktale about the series of events that occurred when a small fly alighted on a leaf of an old weak tree in the jungle causing the tree to crash. Illustrated with appropriate double-spread colored pictures. Ages 4-8.

EMBERLEY, BARBARA. *Drummer Hoff*. Illustrated by Ed Emberley. Englewood Cliffs, N.J.: Prentice-Hall, 1967.

An adaptation in cumulative pattern of a folk verse about the building of a cannon. Illustrations are stylized woodcuts in gay, brilliant shades and are filled with humorous details. Caldecott Medal winner, 1968. Ages 4-8.

———. *One Wide River to Cross*. Illustrated by Ed Emberley. Englewood Cliffs, N.J.: Prentice-Hall, 1966.

A counting book which interprets the folk song about groups of animals moving into Noah's ark. Illustrated with precise black woodcuts on brilliantly colored pages. Words and music for the song are included. Ages 5-8.

ENRIGHT, ELIZABETH. *Tatsinda*. Illustrated by Irene Haas. New York: Harcourt, Brace & World, 1963.

Written in the style of a traditional fairy tale, this original story is exciting and romantic and emphasizes the senselessness of conformity. The illustrations match the mood and action of this charming story and are done with pencil, ink, and watercolor in full color. Ages 9-12.

ESTES, ELEANOR. *Miranda the Great*. Illustrated by Edward Ardizzone. New York: Harcourt, Brace & World, 1967.

A humorous account of what happened to the cat, Miranda, her daughter, and the thirty-three cats they rescued as they fled Rome to avoid the barbarians and made their way to the Colosseum ruins. Illustrated with line drawings that express the pathos and humor of this narrative. Ages 9-12.

ETS, MARIE HALL. *Gilberto and the Wind*. Illustrated by Marie Hall Ets. New York: Viking Press, 1963.

A simple childlike account of the many ways a small boy can "play" with the wind. The drawings are done in black and white (except for the brown-skinned Mexican boy), and they are printed on graph paper. They depict the details and moods of the text very well. Ages 3-5.

E-YEH-SHURE. *I Am a Pueblo Indian Girl*. Illustrated by Quincy Tahoma, Tony Martinez, Alan Houser, and Gerald Nailor. New York: William Morrow & Co., 1939.

An interpretation of the daily life activities of a Pueblo Indian girl, including details about her home, her clothes, corn planting, hairwashing, and making bread. Illustrations were done by four Indian artists and include eleven striking watercolors. Ages 10-14.

FARBER, NORMA. *I Found Them in the Yellow Pages*. Illustrated by Marc Brown. Boston: Little, Brown & Co., Atlantic Monthly Press, 1973.

An alphabet book identifying a gamut of occupations. Illustrations, printed on bright yellow pages, are bold pen-and-ink drawings and are as mind-stretching as the variety of occupations they depict. Ages 4-10.

FEELINGS, MURIEL. *Moja Means One: Swahili Counting Book*. Illustrated by Tom Feelings. New York: Dial Press, 1971.

A unique counting book. The reader is introduced to number concepts, some basic aspects about the ways of the people who live in East Africa today, and a number of Swahili words. Double-spread representational paintings illustrate this concept book. Ages 5-10.

FEELINGS, TOM. *Black Pilgrimage.* Illustrated by Tom Feelings. New York: Lothrop, Lee & Shepard Co., 1972.

Many drawings and paintings (mostly in the representational art style, some in full color and some in black and white) and a first-person verbal statement are merged to present a documentation of the author-artist's decision to leave the United States and make his home in his ancestral African home. Ages 9-16.

FENNER, CAROL. *Christmas Tree on the Mountain.* Illustrated by Carol Fenner. New York: Harcourt, Brace & World, 1966.

Three children climb up snow-covered slopes searching for a perfect Christmas tree. Pastel drawings provoke a joyous response to the sights and the feel of winter. Ages 5-8.

———. *Gorilla Gorilla.* Illustrated by Symeon Shimin. New York: Random House, 1973.

Full page black-and-white representational drawings illustrate this thoroughly researched and informative collection of facts about the gorilla's personality and world. Ages 8-12.

FIEDEL, ROSLYN. *Wild Flowers.* Photographs by Ray Kellman. Boston: Houghton Mifflin Co., 1972.

Simple, brief poetic text and photographs recording the spontaneous feelings of contemporary dancers are combined to tell an allegory about life (birth, change, and rebirth): tiny seedlings grow, reaching to the sky and then are blown to the mountaintop by the wind. Ages 8-13.

FISHER, AILEEN. *Feathered Ones and Furry.* Illustrated by Eric Carle. New York: Thomas Y. Crowell Co., 1971.

Sensitive lyrical verse about woodland birds and animals are illustrated with stunning linoleum-cut prints. Ages 6-14.

———. *My Cat Has Eyes of Sapphire Blue.* Illustrated by Marie Angel. New York: Thomas Y. Crowell Co., 1973.

Meticulous watercolor paintings and twenty-four poems comment humorously and affectionately about the idiosyncratic behavior of all kinds of cats and kittens. Ages 5-12.

FISHER, LEONARD EVERETT. *The Death of Evening Star: The Diary of a Young New England Whaler.* Illustrated by Leonard Everett Fisher. New York: Doubleday & Co., 1972.

This account of adventure and intrigue that a young boy experienced on an ill-fated voyage of a whaling ship is illustrated with exquisitely beautiful, dramatic black-and-white scratcherboard prints.

FLORA, JAMES. *The Day the Cow Sneezed.* Illustrated by James Flora. New York: Harcourt, Brace & World, 1957.

A cumulative tale-type story of what happens when a cow sneezes. The illustrations, done in gouache, are action-packed and match the hilarious chain reaction that occurs when the cow sneezes. Ages 4-8.

FRANCOISE (pseud. FRANCOISE SEIGNOBOSC). *Jeanne-Marie Counts Her Sheep.* Illustrated by Francoise. New York: Charles Scribner's Sons, 1957.

A counting book cleverly concocted—Jeanne-Marie dreams of the many lambs her pet sheep will have and what she could buy from their sale. Drawings are refreshingly childlike and are in bright, opaque colors. Ages 3-6.

FRASCONI, ANTONIO. *See Again, Say Again.* Illustrated by Antonio Frasconi. New York: Harcourt, Brace & World, 1964.

A picture book in which many different familiar things and activities are pictured with the name of each given and phonetically pronounced in four languages—English, Italian, French, and Spanish. Illustrations are printed in strong colors and are strikingly simple woodcut prints. Ages 6-9.

———. *The Snow and the Sun.* Illustrated by Antonio Frasconi. New York: Harcourt, Brace & World, 1961.

A South American cumulative rhyme presented in English and Spanish. Illustrated with woodcuts in bold opaque colors and in black and white. Ages 6-10.

FREEMAN, DON. *Dandelion.* Illustrated by Don Freeman. New York: Viking Press, 1964.

A vain but lovable lion is not recognized by the hostess when he arrives at a party too dressed up. Amusing drawings convey the humor of this entertaining picture-book story. Ages 4-8.

FRENCH, FIONA. *King Tree.* Illustrated by Fiona French. New York: Henry Z. Walck, 1973.

Baroque-style illustrations, richly detailed, oversized, and opulent, depict this story which takes place in the beautiful gardens of Versailles in France in the reign of King Louis XIV. It is a story about courtiers acting in a play, dressed as trees and boasting of their virtues, each vying to be named the King Tree by the ladies of the court. Ages 6-10.

FRESCHET, BERNIECE. *Bear Mouse.* Illustrated by Donald Carrick. New York: Charles Scribner's Sons, 1973.

This is a beautifully told story about a mouse's fight to survive the winter and outlive her predators. The tones of soft brown and gray and generous amounts of white were used by this talented artist to create the detailed drawings with watercolor wash overlays. Ages 7-11.

FUCHS, ERICH. *Journey to the Moon.* Illustrated by Erich Fuchs. New York: Delacorte Press, 1970.

The eight-day mission in space of Apollo 11 is recorded by way of introductory text and beautifully imaginative cubistic paintings that are suggestive of Paul Klee. Ages 5-11.

GÀG, WANDA. *Millions of Cats.* Illustrated by Wanda Gàg. New York: Coward-McCann, 1938.

An imaginative folktale-type story about a lonely little old man and a little old lady who acquire a cat that changes from a scrawny little cat to a creature of beauty. Illustrated with black and white illustrations that match perfectly the simple, direct, and repetitious text. Ages 4-6.

GALDONE, PAUL. *The History of Mother Twaddle and the Marvelous Achievements of Her Son Jack.* Illustrated by Paul Galdone. New York: Seabury Press, 1974.

Humorous and dramatic cartoon-styled illustrations depict this verse version of *Jack and the Beanstalk* written by B.A.T. and published originally in England in 1807 by J. Harris. Ages 4-8.

GALLOB, EDWARD. *City Rocks, City Blocks and the Moon.* Photographs by Edward Gallob. New York: Charles Scribner's Sons, 1973.

Brief, explicit text and detail-filled photographs offer the reader a fantastic wealth of interesting geological information ever present in the city, if one only looks and sees. Ages 7-15.

GARTHWAITE, MARION. *The Twelfth Night Santons.* Illustrated by Winifred Lubell. New York: Doubleday & Co., 1965.

An account of Pierre, a young and reluctant sheepherder from Provence, who is led by a wandering sheep to a clay bed where the boy molds his first santon, a small nativity scene figure. Illustrations are colorful, and aptly portray the village and its famous santons. Ages 7-11.

GASIOROWICZ, NINA and GASIOROWICZ, CATHY. *The Mime Alphabet Book.* Illustrated by Nina and Cathy Gasiorowicz. Minneapolis: Lerner Publishing Co., 1973.

This is an interesting compilation of ideas, feelings, and situations, arranged alphabetically, depicting via simple and stark black-and-white photographs the bodily positions and facial expressions used by a mime artist. Ages 6-10.

GERSON, MARY-JOAN. *Why the Sky Is Far Away.* Illustrated by Hope Merryman. New York: Harcourt Brace Jovanovich, 1974.

Handsome stylized blue and brown woodcut prints illustrate this well-told Bini (Nigeria) tale which tells us that once the sky was so close to the Earth that people could cut parts of it to eat but because of their waste and greed it moved far away out of their reach. Ages 5-10.

GINSBURG, MIRRA. *The Chick and the Duckling.* Translated from the Russian by V. Suteyev. Illustrated by Jose and Ariane Aruego. New York: Macmillan Co., 1972.

Simplistic line drawings with four-color tempera overlays unite with brief text to tell this beguiling story about the chick who can do everything the duck can do except swim. Ages 3-7.

———. *The Proud Maiden, Tungak, and the Sun.* Illustrated by Igor Galanin. New York: Macmillan Co., 1974.

This Russian Eskimo legend tells how the moon came to live in the sky and why the long Arctic day eventually overtakes the long Arctic night. The illustrations are blue and white stylized cross-hatching. Ages 9-12.

GLASGOW, ALICE. *Honschi.* Illustrated by Tony Chen. New York: Parents' Magazine Press, 1972.

Meticulously detailed watercolor pen-and-ink paintings suggestive of Japanese landscapes interpret this story about a fragile, staunch chickadee. Ages 6-10.

GLUBOK, SHIRLEY. *The Art of America in the Gilded Age.* Designed by Gerald Nook. New York: Macmillan Co., 1974.

Copies of paintings and photographs depict various aspects of life in America during the Gilded Age, which lasted from the end of the Civil War to the close of the nineteenth century. Copies of art pieces by such personalities as Thomas Eakins, Winslow Homer, John Singer Sargent, Mary Cassatt, and James Whistler are included. Ages 10 and up.

————. *The Art of Ancient Mexico.* Photographs by Alfred H. Tamarin. New York: Harper & Row, Publishers, 1968.

A description of artifacts that typify the art and culture of the civilizations of ancient Mexico. Photographs of the art objects are clearly reproduced. Ages 9-14.

————. *Discovering Tut-Ankh-Amen's Tomb.* Forward by Eric Young. New York: Macmillan Co., 1968.

Methods of excavation, the preservation of fragile objects, and the Egyptian burial customs are discussed in this abridgment and adaptation of *The Tomb of Tut-Ankh-Amen* by Howard Carter and A. C. Mace. Copiously illustrated with reproductions of photographs taken at the time of the excavation. Ages 11-16.

GOODALL, JOHN. *Paddy's Evening Out.* Illustrated by John Goodall. New York: A Margaret McElderry Book/Atheneum Publishers, 1973.

An hilarious chase on stage and behind the scenes results when Paddy falls into the orchestra pit from his theatre box. Vivid and delicate watercolor paintings, realistic and imaginative in detail, on alternating half and full pages carry the outrageous action of this wordless story. Ages 4-10.

————. *Shrewbettina's Birthday.* Illustrated by John S. Goodall. New York: Harcourt Brace Jovanovich, 1971.

Carefully detailed watercolor paintings in rich colors tell how Shrewbettina prepared for and celebrated her birthday. This wordless book is told by way of illustrations that appear on half-page alternating with full-page illustrations. Ages 7-11.

GOODMAN, ROBERT B. and SPICER, ROBERT A. *Issunbōshi.* Illustrated by George Suyeoka. Honolulu: Island Heritage Books, 1974.

Issunbōshi is a Japanese Thumbling of marvelous powers. His story is told with colorful and detailed double-spread paintings and poetic prose text. The action-filled representational illustrations add much to the story itself and offer the reader an amazing wealth of information about Kyoto, the ancient capital city of Japan. Ages 5-9.

GOODMAN, ROBERT B. and SPICER, ROBERT A. *The Magic Brush.* Edited by Ruth Tabroh. Illustrated by Y. T. Mui. Honolulu: Island Heritage Books, 1974.

Firm-line watercolor landscape paintings in full color in the authentic Chinese tradition along with lyrical prose present this legend of how an orphan boy, Ma Lien, a woodgather, realized his dreams of becoming a painter of pictures. Ages 6-10.

GOUDEY, ALICE E. *Butterfly Time.* Illustrated by Adrienne Adams. New York: Charles Scribner's Sons, 1964.

Simple poetic prose describes various butterflies "flitting and dancing, chasing one another." A happy book, illustrated with beautiful, accurately detailed, representational watercolor paintings. The author's note describes the life cycle of the butterfly. Ages 4-8.

————. *Houses from the Sea.* Illustrated by Adrienne Adams. New York: Charles Scribner's Sons, 1959.

Illustrated by Y. T. Mui for *The Magic Brush* by Robert B. Goodman and Robert A. Spicer. Copyright © 1974 Island Heritage Limited. Reproduced by permission of the publisher.

A quick guide for identification of common seashells. Watercolor paintings that illustrate this picture book are representational, detailed, and exact. Ages 5-9.

GRAHAM, LORENZ. *David He No Fear*. Illustrated by Ann Grifalconi. New York: Thomas Y. Crowell Co., 1971.

Unique woodcut prints and brief text told in a black dialect relate this story of David and Goliath. Ages 8-12.

GRAMATKY, HARDIE. *Little Toot*. Illustrated by Hardie Gramatky. New York: G. P. Putnam's Sons, 1939.

An account of a lazy, irresponsible tugboat that reforms and makes a heroic rescue. Illustrations are cartoon-style, done in watercolor, and match this hilarious personified tale. Ages 5-8.

GREEN, NORMA. *The Hole in the Dike*. Illustrated by Eric Carle. New York: Thomas Y. Crowell Co., 1975.

Collage and painting plus a simple, yet interesting, text are effectively combined to tell this memorable fantasy created by Mary Mapes Dodge about the boy who saved Holland from destruction by using his finger to plug up the leak in the dike until it could be repaired. Ages 4-8.

GREENFELD, HOWARD. *Marc Chagall.* Illustrated with reproductions. Chicago: Follett Publishing Co., 1968.

A personal biography of the contemporary Russian-born painter. Illustrated with sixteen full-color reproductions of the artist's work plus some black-and-white prints. Ages 11-15.

GREGG, ERNEST. *And the Sun God Said: That's Hip.* Illustrated by G. Falcon Beazer. New York: Harper & Row, Publishers, 1972.

A hip poetic version of the creation of *all* God's people. Action-filled paintings in vibrant full color illustrate the narrative told in a black dialect. Ages 9-12.

GRIFALCONI, ANN. *City Rhythms.* Illustrated by Ann Grifalconi. New York: Bobbs-Merrill Co., 1965.

An alert, small Negro boy notices the sights and sounds of the city and re-creates the rhythm of these activities by drumming out the beat on instruments made from buckets, glasses, and sticks. Illustrated with dramatic, colored drawings. Ages 5-8.

———. *The Matter with Lucy.* Illustrated with memorabilia. New York: Bobbs-Merrill Co., 1973.

Illustrated with an array of memorabilia, reproductions of photographs, and full-color drawings by artists of the past. This story about a Victorian child proves in a unique way that women can and do become scholars "researching great questions." A good women's lib book; also fits the current nostalgia craze. Ages 8-11.

GRIMM, JACOB and GRIMM, WILHELM. *The Cat and Mouse Who Shared a House.* Translated from the German by Anthea Bell. Illustrated by Ruth Hurlimann. New York: Henry Z. Walck, 1973.

The cat and the mouse set up a house together but they quarrel when the mouse discovers that the cat cheated him, proving that "cat and mouse can never really be friends." Full-page, dramatic, action-filled, realistic, and detailed paintings retell this unhappy story of greed. Ages 6-10.

———. *The Four Clever Brothers.* Illustrated by Felix Hoffmann. New York: Harcourt, Brace & World, 1967.

The traditional tale of four brothers each of whom becomes a master of his chosen trade. Illustrations are clear-cut and rich-colored line drawings that reflect the wit and vitality of the tale. Ages 4-8.

———. *The Good-for-Nothings.* Illustrated by Hans Fischer. New York: Harcourt, Brace & World, 1957.

A picture-book version of the adventures of Chanticleer, the rooster, and his wife as they are homeward bound in a nutshell carriage drawn by a goose. Detailed pen-and-ink sketches highlight this sprightly and humorous folktale. Ages 4-8.

———. *The Luck Child.* Illustrated by Gaynor Chapman. New York: Atheneum Publishers, 1968.

Vital expressionistic paintings in rich full color and a simple forthright text in the style of an experienced storyteller are artistically combined to present this fairy tale of how goodness and truth triumph over craftiness and evil, of how a humble peasant boy who was a "Luck Child" manages to marry the beautiful princess despite the scheming of her father, a cold-hearted king. Ages 5-9.

———. *Rumpelstiltskin.* Retold by Edith Tarcov. Illustrated by Edward Gorey. New York: Four Winds Press, 1973.

This new version of the familiar folktale is illustrated with antic pen-and-ink sketches in black and white and with strategically placed splashes of yellow. Ages 5-9.

———. *The Sleeping Beauty.* Illustrated by Lieselotte Schwarz. New York: Scroll Press, 1967.

Paintings suggestive of Silesian peasant art and in vivid primary hues interpret this well-known tale and the result is a truly exciting picture book. Ages 6-10.

———. *Snow-White and Rose-Red.* Illustrated by Barbara Cooney. New York: Delacorte Press, 1966.

Spirited full-color drawings convey the charm of this simple adaptation of the familiar fanciful tale. Ages 5-10.

———. *The Twelve Dancing Princesses.* Illustrated by Uri Shulevitz. New York: Charles Scribners Sons, 1966.

A facsimile of the first German edition of the now familiar Munster tale. Two-dimensional sketches in bright colors convey the spirit of this folktale. Ages 5-10.

HAMILTON, VIRGINIA. *Zeely.* Illustrated by Symeon Shimin. New York: Macmillan Co., 1967.

An imaginative eleven-year-old black girl eventually learns to differentiate between her daydreams and reality. The illustrations for this fine study of character and of personal relationships are particularly effective. Ages 10-13.

HARRIS, CHRISTIE. *Raven's Cry.* Illustrated by Bill Reid. New York: Atheneum Publishers, 1966.

A narrative description of Haida customs and beliefs during the reign of the last three great Stastas Eagle chiefs, and the effects of the North American Indian's contact with the white man's civilization. Although relatively few in number, the black-and-white line drawings masterfully illustrate the account. They are done in authentic Haida style. Ages 12-16.

HARRIS, DOROTHY JOAN. *The House Mouse.* Illustrated by Barbara Cooney. New York: Frederick Warne & Co., 1973.

Pleasant account of a friendship between Jonathan, a four-year-old boy, and a field mouse, when the latter moves into the boy's sister's dollhouse and remains all during the winter. A cozy read-aloud book illustrated with detailed, full-color line-and-wash paintings. Ages 6-10.

HAUGAARD, ERIK CHRISTIAN. *Hakon of Rogen's Saga.* Illustrated by Leo and Diane Dillon. Boston: Houghton Mifflin Co., 1963.

A descriptive and gripping first-person narrative that tells how thirteen-year-old Hakon of Rogen regained his birthright to become ruler of the rocky island of Rogen, in Norway, at the end of the Viking period. Illustrations are intricate woodcuts in black and white. Ages 11-15.

HILL, ELIZABETH STARR. *Evan's Corner.* Illustrated by Nancy Grossman. New York: Holt, Rinehart & Winston, 1967.

Evan, a member of a family of six children, provides peace of his own—a corner in a two-room apartment, but finds he is happy only when helping his brother fix up his corner. Illustrations add to the feelings of warmth and sensitivity that prevail throughout this story. Ages 5-8.

HOBAN, RUSSELL. *Bedtime for Frances.* Illustrated by Garth Williams. New York: Harper & Row, Publishers, 1960.

Frances, a little badger, finds many excuses for not going to sleep. Illustrations are carefully detailed, realistically styled black-and-white sketches. Ages 4-7.

HOBAN, TANA. *Circles, Triangles and Squares.* Illustrated with photographs by Tana Hoban. New York: Macmillan Co., 1974.

The unique and imaginative black-and-white photographs of our here-and-now world are bound to alert the child to the array of shapes around him and encourage him to discover even more. Ages 3-5.

———. *Look Again.* Illustrated with photographs by Tana Hoban. New York: Macmillan Co., 1971.

A visual mystery game (two-inch-square openings cut into white pages alternating with full-page black-and-white photographs of animals and plants) challenges the reader to guess what the thing is. A unique wordless book. Ages 6-14.

———. *Shapes and Things.* Illustrated with photograms by Tana Hoban. New York: Macmillan Co., 1970.

Beautifully striking black-and-white photograms dramatize ordinary objects that children can identify and will enjoy talking about. A good wordless book for the very young. Ages 4-9.

HODGES, MARGARET. *The Wave.* Illustrated by Blair Lent. Boston: Houghton Mifflin Co., 1964.

A picture-book version of the Japanese folktale about an old man who sets fire to his rice fields on the mountain in order to save the villagers from a tidal wave. Illustrations are effective cardboard cutout prints in watercolor. Ages 9-12.

HOFFMANN, FELIX. *A Boy Went Out to Gather Pears.* Illustrated by Felix Hoffmann. New York: Harcourt, Brace & World, 1966.

A traditional, gay cumulative verse that tells about a boy who was sent out to gather pears. Illustrated with amusing prints in full color. Ages 4-7.

HOGE, DOROTHY. *The Black Heart of Indri.* Illustrated by Janina Domanska. New York: Charles Scribner's Sons, 1966.

A retelling of the Chinese version of a fantasy about an ugly, frog-shaped creature who changes into a handsome prince through the love of a headman's daughter. Large illustrations done in a style suggestive of Chinese folk art portray the mood and setting of this nineteenth-century folktale. Ages 4-10.

HOLL, ADELAIDE. *The Rain Puddle.* Illustrated by Roger Duvoisin. New York: Lothrop, Lee & Shepard Co., 1965.

A simple folktale describing a little hen and others when they see their reflection in a rain puddle. Illustrated with clear-cut, brightly colored drawings. Ages 3-6.

HOLLING, HOLLING C. *Paddle-to-the-Sea*. Illustrated by Holling C. Holling. Boston: Houghton Mifflin Co., 1941.

A hand-carved boat travels over the Great Lakes and Niagara Falls to the coast of Newfoundland. Large representational paintings in full-color and black-and-white sketches illustrate this episodic story. Ages 9-12.

HORVATH, BETTY. *Be Nice to Josephine*. Illustrated by Pat Grant Porter. New York: Franklin Watts, 1970.

This is an amusing account of the day a little boy reluctantly spends with his cousin Josephine. A good book for "free children." Ages 5-8.

HOYLE, GEOFFREY. *2010: Living in the Future* (revised text). Illustrated by Alasdair Anderson. New York: Parents' Magazine Press, 1974.

An enlightening estimate of how people will live in the year 2010, with a challenge to the reader to decide whether or not he would like it that way and what he might do to make it different. Ages 7-12.

HURLIMANN, BETTINA. *Barry: The Story of a Brave St. Bernard*. Illustrated by Paul Nussbaumer. New York: Harcourt, Brace & World, 1968.

A picture-book presentation of Barry, the St. Bernard dog that won fame for his rescue work with the monks of the great St. Bernard Hospice in the Swiss Alps at the time of Napoleon. Illustrations are black-and-white marginal drawings and full-page paintings which depict mood, scene, and action. Ages 5-10.

———. *William Tell and His Son*. Translated by Elizabeth D. Crawford, Illustrated by Paul Nussbaumer. New York: Harcourt, Brace & World, 1967.

A shortened picture-book version of Tell, the famous Swiss legendary hero. Illustrated with full-color poster paintings and line drawings. Ages 7-11.

HUTCHINS, PAT. *Changes, Changes*. Illustrated by Pat Hutchins. New York: Macmillan Co., 1971.

A series of brightly colored, stylized illustrations cleverly depict a man and a woman constructing with blocks a house, a fire engine, a boat, a truck, an engine, and a house again. A wordless book. Ages 4-8.

———. *Clocks and More Clocks*. Illustrated by Pat Hutchins. New York: Macmillan Co., 1970.

The extreme and simple directness that typifies the action-filled full-color illustrations are beautifully suited to this lighthearted story about a man who tries to figure out why there is a difference in time when he checks his clock from one part of the house to the next. Ages 4-8.

———. *Good-Night Owl!* Illustrated by Pat Hutchins. New York: Macmillan Co., 1972.

Vivid full-color paintings add considerably to this pleasantly humorous tale about what happened when creatures as the buzzing bees, creaking crows, chittering starlings, and the screaming jays kept the owl awake when he tried to sleep. Ages 4-6.

———. *The Silver Christmas Tree*. Illustrated by Pat Hutchins. New York: Macmillan Co., 1974.

Illustration for *Changes, Changes* by Pat Hutchins. Copyright © 1971 by Pat Hutchins. Reprinted with permission of Macmillan Publishing Company, Inc.

The same animals created by this author-artist in *The Surprise Party* engage in a frantic and humorous search for the silver star that disappeared from the tree that Squirrel decorated for Christmas. Illustrations are black line drawings and color separations of yellow, red, and blue tempera. Ages 4-6.

——. *Tom and Sam*. Illustrated by Pat Hutchins. New York: Macmillan Co., 1968.

This tale depicting one-upmanship and envy of two friends ends happily. Illustrated with fast-action drawings in full color. Ages 4-8.

——. *The Wind Blew*. Illustrated by Pat Hutchins. New York: Macmillan Co., 1974.

Full-color tempera paintings (each a double-page spread) tell this cumulative tale about how a gust of wind mixed up such things as an umbrella, a balloon, a hat, a kite, a shirt, a hanky, a wig, letters, a flag, scarves, and newspapers. Then it sailed out to sea. Ages 4-6.

IONESCO, EUGENE. *Story Number 1*. Translated by Calvin K. Towle. Illustrated by Etienne Delessert. New York: Harlin Quist Books, 1968.

Zany surrealistic paintings for this surrealistic wordplay story about a three year old who strives to get the attention of her sleepy, hung-over parents and the maid early in the morning. Ages 4-11.

IRVING, WASHINGTON. *Rip Van Winkle*. Illustrations by Arthur Rackham. Philadelphia: J. B. Lippincott Co., 1967.

A familiar narrative illustrated effectively with full-color drawings and several black-and-white drawings. Ages 11-14.

IWASAKI, CHIHIRO. *Staying Home Alone on a Rainy Day*. Illustrated by Chihiro Iwasaki. New York: McGraw-Hill Book Co., 1968.

Poetic text and impressionistic watercolor paintings reveal the thoughts and feelings of a small child home alone during a thunderstorm. Ages 4-8.

JARRELL, RANDALL. *The Bat-Poet*. Illustrated by Maurice Sendak. New York: Macmillan Co., 1964.

A little brown bat, unable to sleep during the day, notices for the first time details about the owl, the mockingbird, and the chipmunk. He makes poems about them as well as his own bat boyhood. Illustrations are black-and-white fine pen-and-ink drawings that look like steel engravings.

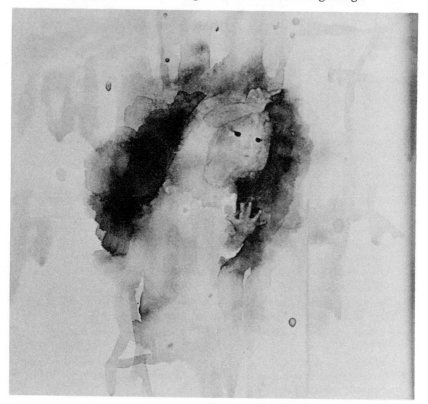

Illustration for *Staying Home Alone on a Rainy Day* written and illustrated by Chihiro Iwasaki. Copyright © 1968 by Shiko-Sha. First distribution in the United States of America by McGraw-Hill Book Company, 1969. Reprinted with permission of McGraw-Hill Book Company.

JEFFERS, SUSAN. *All the Pretty Horses*. Illustrated by Susan Jeffers. New York: Macmillan Co., 1974.

An exquisite graphic interpretation of a well-known lullaby presented as a dream wherein are found beautiful and lively horses cantering gracefully about a lush countryside. Illustrations are black pen-and-ink line drawings with overlays done in acrylic paint in muted shades of yellow, gray, blue, and rust. Ages 6-9.

JESCHKE, SUSAN. *Firerose*. Illustrated by Susan Jeschke. New York: Holt, Rinehart & Winston, 1974.

An "antic gray comedy" about a fire-breathing girl with a curly green tail who is left on the doorstep of Zora, the fortuneteller. Illustrated with black-and-white pencil drawings that complement the humor and warmth of this fanciful tale. Ages 6-10.

JONES, HETTIE. *The Trees Stand Shining: The Poetry of the North American Indians*. Illustrated by Robert Andrew Parker. New York: Dial Press, 1971.

Modern watercolor paintings reflect the attitude and mood of original poetry of many ancient American Indian cultures. Ages 9-15.

Illustration by Robert Andrew Parker. Copyright © 1971 by Robert Andrew Parker. From the book *The Trees Stand Shining: Poetry of the North American Indians*, selected by Hettie Jones. Reproduced with permission of The Dial Press.

KAY, HELEN. *Man and Mastiff: The Story of the St. Bernard Dog Through History.* New York: Macmillan Co., 1967.

A treatise describing the domestication and characteristics of the St. Bernard dog and the role it played in the Switzerland mountain snow rescue work by the monks of St. Bernard's Hospice. The author has used historical, legendary, and scientific sources as references. Illustrations are photographs and old prints. Ages 10-14.

KEATS, EZRA JACK. *Dreams.* Illustrated by Ezra Jack Keats. New York: Macmillan Co., 1974.

Colorful collage and acrylic painting illustrate the story of how Roberto's paper mouse saves Archie's cat from a snarling dog on a hot summer night. Ages 4-7.

———. *Peter's Chair.* Illustrated by Ezra Jack Keats. New York: Harper & Row, Publishers, 1967.

Peter is upset when his new little sister is given his crib and his high chair. He decides to run away and plans to take his dog and his little blue chair with him. He changes his mind when he discovers that he has grown too big for the chair and suggests that it be painted pink for his sister. Illustrations done in collage in bright colors. Ages 4-8.

KEEPING, CHARLES. *Joseph's Yard.* Illustrated by Charles Keeping. New York: Franklin Watts, 1969.

Joseph learns that if it is to survive and flourish, *all life* needs to live in its natural environment. Full-color sophisticated illustrations and carefully written text are effectively merged. Ages 5-9.

———. *Through the Window.* Illustrated by Charles Keeping. New York: Franklin Watts, 1970.

Jacob observes life on the London street from his window and some of the things he sees he does not seem willing to accept if one correctly interprets this moving and very sophisticated book. The full-color illustrations are exceptionally moving. Although the text is brief, it too stirs the reader emotionally. This is in every way an exceptional picture book. Ages 6-10.

KELLOG, STEVEN. *The Mystery of the Missing Red Mitten.* Illustrated by Steven Kellog. New York: Dial Press, 1974.

Annie engages in delightfully imaginative fantasies suggesting where her missing red mitten might be. Eventually she finds that it actually served as the heart of the snowman she made as a surprise for a neighbor lady. Illustrations are black-and-white sketches with splashes of the red occasioned throughout. Ages 3-7.

KEMPADOO, MANGHANITA. *Letters of Thanks.* Illustrated by Helen Oxenbury. New York: Simon & Schuster, 1969.

This is a great spoof—in text and Victorian-period type illustrations. This is a sophisticated take-off on the song "Twelve Days of Christmas." Ages 9-16.

KINGMAN, LEE. *Peter's Long Walk.* Illustrated by Barbara Cooney. Garden City, N.Y.: Doubleday & Co., 1953.

Told that when he is five years old he will be able to go to school and will find playmates there, lonely Peter walks to the village the morning after his fifth birthday. The illustrations capture the spirit of the story told in rhyme, and they comply with the content. Ages 4-7.

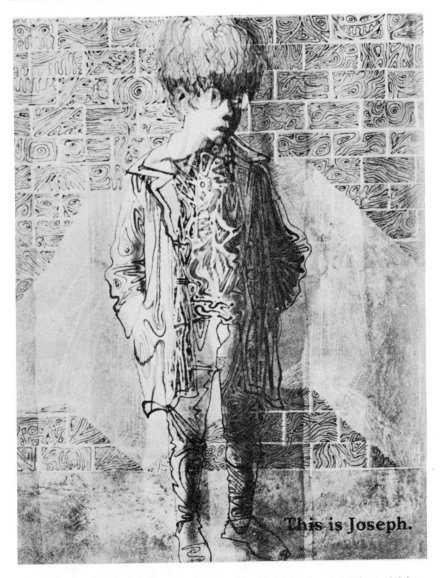

Illustration for *Joseph's Yard* written and illustrated by Charles Keeping. Copyright © 1969 by Charles Keeping. Reprinted with permission of Franklin Watts, Inc.

KIPLING, RUDYARD. *Just So Stories*. Illustrated by Etienne Delessert. New York: Doubleday & Co., 1972.

Colorful and moderately surrealistic paintings illustrate twelve of Kipling's classic tales. This profusely illustrated edition is in recognition of the seventy-fifth anniversary of the publication of *Just So Stories*. Ages 8-12.

KRAHN, FERNANDO. *April Fools.* Illustrated by Fernando Krahn. New York: E. P.
Dutton and Co., 1974.

This humorous wordless story, told with black line-and-wash cartoon
sketches, is about two little boys who create a monster, tease and frighten
the townspeople with it, and get lost in the woods, but, happily, are rescued by the very foolish people they taunted. Ages 5-9.

KRASILOVSKY, PHYLLIS. *The Cow Who Fell in the Canal.* Illustrated by Peter
Spier. Garden City, N.Y.: Doubleday & Co., 1972.

Hendrika, a Dutch cow, falls into the canal, climbs onto a raft, and floats
down to the city. Detailed illustrations are in gay colors; many of them are
double-page spreads. All of them afford a view of Holland's countryside
and city streets and record Hendrika's sight-seeing cruise down the canal.
Ages 4-7.

KRAUS, ROBERT. *Owliver.* Illustrated by Jose Aruego and Arianne Dewey. New
York: Windmill/E. P. Dutton & Co., 1974.

Fresh, peppy drawings and simple text tell this refreshing story about
Owliver who does not become the lawyer, the doctor, or the performer his
parents wanted him to be. Instead he surprises all by becoming the fireman
he wants to be. Ages 4-7.

———. *Pinchpenny Mouse.* Illustrated by Robert Byrd. New York: Windmill
Books/E. P. Dutton & Co., 1974.

Pen-and-ink drawings and the brief but well-written text tell this charming
fantasy of how Pinchpenny, the "miser mouse" rescued his destitute friends,
fellow mice who are out of work, but were employed by the Friendly
Mousetrap Factory. Ages 5-8.

———. *Poor Mister Splinterfritz.* Illustrated by Robert Byrd. New York: E. P.
Dutton & Co., 1973.

Almost a wordless book. Told primarily by means of black-and-white pen-
and-ink crosshatch sketches. This is a slapstick story about a man who gets
splinters wherever and whenever he sits. He resolves his problem when
he sees a bare light bulb hanging down from the ceiling. From then
on he stands (sits) on his head. Ages 3-7.

KRAUSS, RUTH. *The Growing Story.* Illustrated by Phyllis Rowand. New York:
Harper & Row, Publishers, 1947.

A little boy watches the many animals and plants around him grow but
doesn't realize that he has grown, too, until late autumn when he brings
out his last year's warm clothes. Simple illustrations in bright colors. Ages
4-6.

KREDENSER, GAIL and MACK, STANLEY. *One Dancing Drum.* Illustrated by
Stanley Mack. New York: S. G. Phillips, 1971.

Progressing from one to ten, musicians with their instruments accumulate
on each successive page in action-filled cartoon-styled drawings. The text
is pleasantly musical, too: persnickety piccolos, tootling trombones, crashing cymbals, etc. Ages 3-7.

KURELEK, WILLIAM. *Lumberjack.* Illustrated by William Kurelek. Boston:
Houghton-Mifflin Co., 1974.

Twenty-five full-color paintings depicting the varied aspects of the life of the lumberjack and a conglomerate of experiences had by the author-artist in the bush country of Quebec and Ontario. Ages 9-12.

————. *A Prairie Boy's Winter.* Illustrated by William Kurelek. Boston: Houghton Mifflin Co., 1973.

Twenty full-color paintings and a rather brief text written in a matter-of-fact style enables the reader to share this author-artist's experiences of living on the western Canadian prairie in winter. Ages 7-12.

Illustration for *A Prairie Boy's Winter* written and illustrated by William Kurelek. Copyright © 1973 by William Kurelek. Reprinted by permission of the publisher Houghton Mifflin Company.

KUSKIN, KARLA. *In the Flaky Frosty Morning.* Illustrated by Karla Kuskin. New York: Harper & Row, Publishers, 1969.

A snowman tells in verse how he got his arms and legs, hat, and nose, only to lose them. Illustrated with quaint drawings that match the freshness and sparkle of a winter day. Ages 4-7.

LANG, ANDREW. *The Twelve Dancing Princesses.* Illustrated by Adrienne Adams. New York: Holt, Rinehart & Winston, 1966.

An extended romantic version of the famous fairy tale, drawn from French sources. Vividly-colored illustrations convey the gay spirit and are suggestive of Gallic art. Ages 5-10.

LANGSTAFF, JOHN. *Frog Went A-Courtin'.* Illustrated by Feodor Rojankovsky. New York: Harcourt, Brace & World, 1955.

A picture-book version of the old ballad about the frog and the mouse. Illustrations done in crayon, brush, and ink, are gay and colorful. The music for the ballad, which is sung in the southern Appalachian Mountain area, is included. Ages 5-7.

LAWRENCE, JACOB. *Harriet and the Promised Land.* Illustrated by Jacob Lawrence. New York: Simon & Schuster, 1968.

A story in verse about Harriet Tubman, Negro slave who was active in the Underground Railroad Movement. Illustrated with large full-color expressionistic paintings (poster paint). Ages 9-14.

LEAR, EDWARD. *The New Vestments.* Illustrated by Arnold Lobel. New York: Bradbury Press, 1970.

Pencil-line drawings illustrate the nonsense rhymes which describe the disastrous events that occur when a king wears vestments made from good things to eat. Ages 8-12.

———. *Whizz!* Illustrated by Janina Domanska. New York: Macmillan Co., 1973.

Action-filled pen-and-ink line drawings combined with the watercolors help interpret this collection of limericks. Ages 4-6.

LEAR, EDWARD, and NASH, OGDEN. *The Scroobious Pip.* Illustrated by Nancy Ekholm Burkert. New York: Harper & Row, Publishers, 1968.

Rhythmic nonsense verse which tells how all the animals in the world gathered around a strange creature. Quiet, subtle colors are used in representational brush-and-ink drawings that are detailed and exact. Ages 8-12.

LEEKLEY, THOMAS B. *The World of Manabozho: Tales of the Chippewa Indians.* Illustrations by Teffe Kumball. New York: Vanguard Press, 1965.

A compilation of tales and episodic accounts about Manabozho, a legendary hero of the Algonquian Indians, which serves as an example to show how legends may reflect the beliefs, fears, and hopes of a specific culture. Illustrated by appropriate and informative line drawings. Ages 10-12.

LENT, BLAIR. *John Tabor's Ride.* Illustrated by Blair Lent. Boston: Atlantic Monthly Press, 1966.

John Tabor is rescued from a South Sea island by a strange, bearded man and is brought back to New England on the back of a whale. Three-color watercolor prints made from cardboard cutouts illustrate this humorous whaling legend. Ages 6-10.

LEWIS, RICHARD, ed. *Out of the Earth I Sing*. New York: W. W. Norton & Co., 1968.

An anthology of poetry and songs of primitive peoples of the world. Human concerns and emotions expressed by North American and South American Indians, African, Asian, Pacific, and Arctic cultures. Illustrations consist of well-produced and attractively arranged reproductions of primitive art pieces. Ages 10 and up.

LEXAU, JOAN M. *Emily and the Klunky Baby and the Next-Door Dog*. Illustrated by Martha Alexander. New York: Dial Press, 1972.

Expressive pencil and tempera drawings and well-written text tell this believable story about a little girl whose parents are divorced. She is frustrated when her mother is too busy to play with her, so runs away with her little brother in hopes of finding their father. Ages 5-9.

———. *Every Day a Dragon*. Illustrated by Ben Shecter. New York: Harper & Row, Publishers, 1967.

A little boy and his father play a daily game of make-believe, and his mother's invitation to dinner saves him from being eaten by "a fierce dragon." Illustrated with sketches. Ages 3-5.

———. *Striped Ice Cream*. Illustrated by John Wilson. Philadelphia: J. B. Lippincott Co., 1968.

Realistic portrayal of situations faced by a self-reliant, fatherless Negro family. Black-and-white sketches highlight the genuine lifelike emotions depicted in this story. Ages 6-10.

LIFTON, BETTY JEAN. *The Dwarf Pine Tree*. Illustrated by Fuko-Akino. New York: Atheneum Publishers, 1963.

After it has endured months of torturous pain and learns that it will have only six months left on earth, a small straight-as-a-stick pine tree is chosen as the tree that is used to cure a princess of her mysterious malady. Illustrations are beautifully compatible with this moving Japanese folktale. Ages 8-12.

———. *Return to Hiroshima*. Illustrated with photographs by Eikoh Hosoe. New York: Atheneum Publishers, 1970.

A dramatically realistic and emotionally arousing delineation of the immediate and long-lasting effects of the dropping of the atomic bomb on Hiroshima in 1945. Ages 10-16.

———. *The Rice-Cake Rabbit*. Illustrated by Eiichi Mitsui. New York: W. W. Norton & Co., 1966.

A fantasy based on a Japanese folktale about a rabbit, successful baker of rice-cakes, who becomes a master at swordsmanship and is made Samurai of the Moon. Stunning brush and black ink sketches illustrate this tale. Ages 6-9.

LIONNI, LEO. *The Biggest House in the World*. Illustrated by Leo Lionni. New York: Pantheon Books, 1968.

After hearing how one snail grew to such an enormous size that he was unable to move about from cabbage to cabbage and thus slowly faded away, a little snail appreciates his small size and the movability of his house. Illustrations are large colorful and imaginative paintings. Ages 4-8.

————. *Frederick.* Illustrated by Leo Lionni. New York: Pantheon Books, 1967.

Frederick recreates the wonder of the seasons through the magic of imagery-filled language, whereas the other members of a hardworking field-mouse family gather food for the winter. Illustrated with three-dimensional collage pictures. Ages 5-8.

Illustration for *Frederick,* written and illustrated by Leo Lionni. Copyright © 1967 by Leo Lionni. Reprinted with permission of Pantheon Books, a Division of Random House, Inc.

————. *Tico and the Golden Wings.* Illustrated by Leo Lionni. New York: Pantheon Books, 1964.

An Indian folktale about a bird who gives away his golden feathers to bring happiness to those in need. Although he then looks like all the other black birds, he knows he is different for he has his own memories and dreams. Illustrated in muted colors in a style suggestive of the traditional art of India. Ages 5-10.

LOBEL, ANITA. *A Birthday for the Princess.* Illustrated by Anita Lobel. New York: Harper & Row, Publishers, 1973.

An unhappy princess finds love, companionship, and understanding with a young organ grinder and his monkey. Illustrated in pen-and-ink sketches and watercolor wash in three colors. Ages 5-9.

LOBEL, ARNOLD. *Frog and Toad Are Friends.* Illustrated by Arnold Lobel. New York: Harper & Row, Publishers, 1970.

An easy-to-read-book, this is a compilation of five episodes involving a frog and a toad. The droll story is competently illustrated with detailed pencil drawings in three colors. Ages 5-8.

————. *The Man Who Took the Indoors Out.* Illustrated by Arnold Lobel. New York: Harper and Row, Publishers, 1974.

Pen-and-ink line drawings with overlays in watercolor and narrative verse depict this nonsensical tale about the man named Bellwood Bouse who invited everything inside of his house to come outside. Ages 5-8.

MACAULAY, DAVID. *Cathedral: The Story of Its Construction.* Illustrated by David Macaulay. Boston: Houghton Mifflin Co., 1973.

This is a picture-book story relating the construction of Chutreaux Cathedral—a ninety-year-old imaginary structure created by the author-artist to present the many intricate details included in the step-by-step process of a cathedral's growth. The pen-and-ink drawings reproduced as fine line are exemplary of graphics in book illustration. Ages 10 and up.

MacCLINTOCK, DORCAS. *A Natural History of Giraffes.* Illustrated by Ugo Mochi. New York: Charles Scribner's Sons, 1973.

Stunning graphic sculptures and black paper silhouettes illustrate the many fascinating scientific facts included in this comprehensive discourse about giraffes. Ages 9-16.

McCLOSKEY, ROBERT. *Make Way for Ducklings.* Illustrated by Robert McCloskey. New York: Viking Press, 1941.

A large picture book which tells the story about a family of ducks that grew up in the Boston area. Representational drawings highlight the laughable situations and portray some familiar Bostonian landmarks. Ages 4-8.

———. *Time of Wonder.* Illustrated by Robert McCloskey. New York: Viking Press, 1957.

A description of the many moods and interesting terrain of the Maine coast, in poetic prose and full-color watercolor paintings. Ages 7-12.

McDERMOTT, BEVERLY BRODSKY. *The Crystal Apple.* Illustrated by Beverly Brodsky McDermott. Viking Press, 1974.

The retelling of the Russian folktale about "a young girl who sees the world through the power of her imagination" is illustrated in brilliantly bold, colorful abstract-styled paintings. Ages 5-9.

McDERMOTT, GERALD. *Anansi the Spider.* Illustrated by Gerald McDermott. New York: Holt, Rinehart and Winston, 1972.

A stunning picture book! This story about the folk hero Anansi is presented in rhythmic language patterns and sophisticated illustrations of geometric shapes in brilliant colors. Ages 5-10.

———. *Arrow to the Sun.* Illustrated by Gerald McDermott. New York: Viking Press, 1974.

Vivid stylized illustrations suggestive of the Pueblo Indian folk art in rich tones and brief simple text, with the style of a master storyteller, depict this Pueblo Indian legend which tells how the spirit of the Lord of the Sun was brought to the world of men. 1975 Caldecott Award winner. Ages 6-10.

———. *The Stonecutter.* Illustrated by Gerald McDermott. Viking Press, 1975.

The collage technique and brilliant hues in cubistic-styled illustrations are used in this Japanese cyclic folktale about a man's longing for power. Ages 7-10.

McNEER, MAY. *America's Abraham Lincoln.* Illustrated by Lynd Ward. Boston: Houghton Mifflin Co., 1957.

A biography covering the life of Lincoln from age seven to his assassination. Black-and-white and colored lithographs done in a representational art style illustrate the biography. Ages 10-14.

MANUSHKIN, FRAN. *Baby*. Illustrated by Ronald Himler. New York: Harper and Row, Publishers, 1972.

This story is not for the literal level reader or thinker. It is a good off-beat story that stresses love and affection. Illustrated with hilarious pen-and-ink sketches in black and white. Ages 5-10.

MARI, IELA and MARI, ENZO. *The Apple and the Moth*. Illustrated by Iela and Enzo Mari. New York: Pantheon Books, 1970.

Bold vibrant illustrations depict the life cycle of a moth. A simple and beautiful wordless book. Ages 3-5.

MARSHALL, JAMES. *The Guest*. Illustrated by James Marshall. Boston: Houghton Mifflin Co., 1975.

Cartoon-style illustrations in clear and bright shades of yellow, fuchsia, green, and gray wash are used in this refreshing fantasy about a friendship between a moose and a snail. Ages 4-6.

MATHIS, SHARON BELL. *The Hundred Penny Box*. Illustrated by Leo and Diane Dillon. New York: Viking Press, 1975.

This pathos-filled story about a senile woman is told in poetic prose and stunning two-color, full-page paintings. The illustrations were made with watercolors applied with cotton; light areas were created with water and bleach applied with brush. The frames were made with an air brush. Ages 9-14.

MATSUNO, MASAKO. *A Pair of Red Clogs*. Illustrated by Kazue Mizumura. Cleveland: World Publishing Co., 1960.

A little Japanese girl cracks her new red clogs and tries to deceive her mother by walking in the mud. Illustrated with simple and effective sketches that convey the emotions and actions of the characters. Ages 5-7.

MENDOZA, GEORGE. *The Alphabet Boat*. Illustrated by Lawrence Di Fiori. New York: American Heritage Press, 1972.

From A to Z, one gets an earful and eyeful of nautical life. Illustrations are full-color pen-and-ink line drawings and watercolor and are perfectly compatible with this seagoing lyrical alphabet book. Ages 4-10.

———. *And I Must Hurry for the Sea Is Coming In*. Illustrated with photographs by DeWayne Dalrymple. Englewood Cliffs, N.J.: Prentice-Hall, 1969.

Full-color photographs relate this poetic telling of the imaginative play of a black boy in a puddle by a hydrant in an urban ghetto. Ages 9-14.

———. *Goodbye, River, Goodbye*. Illustrated with photographs by George A. Tice. New York: Doubleday & Co. 1971.

Poetic text and black-and-white photographs depict a river which was a refuge for nature and is fast becoming so polluted that it cannot serve as the habitat for wildlife. Ages 9-12.

———. *The Good Luck Spider and Other Bad Luck Stories*. Illustrated by Gahan Wilson. New York: Doubleday and Co., 1970.

Illustration by Gahan Wilson from *The Good Luck Spider and Other Bad Luck Stories* by George Mendoza. Copyright © 1970 by George Mendoza. Reprinted by permission of Doubleday & Co., Inc.

Three gruesome stories of superstition together with cartoon-styled illustrations that highlight the content and mood of these bad luck stories result in a unique and modern picture book. Ages 6-10.

——. *The Inspector*. Illustrated by Peter Parnall. New York: Doubleday & Co., 1970.

This is an intriguing and highly imaginative wordless story about a myopic inspector and his "faithful" hound. Illustrated with line drawings that reveal master draftsmanship. Ages 9-14.

————. *The Scarecrow Clock.* Illustrated by Eric Carle. New York: Holt, Rinehart and Winston, 1971.

A lighthearted and informative graphic statement for how to tell time on a clock. Illustrated with colorful collages. Ages 3-6.

MEYER, RENATE. *Hide-and-Seek.* Illustrated by Renate Meyer. New York: Bradbury Press, 1972.

Action-filled, full-color illustrations in this wordless book tell the story of a girl and boy playing a game of hide-and-seek. Ages 4-9.

————. *Vicki.* Illustrated by Renate Meyer. New York: Atheneum Publishers, 1969.

Detailed, full-color stylized illustrations in this wordless book tell how a lonely little girl finds companionship. Ages 5-9.

MILES, MISKA. *Annie and the Old One.* Illustrated by Peter Parnall. Boston: Little, Brown & Co., 1971.

Detailed pen-ind-ink drawings in black and white illustrate this story of how a little Navaho Indian girl comes to grips with the impending death of her beloved grandmother. Ages 6-10.

————. *Wharf Rat.* Illustrated by John Schoenherr. Boston: Little, Brown & Co., Atlantic Monthly Press, 1972.

Large, representational line drawings and forthright narrative are integrated to tell what happens to a water rat when a disastrous oil slick fouls the waterfront. Ages 7-11.

MINCIELI, ROSE LAURA. *Old Neapolitan Fairy Tales.* Illustrated by Beni Montresor. New York: Alfred A. Knopf, 1963.

A compilation of ten Italian folktales retold from Il Pentamerone, including the Italian versions of *Cinderella, Rapunzel,* and *The Three Citrons.* Illustrations are black-and-white line drawings which comply with the mood and content of these romantic tales. Ages 8-12.

MIZUMURA, KAZUE. *If I Were a Cricket* . . . Illustrated by Kazue Mizumura. New York: Thomas Y. Crowell Co., 1973.

The quiet, sensitive, sensory image-filled prose and the full-color paintings alternating with black ink and wash drawings alert the young reader to the beauties of nature. Ages 4-6.

MOORE, LILIAN. *I Feel the Same Way.* Illustrated by Robert Quackenbush. New York: Atheneum Publishers, 1967.

A compilation of twenty short poems which are characterized by simplicity in imagery, and which interpret childlike responses to the world of nature and to personal experiences. Illustrated with pictures in soft pastels. Ages 3-7.

MOSEL, ARLENE. *The Funny Little Woman.* Illustrated by Blair Lent. New York: E. P. Dutton & Co., 1972.

A new version of the Johnnycake story. This weird and comical version of the tale centers on a rice dumpling which rolls away from its little woman cook, who in turn is forced to work for some gods and demons under the earth. She eventually masters a clever escape back above ground and is free to cook as many rice dumplings as she wishes. Illustrated in two contrasting techniques: pen drawings depict the outside world and soft acrylic paintings depict the demon's world underground. 1973 Caldecott Award winner. Ages 5-9.

MOSES, JOSEPH. *The Great Rain Robbery.* Illustrated by David Levine. Boston: Houghton Mifflin Co., 1975.

A clever play with words and cartoon-styled pen drawings are found in this whimsical mystery about the disappearance of the letter "j" during a prolonged rainfall that occured nearly 200 years ago in the picturesque village of Jpswich (Ipswich!), England. Ages 4-9.

MUNARI, BRUNO. *The Birthday Present.* Illustrated by Bruno Munari. Cleveland: World Publishing Co., 1959.

A "participation" picture book in which various means of transportation are used to bring a birthday present to a three-year-old boy. Illustrated with bold, but simple, flat-colored pictures done with tempera. Ages 3-5.

NESS, EVALINE. *Old Mother Hubbard and Her Dog.* Illustrated by Evaline Ness. New York: Holt, Rinehart and Winston, 1972.

Mother Hubbard's dog is a big sheep dog who engages in an array of boisterous and merry antics. The exciting illustrations are in rich full color. Ages 4-8.

———. *Sam, Bangs and Moonshine.* Illustrated by Evaline Ness. New York: Holt, Rinehart & Winston, 1966.

Sam, a fisherman's daughter, gets her friend Thomas and her cat Bangs into serious difficulties as a result of her tall tales (moonshine). Illustrated effectively with line-and-wash drawings. Recipient of 1967 Caldecott Medal. Ages 5-8.

———. *Tom Tit Tot.* Illustrated by Evaline Ness. New York: Charles Scribner's Sons, 1965.

An English version of the well-known fairy tale, Rumpelstiltskin, presented in picture-book form. Illustrations are woodcuts done in black, blue, and brown shades and emphasize the humor of this tale. Ages 5-8.

NIC LEODHAS, SORCHE (pseud. ALGER LeCLAIRE). *All in the Morning Early.* Illustrated by Evaline Ness. New York: Holt, Rinehart & Winston, 1963.

A retelling of an old Scottish nursery rhyme—a boy on his way to a mill is joined by one huntsman winding his horn, two old ewes by the shepherd shorn, etc. Two- and four-color drawings illustrate this tale which is told in poetic prose and couplets. Ages 5-9.

———. *Always Room for One More.* Illustrated by Nonny Hogrogian. New York: Holt, Rinehart & Winston, 1965.

A picture-book version of an old Scottish folk song about a hospitable man who fills his house with guests until their gaiety causes it to tumble down. Illustrations are black-and-white pen and line drawings with touches of pastel in heather and green for the fields to convey the fresh atmosphere and beauty of Scotland. Recipient of the 1966 Caldecott Medal. Ages 5-9.

NOEL, BERNARD, Adapter. *Sinbad the Sailor.* Translated by C. Ross Smith. Illustrated by Alain Le Foll. New York: Doubleday & Co., 1972.

A humorous and action-filled text accompanied by vital and large black-and-white drawings present an excellent version of one of the classics of mock heroics from *The Arabian Nights*. Ages 9-12.

NUSSBAUMER, MARES. *Away in a Manger: A Story of the Nativity*. Illustrated by Paul Nussbaumer. New York: Harcourt, Brace & World, 1965.

An expanded version of the story of the nativity, set in Switzerland. Illustrated with full-color poster paintings. Musical scores for "Away in a Manger" and "O Come Little Children" are included. Ages 5-9.

OXENBURY, HELEN. *Helen Oxenbury's ABC of Things*. Illustrated by Helen Oxenbury. New York: Franklin Watts, 1972.

Ink and pastel illustrations in full-color depict a wild assortment of things beginning with each respective letter of the alphabet and engaging in humorous situations. Ages 4-9.

PARNALL, PETER. *The Great Fish*. Illustrated by Peter Parnall. New York: Doubleday & Co., 1973.

A dignified fable that tells how the silver salmon saved the Indians from starvation. The concluding statement "But now . . . a mother's tears are not enough," illustrated with a junk-filled waterway, serves as a poignant comment on the problems of pollution and ecology that now plague us. Ages 6-10.

———. *The Mountain*. Illustrated by Peter Parnall. New York: Doubleday & Co., 1971.

Brief text and line drawings are integrated to create an important and serious commentary when an influx of people take over a mountain wilderness. Ages 7-11.

PEET, BILL. *The Wump World*. Illustrated by Bill Peet. Boston: Houghton Mifflin Co., 1970.

Cartoon-style drawings highlight the destruction brought on by the Pollutions, who hail from the planet Pollutus, when they take over planet of the Wumps. Ages 6-10.

PERRINE, MARY. *Salt Boy*. Illustrated by Leonard Weisgard. New York: Houghton Mifflin Co., 1968.

A Navajo Indian boy is forced to lasso a lamb that is swept away in a flash flood. Illustrated in three colors in drawings suggestive of primitive art. Ages 5-8.

PIATTI, CELESTINO. *Celestino Piatti's Animal ABC*. English text by Jon Reid. Illustrated by Celestino Piatti. New York: Atheneum Publishers, 1966. For each letter of the alphabet, four-line rhymes identify animals from alligator to zebra. Bold drawings that are brightly-colored poster paintings illustrate this alphabet book. Ages 3-6.

PILKINGTON, FRANCES M. *The Three Sorrowful Tales of Erin*. Illustrated by Victor Ambrus. New York: Henry Z. Walck, 1966.

Three Irish legends telling about the punishment given three murderers and the tragic destiny of the children of Lir and Deirdre. Drawings reflect the harsh and heroic mood and setting of the legends, which originated around the third century. Ages 11-14.

PLOTZ, HELEN. *Imagination's Other Place.* Illustrated by Clare Leighton. New York: Thomas Y. Crowell Co., 1955.

An anthology of poetry about aspects of science and mathematics. Illustrated with symbolic wood engravings printed in black and white. Ages 12 and up.

POLITI, LEO. *The Nicest Gift.* Illustrated by Leo Politi. New York: Charles Scribner's Sons, 1973.

Typical Politi naive peasant illustrations in full color and unpretentious text are combined to tell this story about a family and their pet dog who live in the "quaint and picturesque" barrio of East Los Angeles. Several Mexican words are used throughout and are appropriately translated for the non-Mexican-American readers. Ages 5-8.

Reprinted by permission of Charles Scribner's Sons from *The Nicest Gift* by Leo Politi. Copyright © 1973 Leo Politi.

————. *Song of the Swallows.* Illustrated by Leo Politi. New York: Charles Scribner's Sons, 1949.

A little boy in the California town of Capistrano, an old gardener, and the bell ringer at the Mission of San Juan Capistrano welcome the swallows as they fly in from the sea on St. Joseph's day. Illustrated with full-color watercolor paintings; figures are primitive and lumbering. Ages 5-8.

POMERANTZ, CHARLOTTE. *The Princess and the Admiral.* Illustrated by Tony Chen. Reading, Mass.: Addison-Wesley Publishing Co., 1974.

Monochromatic drawings carefully detailed in the Chinese tradition illustrate this fable of a princess' efforts to keep the tiny kingdom at peace with the world. This story about a kingdom of poor farmers and fisherfolk is based on Kublai Khan's invasion of Vietnam in the thirteenth century. Ages 4-7.

PRELUTSKY, JACK. *Circus.* Illustrated by Arnold Lobel. New York: Macmillan Co., 1974.

Verse and cartoon-styled pictures done in pen-and-ink and pencil with full-color painted overlay depict in grand style the sounds and sights of the most exciting and thrilling attractions offered at the circus. Ages 5-10.

PRICE, CHRISTINE. *Talking Drums of Africa.* Illustrated by Christine Price. New York: Charles Scribner's Sons, 1973.

Illustrations in bold black line drawings with the gold of the Ashanti and the blue of the Yoruba people are combined with rhythmic text to tell the story of the talking drums—how they are made to talk and the poems and stories they tell. Ages 7-11.

PRODDOW, PENELOPE. *Demeter and Persephone.* Illustrated by Barbara Cooney. New York: Doubleday & Co., 1972.

This is a beautiful version of the ancient Greek myth of the seasons. Stylized paintings reflecting classical Greece are integrated with the competent narrative poem. Ages 9-12.

QUACKENBUSH, ROBERT. *Clementine.* Illustrated by Robert Quackenbush. Philadelphia: J. B. Lippincott Co., 1974.

This tale of Clementine, the miner's daughter, is presented as a melodrama of the 1880s. The author-artist includes some traditional verses and adds some new ones. Also, he offers instructions on how and where to pan for gold. Illustrated with line-and-wash cartoon-type drawings.

RAND, ANN and RAND, PAUL. *I Know a Lot of Things.* Illustrated by Paul Rand. New York: Harcourt, Brace & World, 1956.

A child is helped to notice and view the world around him with an attitude of wonder and delight. Illustrations are brightly colored impressionistic drawings. Ages 4-6.

RASKIN, ELLEN. *Spectacles.* Illustrated by Ellen Raskin. New York: Atheneum Publishers, 1968.

Highly imaginative and amusing things are "seen" by near-sighted Iris Fogel when she does not wear her glasses. The cartoon-styled line drawings are perfectly suited to this story. Ages 6-10.

——. *Who, Said Sue, Said Whoo?* Illustrated by Ellen Raskin. New York: Atheneum Publishers, 1973.

Happy cartoon-styled pen-and-ink drawings with overlays of fresh bright colors plus a chatty repetitive pattern of words have produced a nonsense adventure when the animals and Sue try to find out who said "chitter-chitter chatter." Ages 4-8.

——. *The World's Greatest Freak Show.* Illustrated by Ellen Raskin. New York: Atheneum Publishers, 1971.

Line drawings with flat-color overlays and sardonic text, in which the author employs a marvelous play with words, tell the story of how Alastair

Pflug gets his comeuppance when he takes some "individuals" across the ocean and presents them as the "world's greatest freaks." Ages 6-10.

RAVIELLI, ANTHONY. *Wonders of the Human Body.* Illustrated by Anthony Ravielli. New York: Viking Press, 1954.

The structure of the human body is explained by comparing it to a machine. Graphic and imaginative drawings are anatomically accurate and explicit. Ages 10-14.

REED, PHILIP, ed. *Mother Goose and Nursery Rhymes.* Illustrated by Philip Reed. New York: Atheneum Publishers, 1963.

An anthology of carefully selected nursery rhymes, illustrated with colored wood engravings in a quaint style suggestive of the eighteenth century. Ages 4-8.

RICE, JAMES. *Cajun Night Before Christmas.* Illustrated by James Rice. Gretna, La.: Pelican Publishing Co., 1974.

A parody on the classic tale of Christmas Eve in a bayou setting. Language is Cajun dialect and the illustrations are impressionistic paintings in full color and in black and white. Ages 7-12.

———. *Gaston, the Green-Nosed Alligator.* Illustrated by James Rice. Gretna, La.: Pelican Publishing Co., 1974.

Impressionistic drawings in full color and black and white illustrate this narrative which explains why Santa Claus moved to the moss-draped bayou country and why his reindeer were replaced by a team of flying alligators. Ages 6-10.

RIDDELL, JAMES. *Hit or Myth.* Illustrated by James Riddell. New York: Harper & Row, Publishers, 1949, 1969.

An unusual format; the pages of this book are divided in half horizontally so that the reader can form many different kinds of creatures, (some real and some fanciful) by combining the upper and lower halves of the animals in whatever ways he wishes. Ages 5-10.

RINGI, KJELL. *The Magic Stick.* Illustrated by Kjell Ringi. New York: Harper & Row, Publishers, 1968.

Picture book without words. Brilliantly colored pictures depict the things a little boy imagines he can become—a pirate with a telescope, a weight lifter, and a general leading a parade. Ages 4-7.

———. *The Winner.* Illustrated by Kjell Ringi. New York: Harper & Row, Publishers, 1969.

Comic line drawings in bold color (polychrome crayons) tell this wordless story about one-upmanship. Dwarflike men with cherry cheeks and berry eyes try to outdo each other and are eventually consumed by the creation of their pride and vanity. Ages 5-12.

RIPKINS, MARTIN and STEMPEL, HANS. *Andromedar SR 1.* Illustrated by Heinz Edelman. New York: Harlin Quist Books, 1971.

Illustrations in full color and in black and white, in the style of the surrealist and the symbolist, depict this science fantasy that comments on the struggle of goodness and humanity against the evils and greed of power. Ages 9-12.

RITCHIE, JEAN. *Apple Seeds and Soda Straws.* Illustrated by Don Bolognese. New York: Henry Z. Walck, 1965.

A compilation of love charms and legends collected in Appalachian Mountain area. Pen-and-ink drawings done in cartoon style highlight the lively humor of these superstitious sayings and practices. Ages 8-12.

RIVERA, EDITH VONNEGUT. *Nora's Tale.* Illustrated by Edith Vonnegut Rivera. New York: E. P. Dutton & Co., 1974.

An allegory, imaginatively illustrated in simple pen-and-ink drawings, highlights the power of good over evil. May even serve as an example for the power of women for when she is told that she "can do anything," indeed she does! Beautifully modern, imaginative, and whimsical. Ages 10-14.

ROACH, MARILYNNE K. *The Mouse and the Song.* Illustrated by Joseph Low. New York: Parents' Magazine Press, 1974.

A factual narrative about the female white-footed mouse that lived in the cellar of the cabin Thoreau built at Walden Woods, shared his food, and listened to his flute music. Illustrated with wistful, action-filled line-and-wash expressionistic drawings. Ages 4-8.

ROBBINS, RUTH. *Baboushka and the Three Kings.* Illustrated by Nicolas Sidjakov. Berkeley: Parnassus Press, 1960.

An adaptation of a Russian folktale about an old woman who searches for the Christ Child. Illustrated in brilliantly-colored stylized drawings done in tempera and felt pen. Awarded the 1961 Caldecott Medal. Ages 7-10.

———. *Taliesin and King Arthur.* Illustrated by Ruth Robbins. Berkeley: Parnassus Press, 1970.

Stunning illustrations suggestive of medieval times are quite appropriate for this story about Taliesin, the famous poet in Welsh legend, who wins the poets by singing about the mystery of King Arthur's birth. Ages 7-11.

ROCKWELL, ANNE. *Befana.* Illustrated by Anne Rockwell. New York: Atheneum Publishers, 1974.

A retelling of the legend about a friendless and lonely old lady who refused to join the Three Wise Men and a shepherd in their search for the Christ Child. To this day as she continues to search for Him alone she brings gifts to all children on Christmas night. Ages 5-8.

ROSS, PAT. *Hi Fly.* Illustrated by John C. Wallner. New York: Crown Publishers, 1974.

Wordless picture book which tells of the zany adventures a little girl has from a fly's point of view. Black-and-white line drawings are filled with detail and offer the "reader" an imaginative perspective of his world. Ages 4-9.

ROUNDS, GLEN. *The Boll Weevil.* Illustrated by Glen Rounds. Los Angeles: Golden Gate Junior Books, 1967.

A picture-book presentation of a familiar Southern ballad that tells of a farmer's losing battle with the boll weevil. The faintly-colored drawings are rustic, and emphasize the wry humor of the ballad. Ages 6-11.

———. *Wild Horses of the Red Desert.* Illustrated by Glen Rounds. New York: Holiday House, 1969.

A matter-of-fact description of the activities, trials, and tribulations of the wild horses that roam the Red Desert, an area of "rocky ridges, twisting canyons, and dusty sagebrush flats." Drawings done in rough brush line effectively convey the wildness, spaciousness, and challenging setting of this story. Ages 9-14.

SANDBURG, CARL. *The Wedding Procession of the Rag Doll and the Broom Handle and Who Was in It.* Illustrated by Harriet Pincus. New York: Harcourt, Brace & World, 1967.

A picture-book version of a tale from Sandburg's *The Rootabaga Stories.* Unique and imaginative drawings reflect the humor of the story. Ages 6-9.

SASEK, MIROSLAV. *This Is Historic Britain.* Illustrated by Miroslav Sasek. New York: Macmillan Co., 1974.

Presented herein is a fine expressionistic, panoramic view of the many facets of historic Britain—Stonehenge, Shakespeare's burial place, Yorkshire, Trafalgar Square, Buckingham Palace, and so much more. Ages 9-15.

———. *This Is New York.* Illustrated by Miroslav Sasek. New York: Macmillan Co., 1960.

A sophisticated view of typical landmarks and scenes of New York City. Illustrated with stylized drawings and pointillism. Ages 8-13.

SCHACKBURG, RICHARD. *Yankee Doodle* (song). Illustrated by Ed Emberley. Notes by Barbara Emberley. Englewood Cliffs, N.J.: Prentice-Hall, 1965.

A colorful picture-book interpretation of this ten-verse song about the Yankee soldiers during the Revolutionary War. Illustrations are precise and striking full-color woodcuts. Included are simple arrangements for the verses, brief historical notes about the song, and a recipe for hasty pudding. Ages 4-7.

SCHATZ, LETTA.. *Bolla and the Oba's Drummers.* Illustrated by Tom Feelings. New York: McGraw-Hill Book Co., 1967.

An account of a talented drummer who became an apprentice for the Oba's Royal Drummers. Black-and-white tempera paintings convey the mood and depict the West African setting. Ages 10-13.

SCHEER, JULIAN. *Rain Makes Applesauce.* Illustrated by Marvin Bileck. New York: Holiday House, 1964.

A series of wonderfully nonsensical ideas and the refrains ". . . and rain makes applesauce" and "oh, you just talking silly talk." Intricate and imaginative drawings in pale colors match the nonsense of the text. A careful observer will notice that indeed rain does make applesauce, for the artist has shown, step by step, that from a seedling come bushels of apples with which delicious applesauce is made. Ages 4-8.

SCHMIDERER, DOROTHY. *The Alphabeast Book: An Abecedarium.* Illustrations by Dorothy Schmiderer. New York: Holt, Rinehart and Winston, 1971.

Each letter of the alphabet is presented in four stages: a drawn lowercase letter, a rather abstract shape of that letter, a globlike shape suggestive of some animal and a silhouette image of a recognizable animal the name of which is printed below that figure. Ages 5-8.

SCHOENHERR, JOHN. *The Barn.* Illustrated by John Schoenherr. Boston: Little, Brown & Co., 1968.

A skunk experiences terror when he becomes the prey of a great horned owl during a severe summer drought. Illustrated with black-and-white representational drawings. Ages 7-12.

SEGAL, LORE and SENDAK, MAURICE. *The Juniper Tree and Other Tales from Grimm.* Translated by Lore Segal and Randall Jarrell. Illustrated by Maurice Sendak. New York: Farrar, Straus & Giroux, 1973.

This collection of twenty-seven tales is illustrated with pen-and-ink drawings that measure 3½" x 4½". The illustrations reflect the tradition of fifteenth- and sixteenth-century engravings, the English illustrators of the 1860s, and the stocky peasant shapes so typical of Sendak's own work. All ages.

SEIDELMAN, JAMES E. and MINTONYE, GRACE. *The 14th Dragon.* Drawings by thirteen illustrators. New York: Harlin Quist Books, 1968.

A clever narrative verse that describes the thirteen kinds of dragons found by hunters—the fourteenth dragon is created by the reader. Each of the thirteen dragons was drawn by a different artist. They used full color and a variety of media. Ages 4-10.

SELDEN, GEORGE. *Sparrow Socks.* Illustrated by Peter Lippman. New York: Harper & Row, Publishers, 1965.

A young boy uses his family's knitting machine to make warm socks for the shivering sparrows, and soon every person in town wants to own a pair of "sparrow socks." Illustrations are detailed black-and-white sketches with clever red accents throughout. Ages 4-9.

SENDAK, MAURICE. *The Nutshell Library.* Illustrated by Maurice Sendak. New York. Harper & Row, Publishers, 1962.

A set of four nonsense picture books: "Alligators All Around" (an alphabet book), "Chicken Soup with Rice" (a book about months), "One Was Johnny" (a counting book), and "Pierre" (a cautionary tale in five chapters and a prologue). Illustrated with delightfully humorous cartoon-style sketches. Ages 4-8.

———. *Where the Wild Things Are.* Illustrated by Maurice Sendak. New York: Harper & Row, Publishers, 1963.

A playful fanciful tale about a boy in a wolf suit who sails away to where the wild things are. Illustrations are imaginative, colorful cartoon-style paintings. Excellent use of color and white space to designate the boy's involvement in fantasy and reality. Ages 4-8.

SEUSS, DR. *The 500 Hats of Bartholomew Cubbins.* Illustrated by Dr. Seuss. New York: Vanguard Press, 1938.

A folktale-type story about a small boy who enrages the king because he doesn't (cannot) remove his hat. Effective cartoon-style illustrations match the hilarious story. Ages 5-12.

SHARMAT, MARJORIE WEINMAN. *Walter The Wolf.* Illustrated by Kelly Oechsli. New York: Holiday House, 1975.

A humorous story about a wolf who chooses not to use his fang teeth for biting because he does not want to hurt others. Illustrated in full color with a series of cartoon drawings and double-page spreads. Ages 4-8.

SHECTER, BEN. *Stone House Stories.* Illustrated by Ben Shecter. New York: Harper & Row, Publishers, 1973.

Compilation of four short episodes involving forest creatures: Gray Fox, Owl, Rabbit, Chicken, Porcupine, etc. Stories are simply told and the dialogue tends to be flip, at times even waspish, but offers warm, simple humor. Illustrations are black pen-and-ink drawings and expand nicely upon the action and personalities depicted in the fanciful stories. Ages 4-9.

SHULEVITZ, URI. *Dawn.* Illustrated by Uri Shulevitz. New York: Farrar, Straus & Giroux, 1974.

Based on the ancient Chinese poem by Lui Chung-yuan this is a beautiful graphic portrait depicting the gradual and subtle approach of a pastoral dawn. The illustrations are stunning watercolor paintings in rich shades of blue, yellow, green, and lavender. Ages 5-9.

————. *The Magician.* An adaptation from the Yiddish of I. L. Peretz. Illustrated by Uri Shulevitz. New York: Macmillan Co., 1973.

Detailed, small pen-and-ink illustrations and text nicely in keeping with the style of a master storyteller are effectively combined to tell how Elijah, in the guise of a travelling magician, conjures up a feast on the eve of Passover for a devout and needy couple. Ages 6-12.

————. *One Monday Morning.* Illustrated by Uri Shulevitz. New York: Charles Scribner's Sons, 1967.

A little boy living in a dreary tenement building pretends that a king, a queen, and a little prince had visited him repeatedly during the course of a week, but were able to find him at home only on Sunday. Charming colorful illustrations depict the repetitious story. Ages 4-8.

SILVERBERG, BARBARA, ed. *Phoenix Feathers: A Collection of Mythical Monsters.* Illustrated with old prints. New York: E. P. Dutton & Co., 1973.

This is a fascinating anthology of fanciful and realistic stories about mythical beasts such as griffins, krakens, dragons, rocs, unicorns, basilisks, and the phoenix. Each section is introduced with a black print illustration which is either an old woodcut or engraving. Ages 10-14.

SINGER, ISAAC BASHEVIS. *The Fearsome Inn.* Illustrated by Nonny Hogrogian. New York: Charles Scribner's Sons, 1967.

An exciting account of a young man's using a piece of magic chalk to save himself, his two friends, and three beautiful girls from a wicked witch and her half-devil husband who hold them captive in an inn. Distinctive full-color illustrations interpret mood, characters, and events. Ages 8-12.

————. *Joseph and Koza, or the Sacrifice to the Vistula.* Illustrated by Symeon Shimin. Translated by Isaac B. Singer and Elizabeth Shub. New York: Farrar, Straus & Giroux, 1970.

Line drawings in this oversized picture book, together with poetic prose, create a beautiful and unusual presentation of this story about how a wandering goldsmith and a Jew named Joseph save the Pagan chieftain's daughter Koza from the threat of sacrifice and thereby prove God's might. Ages 8-12.

————. *Mazel and Shlimazel or the Milk of a Lioness.* Illustrated by Margot Zemach. Translated by Isaac B. Singer and Elizabeth Shub. New York: Farrar, Strauss & Giroux, 1967.

A Yiddish fairy tale about Mazel, the spirit of good luck, and Shlimazel, the spirit of bad luck, who vie with each other over the fate of a peasant boy. Full-color illustrations are suggestive of eastern European peasant art. Ages 7-10.

Illustration for *The Magician* adapted and illustrated by Uri Shulevitz. Copyright © 1973 by Uri Shulevitz. Reprinted with permission of Macmillan Publishing Company, Inc.

————. *Why Noah Chose the Dove.* Illustrated by Eric Carle. Translated by Elizabeth Shub. New York: Farrar, Straus & Giroux, 1974.

The dove, because it was the bird of peace, was chosen by Noah to bring back the message indicating that the flood water had receded. This version of Noah's Ark is illustrated with beautiful collage pictures in full color. Ages 4-8.

————. *Zlateh the Goat and Other Stories.* Illustrated by Maurice Sendak. Translated by Isaac B. Singer and Elizabeth Shub. New York: Harper & Row, Publishers, 1966.

A compilation of seven wise and humorous Yiddish folktales. The black-and-white drawings very effectively convey the old middle European atmosphere of the stories. Ages 10-14.

SLEATOR, WILLIAM. *The Angry Moon.* Illustrated by Blair Lent. Boston: Little, Brown & Co., Atlantic Monthly Press, 1970.

With the help of his grandmonther's magic, an Indian boy rescues an Indian girl being held prisoner by the angry moon. Expressionistic illustrations are suggestive of Tlingit motifs. Ages 7-10.

SMITH, IVAN. *The Death of a Wombat.* Illustrated by Clifton Pugh. New York: Charles Scribner's Sons, 1973.

An unforgettable experience—this is a truthful and uncompromising account of how the friendly, waddling wombat meets death during a brush fire by drowning in the river when he attempts to douse the fires burning in his fur. Ages 7-12.

SMUCKER, BARBARA C. *Wigwam in the City.* Illustrated by Gil Miret. New York: E. P. Dutton & Co., 1966.

A sober account of the experiences and emotions of a twelve-year-old Chippewa Indian girl and her family when they leave their impoverished reservation to live and work in Chicago. Although there are only a few woodcut prints included to illustrate this story, they highlight the major events and atmosphere extremely well. Ages 10-13.

SPIER, PETER. *London Bridge Is Falling Down.* Illustrated by Peter Spier. Garden City, N.Y.: Doubleday & Co., 1967.

A picture-book version of the well-known nursery song. Includes many verses plus a brief history of the bridge and music for the song. Illustrated with colorful, detailed drawings that present some well-known landmarks of London. Ages 5-8.

STEPTOE, JOHN. *Stevie.* Illustrated by John Steptoe. New York: Harper and Row, Publishers, 1969.

Robert develops a feeling of rivalry against Stevie, a foster brother staying at his house. Robert's loss is felt immediately, though, when Stevie no longer has to stay with the family. Bold, vibrant pictures illustrate this realistic story. Text includes a small amount of black dialect. Ages 5-9.

STEVENSON, ROBERT LOUIS. *A Child's Garden of Verses.* Illustrated by Brian Wildsmith. New York: Franklin Watts, 1966.

Colorful stylized paintings illustrate this compilation of familiar poems by Robert Louis Stevenson. Ages 4-9.

STOCKTON, FRANK R. *The Bee-Man of Orn.* Illustrated by Maurice Sendak. New York: Holt, Rinehart & Winston, 1964.

A satirical fantasy about a bee man who sets out to discover his original form. Illustrated with colored cartoon-style drawings that match the humor of the story. Ages 8-12.

SUBA, SUSANNE. *The Man with the Bushy Beard.* Illustrated by Susanne Suba. New York: Viking Press, 1969.

Reprinted by permission of Charles Scribner's Sons from *The Death of a Wombat* by Ivan Smith, illustrated by Clifton Pugh. Text copyright © 1972 Ivan Smith. Illustrations copyright © 1972 Clifton Pugh.

A compilation of five short folktales from eastern Europe. The watercolor paintings that illustrate these tales are large and robust. They emphasize the stupidity of the action and the lack of thoughtfulness that is stressed in each tale. Ages 4-8.

SUGITA, YUTAKA. *My Friend Little John.* Illustrated by Yutaka Sugita. New York: McGraw-Hill Book Co., 1973.

A wordless book. Large colorful illustrations depict a series of adventures had by two friends, a droopy-eyed, long-eared St. Bernard and his mischievious and officious master. Ages 3-6.

TEAL, VALENTINE. *The Little Woman Wanted Noise.* Illustrated by Robert Lawson. Chicago: Rand-McNally & Co., 1967.

A woman moves out to the country to get away from the noises of the city but gradually gathers a menagerie of things that make noise. Illustrated with line sketches that highlight the humor of the story. Ages 4-7.

TENNYSON, ALFRED LORD. *The Charge of the Light Brigade.* Illustrated by Alice and Martin Provensen. New York: Golden Press, 1964.

A picture-book version of the well-known poem which commemorates the disastrous British cavalry charge against the Russian batteries in 1854. Stunning double-page, full-color gouache paintings interpret this poem. Ages 8-14.

THAYER, ERNEST L. *The First Book Edition of Casey at the Bat.* Illustrated by Leonard Everett Fisher. Introduction by Casey Stengel. New York: Franklin Watts, 1965.

A picture-book version of the well-known narrative poem. Illustrated with effective scratchboard drawings in black and white. Ages 10-15.

THOMPSON, VIVIAN. *Hawaiian Myths of Earth, Sea, and Sky.* Illustrated by Leonard Weisgard. New York: Holiday House, 1966.

A compilation of twelve ancient Polynesian-Hawaiian folktales pertaining to the origin of the world, to the seasons, and to the natural wonders of the Hawaiian Islands. Black, green, and red drawings illustrate the setting and action of the tales. Ages 9-12.

TOBIAS, TOBI. *Marian Anderson.* Illustrated by Symeon Shimin. New York: Thomas Y. Crowell Co., 1972.

A brief but convincing account of how Marian Anderson came to be recognized as one of the finest contraltos in American history. Stunning, realistic drawings enhance this emotional story. Ages 7-11.

TRESSELT, ALVIN. *Hide and Seek Fog.* Illustrated by Roger Duvoisin. New York: Lothrop, Lee & Shepard Co., 1965.

A mood picture book describing the fog as it rolls in from the sea to veil an Atlantic seacoast village. Exquisite expressionist paintings done in gouache illustrate this book. Ages 4-8.

TRESSELT, ALVIN and CLEAVER, NANCY. *The Legend of the Willow Plate.* Illustrated by Joseph Low. New York: Parents' Magazine Press, 1968.

The tragic love story of the highborn Koong-se and the poor peasant poet, Chang, is the tale behind the Chinese scene that is depicted on the famous blue and white willow-pattern dinnerware, and the topic of this picture book. Illustrated with line drawings colored in soft-hued shades. Ages 6-10.

TUDOR, TASHA. *First Delights: A Book about the Five Senses.* Illustrated by Tasha Tudor. New York: Platt & Munk, 1966.

A little girl who lives on a farm discovers and enjoys through her senses the wonders and pleasures of the different seasons of the year. Realistic watercolor paintings in full color extend the brief text. Ages 5-7.

————. *Take Joy! The Tasha Tudor Christmas Book.* Illustrated by Tasha Tudor. Cleveland: World Publishing Co., 1966.

A compilation of thoughts, poems, stories, lore, and legend focusing on Christmas, plus a description of the Tudor's own Christmas celebration. Illustrated with black-and-white drawings and full-color watercolor paintings. Ages 3-7.

UCHIDA, YOSHIKO. *Sumi's Special Happening.* Illustrated by Kazue Mizumura. New York: Charles Scribner's Sons, 1966.

A little Japanese girl presents her ninety-nine-year-old friend with a birthday gift he will not soon forget—a ride on the village's fire engine jeep with the bells and siren sounding out loud and clear. Illustrations are colored drawings that highlight the Japanese setting. Ages 6-9.

UENO, NORIKO. *Elephant Buttons.* Illustrated by Noriko Ueno. New York: Harper and Row, Publishers, 1973.

Simplistic black-and-white line drawings illustrate this delightful, susprise-filled wordless story. From each stuffed animal another one emerges. Ages 3-6.

UNGERER, TOMI. *Allumette.* Illustrated by Tomi Ungerer. New York: Parents' Magazine Press, 1974.

A sophisticated modernization of Andersen's *The Little Match Girl.* The full-color mod illustrations, fill this wry social commentary with an amazing array of detail. Ages 4-6.

————. *The Beast of Monsieur Racine.* Illustrated by Tomi Ungerer. New York: Farrar, Straus & Giroux, 1971.

A *multi-level* picture book, in graphics as well as in text, this is a colorful and entertaining story about Monsieur Racine who thinks he has discovered a strange, unidentified animal only to learn that his discovery is really two children disguised as an animal. The older and more sophisticated the reader, the more he will surely read into the details included by the author-artist. Ages 4-12.

————. *Moon Man.* Illustrated by Tomi Ungerer. New York: Harper & Row, Publishers, 1967.

Shortly after Moon Man descends to earth on the fiery tail of a comet, he is captured and imprisoned but is able to escape by means of special lunar powers. Eventually, he returns to the moon in a spacecraft. Bold drawings in strong colors illustrate this humorous fantasy. Ages 4-8.

————. *Zeralda's Ogre.* Illustrated by Tomi Ungerer. New York: Harper & Row, Publishers, 1967.

The dietary habits of a child-eating ogre are changed so that he learns to enjoy roast turkey à la Cinderella, chocolate sauce Rasputin, and other such appetizing concoctions. Illustrations are droll sketches in vivid colors. Ages 5-8.

VALENS, EVANS G., JR. *Wildfire.* Illustrated by Clement Hurd. Cleveland: World Publishing Co., 1963.

A moving account of the reactions of the birds and animals of the forest to a fire caused by lightning. The story tells how life in the forest is resumed again after the fire. Illustrated with woodcuts printed on rice paper. Ages 9-12.

VAN WOERKOM, DOROTHY. *The Queen Who Couldn't Bake Gingerbread.* Illustrated by Paul Galdone. New York: Alfred A. Knopf, 1975.

Line-and-wash cartoon-styled illustrations add zest and humor to this German folktale that stresses that one will find happiness only if he focuses on the "important" things and unique talents of people. Ages 4-8.

VARNER, VELMA. *The Animal Frolic.* Illustrated by Kakuyu (pseud. Toba Sojo). New York: G. P. Putnam's Sons, 1967.

Picture-book form reproduction of a thirty-six-foot scroll, entitled "Choju Giga" or "Scroll of Animals," an early masterpiece of Japanese art and humor. The pictures of animals playing and feasting in the forest are done in caricature art style and are printed in duotone. Ages 5-9.

VELTHUIJS, MAX. *The Painter and the Bird.* Translated by Ray Broekel. Illustrated by Ray Broekel. Reading, Mass.: Addison-Wesley Publishing Co., 1975.

This story of a firm friendship between a bird and the painter who created it is illustrated with bold and vibrant poster paintings suggestive of the naive style. Ages 5-8.

VIORST, JUDITH. *Alexander and the Terrible, Horrible, No Good, Very Bad Day.* Illustrated by Ray Cruz. New York: Atheneum Publishers, 1972.

Everything went wrong for Alexander from the time he got up in the morning to the moment he went to bed. His grumpy mood and his mishaps are expressively illustrated with crosshatch drawings in black and white. Ages 4-8.

WABER, BERNARD. *An Anteater Named Arthur.* Illustrated by Bernard Waber. Boston: Houghton Mifflin Co., 1967.

Arthur, an anteater, is messy, choosy, bored, curious, and loveable. Illustrations are droll cartoon-style sketches colored in pink and brown. Ages 4-8.

———. *Lyle and the Birthday Party.* Illustrated by Bernard Waber. Boston: Houghton Mifflin Co., 1966.

Lyle, usually an amiable crocodile, suddenly becomes despondent and overcome with jealousy during a birthday party. He is sent to the hospital where he forgets his jealousy by helping others. Illustrated with superb cartoon-style sketches. Ages 4-8.

WARD, LYND. *The Biggest Bear.* Illustrated by Lynd Ward. Boston: Houghton Mifflin Co., 1952.

A dramatic account of a little bear that grew to be a big bear and a nuisance to the valley. The realistic sepia drawings portray the compassion, humor, and suspense of this story amazingly well. Ages 4-8.

———. *The Silver Pony: A Story in Pictures.* Boston: Houghton Mifflin Co., 1973.

A lengthy wordless book in which handsome black-and-white opaque tempera paintings depict heroic and grand episodes dreamed by a farm boy. Ages 7-12.

WEIK, MARY HAYS. *The Jazz Man.* Illustrated by Ann Grifalconi. New York: Atheneum Publishers, 1966.

Nine-year-old Zeke lives in an old brownstone house in Harlem. How he spends his day, the warm relationship that exists between Zeke and his parents, and his temporary abandonment by his parents are related realistically and with exquisite poetic prose. Superb expressionistic woodcuts illustrate this sensitive imagery-filled narrative. Ages 7-11.

WERSBA, BARBARA. *Amanda, Dreaming.* Illustrated by Mercer Mayer. New York: Atheneum Publishers, 1973.

Illustrations copyright © 1973 by Mercer Mayer. From *Amanda, Dreaming* by Barbara Wersba. Used by permission of Atheneum Publishers.

Surrealistic reaction to phenomenon of dreams—in text and style of illustrations. Way out, but timely in terms of young people's current interest in the psyche. Ages 11-16.

WEZEL, PETER. *The Good Bird.* Illustrated by Peter Wezel. New York: Harper & Row, Publishers, 1966.

This wordless book, consisting of fourteen full-color illustrations done in a style suggestive of Matisse, tells the story of the friendship between a red bird and a goldfish. Ages 4-10.

WIESNER, WILLIAM. *Moon Stories.* Illustrated by William Wiesner. New York: Seabury Press, 1973.

A picture-book anthology of three folktales about the moon, each story from a different culture: Czechoslovakia, Persia, and England. Illustrated in vibrant full-color paintings in expressionistic cartoon style. Ages 5-9.

WILDSMITH, BRIAN. *Brian Wildsmith's Birds.* Illustrated by Brian Wildsmith. New York: Franklin Watts, 1967.

A compilation of double-spread pictures of brilliantly colored groups of birds identified by clever single-line captions. Illustrations are poster paintings. Ages 4-9.

———. *Hare and the Tortoise.* Illustrated by Brian Wildsmith. New York: Franklin Watts, 1967.

A picture-book interpretation of La Fontaine's fable about the race between the hare and the tortoise. Imaginative and bright-colored paintings depict the humor and action of this well-known fable. Ages 5-9.

———. *Squirrels.* Illustrated by Brian Wildsmith. New York: Franklin Watts, 1975.

An informative book filled with full-color representational gouache paintings and simple text that will alert young readers to the character and way of life of squirrels. Ages 4-8.

WILLIAMS, BARBARA. *Albert's Toothache.* Illustrated by Kay Chorao. New York: E. P. Dutton & Co., 1974.

Albert is a toothless turtle, so when he complains of a "toothache" no one believes him. Eventually the reader discovers that the toothache is on Albert's left toe where a gopher bit him when he stepped in its hole. Cartoon-style, soft pencil drawings, delicately shaded are beautifully compatible with this pleasant animal fantasy. Ages 4-6.

WITHERS, CARL. *Painting the Moon: A Folktale from Estonia.* Illustrated by Adrienne Adams. New York: E. P. Dutton & Co., 1970.

Large gouache paintings in full color are integrated with the text to tell this story of how the devil attempts to paint the moon with pitch because the bright moonlight prevents him from doing evil. Ages 3-9.

WONDRISKA, WILLIAM. *The Stop.* Illustrated by William Wondriska. New York: Holt, Rinehart & Winston, 1972.

With dramatic illustrations done in a style suggestive of the surrealists and a brief, simple text, a moving story is told about the rescue of a wounded colt as executed by two young brothers. Ages 6-10.

WYNDHAM, ROBERT. *Chinese Mother Goose Rhymes.* Illustrated by Ed Young. Cleveland: World Publishing Co., 1968.

A collection of Mandarin Chinese nursery rhymes, riddles, games, and nonsense verses. Illustrated with paintings suggestive of classical Chinese art. The original Chinese version of each rhyme is also presented in

From *The Stop* by William Wondriska. Copyright © 1972 by William Wondriska. Reprinted by permission of Holt, Rinehart and Winston, Inc.

Chinese calligraphy. The book is to be read vertically like an Oriental scroll. Ages 5-9.

YAROSLAVA (YAROSLAVA SURMACH).*Tusya and the Pot of Gold*. Illustrated by Yaroslava. New York: Atheneum Publishers, 1971.

In this humorous retelling of an old Ukranian folktale that negates the habit of gossiping, the artist used the old Ukranian style of reverse glass painting. Ages 4-9.

YASHIMA, TARO. *Crow Boy*. Illustrated by Taro Yashima. New York: Viking Press, 1955.

An expressive picture-book account of a lonely little Japanese boy who attends a village school, is ridiculed and ignored by his classmates, but who is eventually appreciated for his unique talent. Illustrated with expressionistic full-color paintings done in brush and pencil. Ages 5-9.

YOLEN, JANE. *The Girl Who Loved the Wind*. Illustrated by Ed Young. New York: Thomas Y. Crowell Co., 1972.

This story about a king who wished to protect his beautiful daughter from life's harsh realities is illustrated suitably and effectively with collage art that suggests Persian miniatures. Ages 5-9.

————. *The Little Spotted Fish*. Illustrated by Friso Henstra. New York: Seabury Press, 1974.

An original fairy tale motivated by combining such sources as elements in the poem "The Song of Wandering Aengus" by William Butler Yeats, an Irish legend of the spotted trout, and a Scottish tale *Mabinogion*. Illustrations alternate in full-color pen and wash paintings and black-and-white pen-and-ink drawings. Ages 5-9.

———. *Rainbow Rider.* Illustrated by Michael Foreman. New York: Thomas Y. Crowell Co., 1974.

Suggestive of the creation myths of the North and South American Indians, this original creation myth is illustrated with watercolor impressionistic paintings and portrays the ever-changing colors of the Arizona desert and the Western sky. Ages 5-9.

———. *The Wizard Islands.* Illustrated by Robert Quackenbush. New York: Thomas Y. Crowell Co., 1973.

A marvelous collection of factual, legendary, and fanciful tales about various new and ancient islands throughout the world. Illustrated with photographs, copies of old documents and maps, and original black charcoal pencil drawings. Ages 9-15.

ZEMACH, HARVE. *Mommy, Buy Me a China Doll.* Illustrated by Margot Zemach. Chicago: Follet Publishing Co., 1966.

Humorous cumulative verse pertaining to ridiculous swapping of sleeping places after Eliza Lou suggests that her Daddy made his feather bed in order to get her a china doll. Illustrated in line-and-wash drawings that emphasize the folk quality of this Ozark Mountain-area children's song. Ages 4-8.

ZINDEL, PAUL. *Let Me Hear You Whisper.* Illustrated by Stephen Gammell. New York: Harper & Row, Publishers, 1974.

This memorable and compassionate dramatic commentary about people's relationships with other species is illustrated with full-page surrealistic paintings in black line and wash. Ages 10-15.

ZOLOTOW, CHARLOTTE. *Big Sister and Little Sister.* Illustrated by Martha Alexander. New York: Harper & Row, Publishers, 1966.

Two sisters learn to take care of one another. Illustrated with pleasant, realistic drawings in delicate shades of pink and green. Ages 4-7.

———. *William's Doll.* Illustrated by William Pène du Bois. New York: Harper & Row, Publishers, 1972.

This is a convincing statement as to why William should have the doll that he wants—convincing in text as well as in the pastel drawings. Ages 4-8.

some wordless books
worthy of note

Unless otherwise indicated the books were created and illustrated by the author-artist.

ALEXANDER, MARTHA. *Bobo's Dream*. New York: Dial Press, 1970.
———. *Out! Out! Out!* New York: Dial Press, 1968.
AMOSS, BERTHA. *By the Sea*. New York: Parents' Magazine Press, 1969.
ANNO, MITSUMASA. *Topsy-Turvies: Pictures to Stretch the Imagination*. New York: Walker/Weatherhill, 1970.
ARDIZZONE, EDWARD. *The Wrong Side of the Bed*. New York: Doubleday & Co. 1970.
BAUM, WILLI. *Birds of a Feather*. Reading, Mass.: Addison-Wesley Publishing Co., 1969.
BOLLIGER-SAVELLI, ANTONELLA. *The Knitted Cat*. New York: Macmillan Co., 1971.
———. *The Mouse and the Knitted Cat*. New York: Macmillan Co., 1974.
CARLE, ERIC. *Do You Want to be My Friend?* New York: Thomas Y. Crowell Co., 1971.
———. *1, 2, 3 to the Zoo*. New York: World Publishing Co., 1968.
CARRICK, DONALD. *Drip, Drop*. New York: Macmillan Co., 1973.
CARROLL, RUTH. *The Chimp and the Clown*. New York: Henry Z. Walck, 1968.
———. *The Christmas Kitten*. New York: Henry Z. Walck, 1970.
———. *What Whiskers Did*. New York: Henry Z. Walck, 1965.
FUCHS, ERICH. *Journey to the Moon*. New York: Delacorte Press, 1969.
GOODALL, JOHN S. *The Adventures of Paddy Pork*. New York: Harcourt Brace Jovanovich, 1968.
———. *The Ballooning Adventures of Paddy Pork*. New York: Harcourt Brace Jovanovich, 1969.
———. *Jacko*. New York: Harcourt Brace Jovanovich, 1971.
———. *Paddy's Evening Out*. New York: A Margaret McElderry Book/Atheneum Publishers, 1973.
———. *Shrewbettina's Birthday*. New York: Harcourt Brace Jovanovich, 1971.
HOBAN, TANA. *Look Again*. New York: Macmillan Co., 1971.
———. *Shapes and Things*. New York: Macmillan Co., 1970.
HUTCHINS, PAT. *Changes, Changes*. New York: Macmillan Co., 1971.

KRAHN, FERNANDO. *A Flying Saucer Full of Spaghetti*. New York: E. P. Dutton & Co., 1970.

———. *How Santa Had a Long and Difficult Journey Delivering His Presents*. New York: Delacorte Press, 1970.

KRAUS, ROBERT. *Poor Mister Splinterfritz*. Illustrated by Robert Byrd. New York: E. P. Dutton & Co., 1973.

LISKER, SONIA O. *The Attic Witch*. New York: Four Winds Press, 1973.

MARI, IELA. *The Magic Balloon*. New York: S. G. Phillips, 1969.

MARI, IELA and MARI, ENZO. *The Apple and the Moth*. New York: Pantheon Books, 1970.

———. *The Chicken and the Egg*. New York: Pantheon Books, 1970.

MAYER, MERCER. *A Boy, a Dog and a Frog*. New York: Dial Press, 1967.

———. *Frog on His Own*. New York: Dial Press, 1973.

———. *Frog, Where Are You?* New York: Dial Press, 1969.

MENDOZA, GEORGE. *The Inspector*. New York: Doubleday & Co., 1970.

MEYER, RENATE. *Hide-and-Seek*. Scarsdale, New York: Bradbury Press, 1972.

———. *Vicki*. New York: Atheneum Publishers, 1969.

MILLER, BARRY. *Alphabet World*. New York: Macmillan Co., 1971.

RINGI, KJELL. *The Magic Stick*. New York: Harper & Row, Publishers, 1968.

———. *The Winner*. New York: Harper & Row, Publishers, 1969.

ROSS, PAT. *Hi Fly*. Illustrated by John C. Wallner. New York: Crown Publishers, 1974.

SCHICK, ELEANOR. *Making Friends*. New York: Macmillan Co., 1969.

SUGITA, YUTAKA. *My Friend Little John*. New York: McGraw-Hill Book Co., 1973.

UENO, NORIKO. *Elephant Buttons*. New York: Harper & Row, Publishers, 1973.

UNGERER, TOMI. *One, Two, Three*. New York: Harper & Row, Publishers, 1964.

———. *One, Two, Where's My Shoe?* New York: Harper & Row, Publishers, 1964.

———. *Snail, Where are You?* New York: Harper & Row, Publishers, 1962.

WARD, LYND. *The Silver Pony: A Story in Pictures*. Boston: Houghton Mifflin Co., 1973.

WEZEL, PETER. *Good Bird*. New York: Harper & Row, Publishers, 1966.

the caldecott medal

The Caldecott Medal is named in honor of Randolph Caldecott, a prominent English illustrator of children's books during the nineteenth century. This award is presented each year to "the artist of the most distinguished American picture book for children." The winner is selected by the same committee that chooses the Newbery winner.

1938 Award: *Animals of The Bible, A Picture Book.* Text selected from the King James Bible by Helen Dean Fish. Illustrated by Dorothy O. Lathrop. Stokes (Lippincott).

Honor Books: *Seven Simeons.* Written and illustrated by Boris Artzybasheff. Viking.
Four and Twenty Blackbirds. Compiled by Helen Dean Fish. Illustrated by Robert Lawson. Stokes (Lippincott).

1939 Award: *Mei Li.* Written and illustrated by Thomas Handforth. Doubleday.

Honor Books: *The Forest Pool.* Written and illustrated by Laura Adams Armer. Longmans, Green (McKay).
Wee Gillis. Written by Munro Leaf. Illustrated by Robert Lawson. Viking.
Snow White and the Seven Dwarfs. Translated and illustrated by Wanda Gàg. Coward-McCann.
Barkis. Written and illustrated by Clare Turlay Newberry. Harper (Harper & Row).
Andy and the Lion. Written and illustrated by James Daugherty. Viking.

1940 Award: *Abraham Lincoln.* Written and illustrated by Ingri and Edgar Parin d'Aulaire. Doubleday.

Honor Books: *Cock-a-Doodle-Doo.* Written and illustrated by Berta and Elmer Hader. Macmillan.
Madeline. Written and illustrated by Ludwig Bemelmans. Simon and Schuster.
The Ageless Story. Written and illustrated by Lauren Ford. Dodd, Mead.

1941 Award: *They Were Strong and Good*. Written and illustrated by Robert Lawson. Viking.

Honor Books: *April's Kittens*. Written and illustrated by Clare Turlay Newberry. Harper (Harper & Row).

1942 Award: *Make Way for Ducklings*. Written and illustrated by Robert McCloskey. Viking.

Honor Books: *An American ABC*. Written and illustrated by Maud and Miska Petersham. Macmillan.
In My Mother's House. Written by Ann Nolan Clark. Illustrated by Velino Herrera. Viking.
Paddle-to-the-Sea. Written and illustrated by Holling Clancy Holling. Houghton Mifflin.
Nothing at All. Written and illustrated by Wanda Gàg. Coward-McCann.

1943 Award: *The Little House*. Written and illustrated by Virginia Lee Burton. Houghton Mifflin.

Honor Books: *Dash and Dart*. Written and illustrated by Mary and Conrad Buff. Viking.
Marshmallow. Written and illustrated by Clare Turlay Newberry. Harper (Harper & Row).

1944 Award: *Many Moons*. Written by James Thurber. Illustrated by Louis Slobodkin. Harcourt.

Honor Books: *Small Rain*. Text arranged from the Bible by Jessie Orton Jones. Illustrated by Elizabeth Orton Jones. Viking.
Pierre Pidgeon. Written by Lee Kingman. Illustrated by Arnold Edwin Bare. Houghton Mifflin.
Good-Luck Horse. Written by Chih-Yi Chan. Illustrated by Plato Chan. Whittlesey.
Mighty Hunter. Written and illustrated by Berta and Elmer Hader. Macmillan.
A Child's Good Night Book. Written by Margaret Wise Brown. Illustrated by Jean Charlot. W. R. Scott.

1945 Award: *Prayer for a Child*. Written by Rachel Field. Pictures by Elizabeth Orton Jones. Macmillan.

Honor Books: *Mother Goose*. Compiled and illustrated by Tasha Tudor. Oxford.
In the Forest. Written and illustrated by Marie Hall Ets. Viking.
Yonie Wondernose. Written and illustrated by Marguerite de Angeli. Doubleday.
The Christmas Anna Angel. Written by Ruth Sawyer. Illustrated by Kate Seredy. Viking.

1946 Award: *The Rooster Crows*. Written and illustrated by Maud and Miska Petersham. Macmillan.

Honor Books: *Little Lost Lamb*. Written by Margaret Wise Brown. Illustrated by Leonard Weisgard. Doubleday.
Sing Mother Goose. Music by Opal Wheeler. Illustrated by Marjorie Torrey. Dutton.

My Mother Is the Most Beautiful Woman in the World. Written by Becky Reyher. Illustrated by Ruth C. Gannett. Lothrop.
You Can Write Chinese. Written and illustrated by Kurt Wiese. Viking.

1947 Award: *The Little Island.* Written by Golden MacDonald. Illustrated by Leonard Weisgard. Doubleday.

Honor Books: *Rain Drop Splash.* Written by Alvin R. Tresselt. Illustrated by Leonard Weisgard. Lothrop.
Boats on the River. Written by Marjorie Flack. Illustrated by Jay Hyde Barnum. Viking.
Timothy Turtle. Written by Al Graham. Illustrated by Tony Palazzo. Robert Welch (Viking).
Pedro, Angel of Olvera Street. Written and illustrated by Leo Politi. Scribner.
Sing in Praise. Written by Opal Wheeler. Illustrated by Marjorie Torrey. Dutton.

1948 Award: *White Snow, Bright Snow.* Written by Alvin Tresselt. Illustrated by Roger Duvoisin. Lothrop.

Honor Books: *Stone Soup.* Told and illustrated by Marcia Brown. Scribner.
McElligot's Pool. Written and illustrated by Theodor S. Giesel (Dr. Seuss). Random House.
Bambino the Clown. Written and illustrated by George Schreiber. Viking.
Roger and the Fox. Written by Lavinia R. Davis. Illustrated by Hildegard Woodward. Doubleday.
Song of Robin Hood. Edited by Anne Malcolmson. Illustrated by Virginia Lee Burton. Houghton Mifflin.

1949 Award: *The Big Snow.* Written and illustrated by Berta and Elmer Hader. Macmillan.

Honor Books: *Blueberries for Sal.* Written and illustrated by Robert McCloskey. Viking.
All Around the Town. Written by Phyllis McGinley. Illustrated by Helen Stone. Lippincott.
Juanita. Written and illustrated by Leo Politi. Scribner.
Fish in the Air. Written and illustrated by Kurt Wiese. Viking.

1950 Award: *Song of the Swallows.* Written and illustrated by Leo Politi. Scribner.

Honor Books: *America's Ethan Allen.* Written by Stewart Holbrook. Illustrated by Lynd Ward. Houghton Mifflin.
The Wild Birthday Cake. Written by Lavinia R. Davis. Illustrated by Hildegard Woodward. Doubleday.
Happy Day. Written by Ruth Krauss. Illustrated by Marc Simont. Harper (Harper & Row).
Henry-Fisherman. Written and illustrated by Marcia Brown. Scribner.
Bartholomew and the Oobleck. Written and illustrated by Theodor S. Geisel (Dr. Seuss). Random House.

1951 Award: *The Egg Tree.* Written and illustrated by Katherine Milhous. Scribner.

Honor Books: *Dick Whittington and His Cat.* Told and illustrated by Marcia Brown. Scribner.
The Two Reds. Written by Will (William Lipkind). Illustrated by Nicolas (Mordvinoff). Harcourt.
If I Ran the Zoo. Written and illustrated by Theodor S. Geisel (Dr. Seuss). Random House.
T-Bone, the Baby-Sitter. Written and illustrated by Clare Turlay Newberry. Harper (Harper & Row).
The Most Wonderful Doll in the World. Written by Phyllis Mc-Ginley. Illustrated by Helen Stone. Lippincott.

1952 Award: *Finders Keepers.* Written by Will (William Lipkind). Illustrated by Nicolas (Mordvinoff). Harcourt, Brace.

Honor Books: *Mr. T. W. Anthony Woo.* Written and illustrated by Marie Hall Ets. Viking.
Skipper John's Cook. Written and illustrated by Marcia Brown. Scribner.
All Falling Down. Written by Gene Zion. Illustrated by Margaret Bloy Graham. Harper (Harper & Row).
Bear Party. Written and illustrated by William Pène du Bois. Viking.
Feather Mountain. Written and illustrated by Elizabeth Olds. Houghton Mifflin.

1953 Award: *The Biggest Bear.* Written and illustrated by Lynd Ward. Houghton Mifflin.

Honor Books: *Puss in Boots.* Told and illustrated by Marcia Brown. Scribner.
One Morning in Maine. Written and illustrated by Robert Mc-Closkey. Viking.
Ape in a Cape. Written and illustrated by Fritz Eichenberg. Harcourt.
The Storm Book. Written by Charlotte Zolotow. Illustrated by Margaret Bloy Graham. Harper (Harper & Row).
Five Little Monkeys. Written and illustrated by Juliet Kepes. Houghton Mifflin.

1954 Award: *Madeline's Rescue.* Written and illustrated by Ludwig Bemelmans. Viking.

Honor Books: *Journey Cake, Ho!* Written by Ruth Sawyer. Illustrated by Robert McCloskey. Viking.
When Will the World Be Mine? Written by Miriam Schlein. Illustrated by Jean Charlot. W. R. Scott.
The Steadfast Tin Soldier. Translated by M. R. James. Adapted from Hans Christian Andersen. Illustrated by Marcia Brown. Scribner.
A Very Special House. Written by Ruth Krauss. Illustrated by Maurice Sendak. Harper (Harper & Row).
Green Eyes. Written and illustrated by Abe Birnbaum. Capitol.

1955 Award: *Cinderella*. Written by Charles Perrault. Illustrated by Marcia Brown. Harper (Harper & Row).

Honor Books: *Book of Nursery and Mother Goose Rhymes*. Compiled and illustrated by Marguerite de Angeli. Doubleday.
Wheel on the Chimney. Written by Margaret Wise Brown. Illustrated by Tibor Gergely. Lippincott.

1956 Award: *Frog Went A-Courtin'*. Written by John Langstaff. Illustrated by Feodor Rojankovsky. Harcourt.

Honor Books: *Play with Me*. Written and illustrated by Marie Hall Ets. Viking.
Crow Boy. Written and illustrated by Taro Yashima. Viking.

1957 Award: *A Tree Is Nice*. Written by Janice May Udry. Illustrated by Marc Simont. Harper (Harper & Row).

Honor Books: *Mr. Penny's Race Horse*. Written and illustrated by Marie Hall Ets. Viking.
1 Is One. Written and illustrated by Tasha Tudor. Oxford (Walck).
Anatole. Written by Eve Titus. Illustrated by Paul Galdone. Whittlesey.
Gillespie and the Guards. Written by Benjamin Elkin. Illustrated by James Daugherty. Viking.
Lion. Written and illustrated by William Pène du Bois. Viking.

1958 Award: *Time of Wonder*. Written and illustrated by Robert McCloskey. Viking.

Honor Books: *Fly High, Fly Low*. Written and illustrated by Don Freeman. Viking.
Anatole and the Cat. Written by Eve Titus. Illustrated by Paul Galdone. Whittlesey.

1959 Award: *Chanticleer and the Fox*. Edited and illustrated by Barbara Cooney. Crowell.

Honor Books: *The House That Jack Built*. Written and illustrated by Antonio Frasconi. Crowell.
What Do You Say, Dear? Written by Sesyle Joslin. Illustrated by Maurice Sendak. W. R. Scott.
Umbrella. Written and illustrated by Taro Yashima. Viking.

1960 Award: *Nine Days to Christmas*. Written and illustrated by Marie Hall Ets and Aurora Labastida. Viking.

Honor Books: *Houses from the Sea*. Written by Alice E. Goudey. Illustrated by Adrienne Adams. Scribner.
The Moon Jumpers. Written by Janice May Udry. Illustrated by Maurice Sendak. Harper (Harper & Row).

1961 Award: *Baboushka and the Three Kings*. Written by Ruth Robbins. Illustrated by Nicolas Sidjakov. Parnassus.

Honor Books: *Inch by Inch*. Written and illustrated by Leo Lionni. Obolensky.

1962 Award: *Once A Mouse*. Written and illustrated by Marcia Brown. Scribner.

Honor Books: *The Fox Went Out on a Chilly Night*. Written and illustrated by
Peter Spier. Doubleday.
Little Bear's Visit. Written by Else Minarik. Illustrated by
Maurice Sendak. Harper (Harper & Row).
The Day We Saw the Sun Come Up. Written by Alice E. Goudey. Illustrated by Adrienne Adams. Scribner.

1963 Award: *The Snowy Day*. Written and illustrated by Ezra Jack Keats.
Viking.
Honor Books: *The Sun Is a Golden Earring*. Written by Natalia Belting. Illustrated by Bernarda Bryson. Holt, Rinehart and Winston.
Mr. Rabbit and the Lovely Present. Written by Charlotte Zolotow. Illustrated by Maurice Sendak. Harper & Row.

1964 Award: *Where the Wild Things Are*. Written and illustrated by Maurice
Sendak. Harper & Row.
Honor Books: *Swimmy*. Written and illustrated by Leo Lionni. Pantheon.
All in the Morning Early. Written by Sorche Nic Leodhas. Illustrated by Evaline Ness. Holt, Rinehart and Winston.
Mother Goose and Nursery Rhymes. Written and illustrated by
Philip Reed. Atheneum.

1965 Award: *May I Bring A Friend?* Written by Beatrice Schenk de Regniers.
Illustrated by Beni Montresor. Atheneum.
Honor Books: *Rain Makes Applesauce*. Written by Julian Scheer. Illustrated
by Marvin Bileck. Holiday.
The Wave. Written by Margaret Hodges. Illustrated by Blair
Lent. Houghton Mifflin.
A Pocketful of Cricket. Written by Rebecca Caudill. Illustrated
by Evaline Ness. Holt, Rinehart and Winston.

1966 Award: *Always Room For One More*. Written by Sorche Nic Leodhas.
Illustrated by Nonny Hogrogian. Holt, Rinehart and Winston.
Honor Books: *Hide and Seek Fog*. Written by Alvin Tresselt. Illustrated by
Roger Duvoisin. Lothrop.
Just Me. Written and illustrated by Marie Hall Ets. Viking.
Tom Tit Tot. Edited by Joseph Jacobs. Illustrated by Evaline
Ness. Scribner.

1967 Award: *Sam, Bangs and Moonshine*. Written and illustrated by Evaline
Ness. Holt, Rinehart and Winston.
Honor Books: *One Wide River to Cross*. Written by Barbara Emberley. Illustrated by Ed Emberley. Prentice-Hall.

1968 Award: *Drummer Hoff*. Written by Barbara Emberley. Illustrated by
Ed Emberley. Prentice-Hall.
Honor Books: *Frederick*. Written and illustrated by Leo Lionni. Pantheon.
Seashore Story. Written and illustrated by Taro Yashima. Viking.
The Emperor and the Kite. Written by Jane Yolen. Illustrated
by Ed Young. World Publishing.

1969 Award: *The Fool of the World and the Flying Ship.* Written by Arthur Ransome. Illustrated by Uri Shulevitz. Farrar.

Honor Books: *Why the Sun and the Moon Live in the Sky.* Retold by Elphinstone Dayrell. Illustrated by Blair Lent. Houghton.

1970 Award: *Sylvester and the Magic Pebble.* Written and illustrated by William Steig. Windmill.

Honor Books: *Goggles.* Written and illustrated by Ezra Jack Keats. Macmillan.
Alexander and the Wind-Up Mouse. Written and illustrated by Leo Lionni. Pantheon.
Pop Corn and Ma Goodness. Written by Edna Mitchell Preston. Illustrated by Robert Andrew Parker. Viking.
Thy Friend, Obadiah. Written and illustrated by Brinton Turkle. Viking.
The Judge. Written by Harve Zemach. Illustrated by Margot Zemach. Farrar.

1971 Award: *A Story—A Story.* Written and illustrated by Gail E. Haley. Atheneum.

Honor Books: *The Angry Moon.* Written by William Sleator. Illustrated by Blair Lent. Atlantic/Little.
Frog and Toad Are Friends. Written and illustrated by Arnold Lobel. Harper.
In the Night Kitchen. Written and illustrated by Maurice Sendak. Harper.

1972 Award: *One Fine Day.* Written and illustrated by Nonny Hogrogian. Macmillan.

Honor Books: *If All the Seas Were One Sea.* Written and illustrated by Janina Domanska. Macmillan.
Moja Means One: Swahili Counting Book. Written by Muriel Feelings. Illustrated by Tom Feelings. Dial.
Hildilid's Night. Written by Cheli Duran Ryan. Illustrated by Arnold Lobel. Macmillan.

1973 Award: *The Funny Little Woman.* Written by Arlene Mosel. Illustrated by Blair Lent. E. P. Dutton.

Honor Books: *Hosie's Alphabet.* Written by Hosea, Tobias and Lisa Baskin. Illustrated by Leonard Baskin. Viking.
Anansi the Spider: A Tale from Ashanti. Told and illustrated by Gerald McDermott. Holt.
When Clay Sings. Written by Byrd Baylor. Illustrated by Tom Bahti. Scribner.
Snow-White and the Seven Dwarfs. Retold by Randall Jarrell. Illustrated by Nancy Ekholm Burkert. Farrar, Straus & Giroux.

1974 Award: *Duffy and the Devil.* Written by Harve Zemach. Illustrated by Margot Zemach. Farrar, Straus & Giroux.

Honor Books: *Three Jovial Huntsmen: A Mother Goose Rhyme.* Written and illustrated by Susan Jeffers. Bradbury Press.

Cathedral: The Story of Its Construction. Written and illustrated by David Macaulay. Houghton Mifflin Company.

1975 Award: *Arrow to the Sun*. Written and illustrated by Gerald McDermott. Viking Press.

Honor Books: *Jambo Means Hello: Swahili Alphabet Book*. Written by Muriel Feelings. Illustrated by Tom Feelings. Dial Press.

1976 Award: *Why Mosquitoes Buzz in People's Ears*. Written by Verna Aardema. Illustrated by Leo and Diane Dillon. Dial Press.

Honor Books: *The Desert Is Theirs*. Written by Byrd Baylor. Illustrated by Peter Parnall. Scribner.
Strega Nona. Written and illustrated by Tomie de Paola. Prentice-Hall.

the children's book showcase

1972

ALEXANDER, MARTHA. *Nobody Asked Me If I Wanted a Baby Sister*. Illustrated by Martha Alexander. New York: Dial Press, 1971.

ARUEGO, JOSE. *Look What I Can Do*. Illustrated by Jose Aruego. New York: Charles Scribner's Sons, 1971.

BABBITT, NATALIE. *Goody Hall*. Illustrated by Natalie Babbitt. New York: Farrar, Straus & Giroux, 1971.

BARTHELME, DONALD. *The Slightly Irregular Fire Engine or the Hithering Thithering Djinn*. Illustrated by Donald Barthelme. New York: Farrar, Straus & Giroux, 1971.

BIEHORST, JOHN, ed. *In the Trail of the Wind*. Illustrated with engravings selected by John Biehorst. New York: Farrar, Straus & Giroux, 1971.

BROOKS, LESTER J. *Great Civilizations of Ancient Africa*. Illustrated by Lester J. Brooks. New York: Four Winds Press, 1971.

BURNINGHAM, JOHN. *Mr. Grumpy's Outing*. Illustrated by John Burningham. New York: Holt, Rinehart & Winston, 1971.

CAVALLO, DIANA. *The Lower East Side: A Portrait in Time*. Illustrated with photographs by Leo Stashin. New York: Crowell-Collier Press, 1971.

deKAY, ORMONDE JR., trans. *Rimes de la Mere Oie*. Illustrated by Push Pin Studios. Boston: Little, Brown & Co., 1971.

DU BOIS, WILLIAM PÈNE. *Bear Circus*. Illustrated by William Pène du Bois. New York: Viking Press, 1971.

HEIDE, FLORENCE PARRY. *The Shrinking of Treehorn*. Illustrated by Edward Gorey. New York: Holiday House, 1971.

HOBAN, TANA. *Look Again!* Illustrated with photographs by Tana Hoban. New York: Macmillan Co., 1971.

HURD, EDITH THACHER. *The Mother Beaver*. Illustrated by Clement Hurd. Boston: Little, Brown & Co., 1971.

HUTCHINS, PAT. *Changes, Changes*. Illustrated by Pat Hutchins. New York: Macmillan Co., 1971.

IONESCO, EUGENE. *Story Number 3*. Illustrated by Philippe Corentin. New York: Harlin Quist Books, 1971.

KREDENSER, GAIL. *One Dancing Drum*. Illustrated by Stanley Mack. New York: S. G. Phillips, 1971.

LIST, ILKA KATHERINE. *Questions and Answers about Seashore Life.* Illustrated by Ilka Katherine List and Arabelle Wheatley. New York: Four Winds Press, 1971.

LOBEL, ARNOLD. *On the Day Peter Stuyvesant Sailed into Town.* Illustrated by Arnold Lobel. New York: Harper & Row, Publishers, 1971.

MILLER, MITCHELL. *One Misty Moisty Morning: Rhymes from Mother Goose.* Illustrated by Mitchell Miller. New York: Farrar, Straus & Giroux, 1971.

NELSON, DONALD. *Sam and Emma.* Illustrated by Edward Gorey. New York: Parents' Magazine Press, 1971.

RASKIN, ELLEN. *The Mysterious Disappearance of Leon (I Mean Noel).* Illustrated by Ellen Raskin. New York: E. P. Dutton & Co., 1971.

REAVIN, SAM. *Hurray for Captain Jane!* Illustrated by Emily McCully. New York: Parents' Magazine Press, 1971.

REES, ENNIS. *Lions and Lobsters and Foxes and Frogs: Fables from Aesop.* Illustrated by Edward Gorey. Reading, Mass.: Young Scott Books/Addison-Wesley Publishing Co., 1971.

RYAN, CHELI DURAN. *Hildilid's Night.* Illustrated by Arnold Lobel. New York: Macmillan Co., 1971.

SCHMIDERER, DOROTHY. *The Alphabeast Book.* Illustrated by Dorothy Schmiderer. New York: Holt, Rinehart & Winston, 1971.

SENDAK, JACK. *The Magic Tears.* Illustrated by Mitchell Miller. New York: Harper & Row, Publishers, 1971.

SIMON, SEYMOUR. *The Paper Airplane Book.* Illustrated by Byron Barton. New York: Viking Press, 1971.

SINGER, ISAAC B. *Alone in the Wild Forest.* Illustrated by Margot Zemach. New York: Farrar, Straus & Giroux, 1971.

SOLBERT, RONNI. *I Wrote My Name on the Wall: Sidewalk Songs.* Illustrated with photographs by Ronni Solbert. Boston: Little, Brown & Co., 1971.

STEIG, WILLIAM. *Amos and Boris.* Illustrated by William Steig. New York: Farrar, Straus & Giroux, 1971.

UNGERER, TOMI. *The Beast of Monsieur Racine.* Illustrated by Tomi Ungerer. New York: Farrar, Straus & Giroux, 1971.

WATSON, CLYDE. *Father Fox's Pennyrhymes.* Illustrated by Wendy Watson. New York: Thomas Y. Crowell Co., 1971.

ZEMACH, HARVE. *A Penny a Look.* Illustrated by Margot Zemach. New York: Farrar, Straus & Giroux, 1971.

1973

ARUEGO, JOSE and ARUEGO, ARIANE. *A Crocodile's Tale:A Philippine Folk Tale.* Illustrated by Jose and Ariane Aruego. New York: Charles Scribner's Sons, 1972.

ASCH, FRANK. *Rebecka.* Illustrated by Frank Asch. New York: Harper & Row, Publishers, 1972.

BARTON, BYRON. *Where's Al?* Illustrated by Byron Barton. New York. Seabury Press, 1972.

BERSON, HAROLD. *Balarin's Goat.* Illustrated by Harold Berson. New York: Crown Publishers, 1972.

BOLLIGER, MAX. *Noah and the Rainbow.* Translated by Clyde Robert Bulla. Illustrated by Helga Aichinger. New York: Thomas Y. Crowell Co., 1972.

COHEN, PETER ZACHARY. *Authorized Autumn Charts of the Upper Red Canoe River Country.* Illustrated by Tomie de Paola. New York: Atheneum Publishers, 1972.

DE REGNIERS, BEATRICE SCHENK. *Red Riding Hood.* Illustrated by Edward Gorey. New York: Atheneum Publishers, 1972.

DOWDEN, ANNE OPHELIA. *Wild Green Things in the City.* Illustrated by Anne Ophelia Dowden. New York: Thomas Y. Crowell Co., 1972.

FRENCH, FIONA. *The Blue Bird.* Illustrated by Fiona French. New York: Henry Z. Walck, 1972.

GLASGOW, ALINE. *Honschi.* Illustrated by Tony Chen. New York: Parents' Magazine Press, 1972.

GOODALL, JOHN S. *Jacko.* Illustrated by John S. Goodall. New York: Harcourt Brace Jovanovich, 1972.

HARTWICK, HARRY. *Farewell to the Farivox.* Illustrated by Ib Ohlsson. New York: Four Winds Press, 1972.

KNOTTS, HOWARD. *The Winter Cat.* Illustrated by Howard Knotts. New York: Harper & Row, Publishers, 1972.

KOHN, BERNICE. *The Busy Honeybee.* Illustrated by Mel Furukawa. New York: Four Winds Press, 1972.

LEVOY, MYRON. *The Witch of Fourth Street.* Illustrated by Gabriel Lisowski. New York: Harper & Row, Publishers, 1972.

LOBEL, ARNOLD. *Frog and Toad Together.* Illustrated by Arnold Lobel. New York: Harper & Row, Publishers, 1972.

MARSHALL, JAMES. *George and Martha.* Illustrated by James Marshall. Boston: Houghton Mifflin Co., 1972.

MORRIS, ROBERT A. *Seahorse.* Illustrated by Arnold Lobel. New York: Harper & Row, Publishers, 1972.

MOSEL, ARLENE. *The Funny Little Woman.* Illustrated by Blair Lent. New York: E. P. Dutton & Co., 1972.

ROCKWELL, ANNE. *Toad.* Illustrated by Harlow Rockwell. New York: Doubleday & Co., 1972.

SCHNEIDER, GERLINDE. *Uncle Harry.* Translated by Elizabeth Shub. Illustrated by Lilo Fromm. New York: Macmillan Co., 1972.

SIMON, HILDA. *Dragonflies.* Illustrated by Hilda Simon. New York: Viking Press, 1972.

STALDER, VALERIE. *Even the Devil Is Afraid of a Shrew: A Folktale of Lapland.* Adapted by Ray Broekel. Illustrated by Richard Brown. Reading, Mass.: Addisonian Press, Addison-Wesley Publishing Co., 1972.

SUHL, YURI. *Simon Boom Gives a Wedding.* Illustrated by Margot Zemach. New York: Four Winds Press, 1972.

SUTEYEV, V. *The Chick and the Duckling.* Translated by Mirra Ginsburg. Illustrated by Jose and Ariane Aruego. New York: Macmillan Co., 1972.

WABER, BERNARD. *Ira Sleeps Over.* Illustrated by Bernard Waber. Boston: Houghton Mifflin Co., 1972.

YOLEN, JANE. *The Girl Who Loved the Wind.* Illustrated by Ed Young. New York: Thomas Y. Crowell Co., 1972.

1974

AARDEMA, VERNA. *Behind the Back of the Mountain: Black Folktales from Southern Africa.* Illustrated by Leo and Diane Dillon. New York: Dial Press, 1973.

ADKINS, JAN. *Toolchest: A Primer of Woodcraft*. Illustrated by Jan Adkins. New York: Walker & Co., 1973.

BRANLEY, FRANKLYN M. *Eclipse: Darkness in Daytime*. Illustrated by Donald Crews. New York: Thomas Y. Crowell Co., 1973.

BRIGGS, RAYMOND. *Father Christmas*. Illustrated by Raymond Briggs. New York: Coward, McCann and Geoghegan, 1973.

CHASEK, JUDITH. *Have You Seen Wilhelmina Krumpf?* Illustrated by Sal Murdocca. New York: Lothrop, Lee & Shepard Co., 1973.

FRESCHET, BERNIECE. *Bear Mouse*. Illustrated by Donald Carrick. New York: Charles Scribner's Sons, 1973.

GOODALL, JOHN S. *Paddy's Evening Out*. Illustrated by John S. Goodall. New York: A Margaret McElderry Book/Atheneum Publishers, 1973.

GREENFELD, HOWARD. *Gertrude Stein: A Biography*. Illustrated with photographs. New York: Crown Publishers, 1973.

JAMESON, CYNTHIA. *The Clay Pot Boy*. Illustrated by Arnold Lobel. New York: Coward, McCann and Geoghegan, 1973.

JEFFERS, SUSAN. *Three Jovial Huntsmen: A Mother Goose Rhyme*. Illustrated by Susan Jeffers. Scarsdale, N.Y.: Bradbury Press, 1973.

KINGMAN, LEE. *Escape from the Evil Prophecy*. Illustrated by Richard Cuffari. Houghton Mifflin Co., 1973.

KURELEK, WILLIAM. *A Prairie Boy's Winter*. Illustrated by William Kurelek. Boston: Houghton Mifflin Co., 1973.

LOBEL, ANITA. *A Birthday for the Princess*. Illustrated by Anita Lobel. New York: Harper & Row, Publishers, 1973.

LUNDBERGH, HOLGER, trans. *Great Swedish Fairy Tales*. Illustrated by John Bauer. New York: Delacorte Press/Seymour Lawrence, 1973.

MACAULAY, DAVID. *Cathedral: The Story of Its Construction*. Illustrated by David Macaulay. Boston: Houghton Mifflin Co., 1973.

MacCLINTOCK, DORCAS. *A Natural History of Giraffes*. Illustrated by Ugo Mochi. New York: Charles Scribner's Sons, 1973.

McKILLIP, PATRICIA A. *The Throne of the Erril of Sherill*. Illustrated by Julia Noonan. New York: Atheneum Publishers, 1973.

POLSENO, JO. *Secrets of Redding Glen*. Illustrated by Jo Polseno. Racine, Wis.: Western Publishing Company/Golden Press, 1973.

PUTNAM, PETER BROCK. *Peter, the Revolutionary Tsar*. Illustrated by Laszlo Kubinyi. New York: Harper & Row, Publishers, 1973.

RASKIN, ELLEN. *Who, Said Sue, Said Whoo?* Illustrated by Ellen Raskin. New York: Atheneum Publishers, 1973.

SEGAL, LORE. *All the Way Home*. Illustrated by James Marshall. New York: Farrar, Straus & Giroux, 1973.

SEGAL, LORE and SENDAK, MAURICE. *The Juniper Tree and Other Tales from Grimm*. Translated by Lore Segal and Randall Jarrell. Illustrated by Maurice Sendak. New York: Farrar, Straus & Giroux, 1973.

SHULEVITZ, URI and PERETZ, I. L. *The Magician*. Illustrated by Uri Shulevitz. New York: Macmillan Co., 1973.

SILVERBERG, BARBARA, ed. *Phoenix Feathers: A Collection of Mythical Monsters*. Illustrated with old woodcuts and engravings. New York: E. P. Dutton & Co., 1973.

TAYLOR, EDGAR, trans. *King Grisley-Beard: A Tale from the Brothers Grimm*. Illustrated by Maurice Sendak. New York: Farrar, Straus & Giroux, 1973.

TUNIS, EDWIN. *The Tavern at the Ferry*. Illustrated by Edwin Tunis. New York: Thomas Y. Crowell Co., 1973.

WARD, LYND. *The Silver Pony*. Illustrated by Lynd Ward. Boston: Houghton Mifflin Co., 1973.

WATTS, MABEL. *While the Horses Galloped to London*. Illustrated by Mercer Mayer. New York: Parents' Magazine Press, 1973.

WELLS, ROSEMARY. *Noisy Nora*. Illustrated by Rosemary Wells. New York: Dial Press, 1973.

WILLIAMS, JAY. *Petronella*. Illustrated by Friso Henstra. New York: Parents' Magazine Press, 1973.

ZEMACH, HARVE. *Duffy and the Devil*. Illustrated by Margot Zemach. New York: Farrar, Straus & Giroux, 1973.

1975

ALLARD, HARRY. *The Stupids Step Out*. Illustrated by James Marshall. Boston: Houghton Mifflin Co., 1974.

BARRETT, JUDI. *Benjamin's 365 Birthdays*. Illustrated by Ron Barrett. New York: Atheneum Publishers, 1974.

BELTING, NATALIA. *Whirlwind Is a Ghost Dancing*. Illustrated by Leo and Diane Dillon. New York: E. P. Dutton & Co., 1974.

BODECKER, N. M. *The Mushroom Center Disaster*. Illustrated by Erik Blegvad. New York: A Margaret McElderry Book/Atheneum Publishers, 1974.

CARRICK, CAROL. *Lost in the Storm*. Illustrated by Donald Carrick. New York: Seabury Press, 1974.

CARTER, DOROTHY SHARP. *Greedy Mariani*. Illustrated by Trina Schart Hyman. New York: A Margaret McElderry Book/Atheneum Publishers, 1974.

CUMBERLEGE, VERA. *Shipwreck*. Illustrated by Charles Mikolaycak. Chicago: Follett Publishing Co., 1974.

DE PAOLA, TOMIE. *Charlie Needs a Cloak*. Illustrated by Tomie de Paola. Englewood Cliffs, N.J.: Prentice-Hall, 1974.

DORNBERG, JOHN. *The Two Germanys*. Illustrated by John Dornberg. New York: Dial Press, 1974.

FARBER, NORMA. *Where's Gomer*. Illustrated by William Pène du Bois. New York: E. P. Dutton & Co., 1974.

GRIMM, WILLIAM. *Indian Harvests*. Illustrated by Ronald Himler. New York: McGraw-Hill Book Co., 1974.

KELLOGG, STEVEN. *The Mystery of the Missing Red Mitten*. Illustrated by Steven Kellogg. New York: Dial Press, 1974.

KRAHN, FERNANDO. *April Fools*. Illustrated by Fernando Krahn. New York: E. P. Dutton & Co., 1974.

KRAUS, ROBERT. *Owliver*. Illustrated by Jose Aruego and Ariane Dewey. New York: Windmill Books, 1974.

———. *Pinchpenny Mouse*. Illustrated by Robert Byrd. New York: Windmill Books, 1974.

KURELEK, WILLIAM. *Lumberjack*. Illustrated by William Kurelek. Boston: Houghton Mifflin Co., 1974.

LOBEL, ARNOLD. *The Man Who Took the Indoors Out*. Illustrated by Arnold Lobel. New York: Harper & Row, Publishers, 1974.

MACAULAY, DAVID. *City*. Illustrated by David Macaulay. Boston: Houghton Mifflin Co., 1974.

POPE, ELIZABETH. *The Perilous Gard*. Illustrated by Richard Cuffari. Boston: Houghton Mifflin Co., 1974.

RASKIN, ELLEN. *Figgs and Phantoms*. Illustrated by Ellen Raskin. New York: E. P. Dutton & Co., 1974.

ROACH, MARILYNNE K. *The Mouse and the Song*. Illustrated by Joseph Low. New York: Parents' Magazine Press, 1974.

ROCKWELL, ANNE. *Befana*. Illustrated by Anne Rockwell. New York: Atheneum Publishers, 1974.

RUDSTROM, LENNART. *A Home*. Illustrated by Carl Larsson. New York: G. P. Putnam's Sons, 1974.

SHULEVITZ, URI. *Dawn*. Illustrated by Uri Shulevitz. New York: Farrar, Straus & Giroux, 1974.

UNGERER, TOMI. *Allumette*. Illustrated by Tomi Ungerer. New York: Parents' Magazine Press, 1974.

WILLIAMS, BARBARA. *Albert's Toothache*. Illustrated by Kay Chorao. New York: E. P. Dutton & Co., 1974.

WOLF, BERNARD. *Don't Feel Sorry for Paul*. Illustrated with photographs by Bernard Wolf. Philadelphia: J. B. Lippincott Co., 1974.

1976

ADKINS, JAN. *Inside: Seeing Beneath the Surface*. Illustrated by Jan Adkins. New York: Walker and Company, 1975.

ANNO, MITSUMASA. *Anno's Alphabet: An Adventure in Imagination*. New York: Thomas Y. Crowell Co., 1975.

CARRICK, CAROL. *The Blue Lobster: A Life Cycle*. Illustrated by Donald Carrick. New York: Dial Press, 1975.

CARROLL, LEWIS. *The Pig-Tale*. Illustrated by Leonard B. Lubin. Boston: Little, Brown & Co., 1975.

CHIRINOS, LITO. *Lito, the Shoeshine Boy*. Translated by David Mangurian. Illustrated with photographs by David Mangurian. New York: Four Winds Press, 1975.

CRAFT, RUTH. *The Winter Bear*. Illustrated by Erik Blevad. New York: A Margaret McElderry Book/Atheneum Publishers, 1975.

DOWDEN, ANNE OPHELIA. *The Blossom on the Bough: A Book of Trees*. Illustrated by Anne Ophelia Dowden. New York: Thomas Y. Crowell Co., 1975.

FARBER, NORMA. *As I Was Crossing Boston Common*. Illustrated by Arnold Lobel. New York: E. P. Dutton & Co., 1975.

GARELICK, MAY. *About Owls*. Illustrated by Tony Chen. New York: Four Winds Press, 1975.

GLUBOK, SHIRLEY. *The Art of the Norhtwest Coast Indians*. Illustrated with photographs. New York: Macmillan Co., 1975.

GOODALL, JOHN S. *Creepy Castle*. Illustrated by John S. Goodall. New York: A Margaret McElderry Book/Atheneum Publishers, 1975.

GRAHAM, LORENZ. *Song of the Boat*. Illustrated by Leo and Diane Dillon. New York: Thomas Y. Crowell Company, 1975.

HAAS, IRENE. *The Maggie B*. Illustrated by Irene Haas. New York: A Margaret McElderry Book/Atheneum Publishers, 1975.

HOFFMANN, FELIX. *The Story of Christmas*. Illustrated by Felix Hoffmann. New York: A Margaret McElderry Book/Atheneum Publishers, 1975.

HUGHES, TED. *Season Songs*. Illustrated by Leonard Baskin. New York: Viking Press, Inc., 1975.

KATZ, WILLIAM LOREN and KATZ, JACQUELINE HUNT, compilers. *Making Our Way: America at the Turn of the Century in the Words of the Poor and Powerless*. Illustrated with photographs. New York: Dial Press, 1975.

KIMMEL, MARGARET MARY. *Magic in the Mist*. Illustrated by Trina Schart Hyman. New York: A Margaret McElderry Book/Atheneum Publishers, 1975.

KURELEK, WILLIAM. *A Prairie Boy's Summer*. Illustrated by William Kurelek. Boston: Houghton Mifflin Co., 1975.

LAWRENCE, JOHN. *Rabbit and Pork: Rhyming Talk*. Illustrated by John Lawrence. New York: Thomas Y. Crowell Co., 1975.

LOW, JOSEPH. *Boo to a Goose*. Illustrated by Joseph Low. New York: A Margaret McElderry Book/Atheneum Publishers, 1975.

MACAULAY, DAVID. *Pyramid*. Illustrated by David Macaulay. Boston: Houghton Mifflin Co., 1975.

PUSHKIN, ALEXANDER. *The Tale of Czar Saltan*. Translated and retold by Patricia Tracy Lowe. Illustrated by I. Bilibin. New York: Thomas Y. Crowell Co., 1975.

STREATFEILD, NOEL. *A Young Person's Guide to Ballet*. Illustrated with drawings by Georgette Bordier and with photographs. New York: Frederick Warne & Co., 1975.

TAYLOR, MILDRED D. *Song of the Trees*. Illustrated by Jerry Pinkney. New York: Dial Press, 1975.

THUM, MARCELLA. *Exploring Black America: A History and Guide*. Illustrated with photographs. New York: Atheneum Publishers, 1975.

VELTHUIJS, MAX. *The Painter and the Bird*. Translated by Ray Broekel. Illustrated by Max Velthuijs. Reading, Mass.: Addison-Wesley Publishing Co., 1975.

YOLEN, JANE. *The Little Spotted Fish*. Illustrated by Friso Henstra. New York: Seabury Press, 1975.

ZEMACH, HARVE and ZEMACH, KAETHE. *The Princess and Froggie*. Illustrated by Margot Zemach. New York: Farrar, Straus & Giroux, 1975.

selected professional references

BRUNNER, FELIX. *A Handbook of Graphic Reproduction Processes.* New York: Hastings House Publishers, 1968.

BLAND, DAVID. *The Illustration of Books.* London: Faber & Faber, 1962.

COLBY, JEAN POINDEXTER. *Writing, Illustrating and Editing Children's Books.* New York: Hastings House Publishers, 1967.

CROY, PETER. *Graphic Design and Reproduction Techniques.* New York: Hastings House Publishers, 1968.

HUCK, CHARLOTTE S., and KUHN, DORIS YOUNG. *Children's Literature in the Elementary School.* New York: Holt, Rinehart & Winston, 1968.

KINGMAN, LEE; FOSTER, JOANNA; and LONTOFT, RUTH GILES. *Illustrators of Children's Books, 1957-1966.* Boston: Horn Book, 1968.

LEWIS, JOHN. *Twentieth Century Book; Its Illustration and Design.* New York: Reinhold Publishing Corp., 1967.

PITZ, HENRY C. *Illustrating Children's Books: History, Technique, Production.* New York: Watson-Guptill Publications, 1963.

POPE, ARTHUR. *The Language of Drawing and Painting.* New York: Russell & Russell, 1948.

RAND, PAUL. *Thoughts on Design.* New York: Van Nostrand Reinhold Co., 1970.

REED, WALT, ed. *Illustrator in America, 1900-1960s.* New York: Reinhold Publishing Corp., 1967.

SHAHN, BEN. *The Shape of Content.* Cambridge: Harvard University Press, 1957.

STONE, BERNARD, and ECKSTEIN, ARTHUR. *Preparing Art for Printing.* New York: Reinhold Publishing Corp., 1965.

WEITTENKAMPF, FRANK. *The Illustrated Book.* Cambridge: Harvard University Press, 1938.

Periodicals:

American Artist
Bulletin of the Center for Children's Books
Children's Literature in Education
Elementary English
Graphis
The Horn Book Magazine

Junior Bookshelf
Publishers' Weekly
School Librarian
Top of the News
The Writer

index